PLAYS: ONE

Harold Pinter was born in London in 1930. He is married
to Antonia Fraser.

PLAYS: ONE

HAROLD PINTER

The Birthday Party
The Room
The Dumb Waiter
A Slight Ache
The Hothouse
A Night Out
The Black and White
The Examination

With an introduction:
'Writing for the Theatre'

faber and faber
LONDON·BOSTON

First published in this edition in 1991
by Faber and Faber Limited
3 Queen Square London WCIN 3AU
The first paperback edition of this collection
was published in 1976
by Eyre Methuen Limited
Reprinted 1983
Revised 1986
(to include *The Hothouse*)
Reprinted 1987, 1989 (by Methuen Drama)

Printed in England by Clays Ltd, St Ives plc

The Birthday Party, *The Room*, *The Dumb Waiter* first published by
Methuen & Co. 1960
A Slight Ache, *A Night Out* first published by Methuen & Co. in 1961
The Hothouse first published by Eyre Methuen Ltd in 1980
The Black and White first appeared in *Transatlantic Review* in 1966
The Examination first published by Methuen & Co. in 1963
'Writing for the Theatre' first appeared as 'Between the Lines' in
The Sunday Times 4 March 1962; this revised version first published in
The New British Drama, Grove Press, New York, 1964

A CIP record for this book is available from the British Library
ISBN 0–571–16074–3

4 6 8 10 9 7 5 3

CONTENTS

INTRODUCTION

Writing for the Theatre

A speech made by Harold Pinter at the National Student Drama Festival in Bristol in 1962.

I'm not a theorist. I'm not an authoritative or reliable commentator on the dramatic scene, the social scene, any scene. I write plays, when I can manage it, and that's all. That's the sum of it. So I'm speaking with some reluctance, knowing that there are at least twenty-four possible aspects of any single statement, depending on where you're standing at the time or on what the weather's like. A categorical statement, I find, will never stay where it is and be finite. It will immediately be subject to modification by the other twenty-three possibilities of it. No statement I make, therefore, should be interpreted as final and definitive. One or two of them may sound final and definitive, they may even be *almost* final and definitive, but I won't regard them as such tomorrow, and I wouldn't like you to do so today.

I've had two full-length plays produced in London. The first ran a week and the second ran a year. Of course, there are differences between the two plays. In *The Birthday Party* I employed a certain amount of dashes in the text, between phrases. In *The Caretaker* I cut out the dashes and used dots instead. So that instead of, say: 'Look, dash, who, dash, I, dash, dash, dash,' the text would read: 'Look, dot, dot, dot, who, dot, dot dot, I, dot, dot, dot, dot.' So it's possible to deduce from this that dots are more popular than dashes and that's why *The Caretaker* had a longer run than *The Birthday Party*. The fact that in neither case could you hear the dots and dashes in performance is beside the point. You can't fool the critics for long. They can tell a dot from a dash a mile off, even if they can hear neither.

It took me quite a while to grow used to the fact that critical and public response in the theatre follows a very erratic temperature chart. And the danger for a writer is where he becomes easy prey for the old bugs of apprehension and expectation in this connection. But I think Düsseldorf cleared the air for me. In Düsseldorf about two years ago I took, as is the Continental custom, a bow with a German cast of *The Caretaker* at the end of the play on the first night. I was at once booed violently by what must have been the finest collection of booers in the world. I thought they were using megaphones, but it was pure mouth. The cast was as dogged as the audience, however, and we took thirty-four curtain calls, all to boos. By the thirty-fourth there were only two people left in the house, still booing. I was strangely warmed by all this, and now, whenever I sense a tremor of the old apprehension or expectation, I remember Düsseldorf, and am cured.

The theatre is a large, energetic, public activity. Writing is, for me, a completely private activity, a poem or a play, no difference. These facts are not easy to reconcile. The professional theatre, whatever the virtues it undoubtedly possesses, is a world of false climaxes, calculated tensions, some hysteria, and a good deal of inefficiency. And the alarms of this world which I suppose I work in become steadily more widespread and intrusive. But basically my position has remained the same. What I write has no obligation to anything other than to itself. My responsibility is not to audiences, critics, producers, directors, actors or to my fellow men in general, but to the play in hand, simply. I warned you about definitive statements but it looks as though I've just made one.

I have usually begun a play in quite a simple manner; found a couple of characters in a particular context, thrown them together and listened to what they said, keeping my nose to the ground. The context has always been, for me, concrete and particular, and the characters concrete also. I've never started a play from any kind of abstract idea or theory and never envisaged my own characters as messengers of death, doom, heaven or the milky way or, in other words, as allegorical representations of any particular force, whatever that may mean. When a character cannot be comfortably defined or understood in terms of the familiar, the tendency is to perch him on a symbolic shelf, out of harm's way. Once there, he can be talked about but need not be lived with. In this way, it is easy to put up a pretty efficient smoke screen, on the part of the critics or the audience, against recognition, against an active and willing participation.

We don't carry labels on our chests, and even though they are continually fixed to us by others, they convince nobody. The desire for verification on the part of all of us, with regard to our own experience and the experience of others, is understandable but cannot always be satisfied. I suggest there can be no hard distinctions between what is real and what is unreal, nor between what is true and what is false. A thing is not necessarily either true or false; it can be both true and false. A character on the stage who can present no convincing argument or information as to his past experience, his present behaviour or his aspirations, nor give a comprehensive analysis of his motives is as legitimate and as worthy of attention as one who, alarmingly, can do all these things. The more acute the experience the less articulate its expression.

Apart from any other consideration, we are faced with the immense difficulty, if not the impossibility, of verifying the past. I don't mean merely years ago, but yesterday, this morning. What took place, what was the nature of what took place, what happened? If one can speak of the difficulty of knowing what in fact took place yesterday, one can I think treat the present in the same way. What's happening now? We won't know until tomorrow or in six months' time, and we won't know then, we'll have forgotten, or our imagination will have attributed quite false characteristics to today. A moment is sucked away and distorted, often even at the time of its birth. We will all interpret a common experience quite differently, though we prefer to subscribe to the view that there's a shared common ground, a known ground. I think there's a shared common ground all right, but that it's more like a quicksand. Because 'reality' is quite a strong firm word we tend to think, or to hope, that the state to which it refers is equally firm, settled and unequivocal. It doesn't seem to be, and in my opinion, it's no worse or better for that.

A play is not an essay, nor should a playwright under any exhortation damage the consistency of his characters by injecting a remedy or apology for their actions into the last act, simply because we have been brought up to expect, rain or sunshine, the last act 'resolution'. To supply an explicit moral tag to an evolving and compulsive dramatic image seems to be facile, impertinent and dishonest. Where this takes places it is not theatre but a crossword puzzle. The audience holds the paper. The play fills in the blanks. Everyone's happy.

There is a considerable body of people just now who are asking for some kind of clear and sensible engagement to be evidently disclosed in contemporary plays. They want the playwright to be a prophet. There is certainly a good deal of prophecy indulged in by playwrights these days, in their plays and out of them. Warnings, sermons, admonitions, ideological exhortations, moral judgements, defined problems with built-in solutions; all can camp under the banner of prophecy. The attitude behind this sort of thing might be summed up in one phrase: '*I'm telling you!*'

It takes all sorts of playwrights to make a world, and as far as I'm concerned 'X' can follow any course he chooses without my acting as his censor. To propagate a phoney war between hypothetical schools of playwrights doesn't seem to me a very productive pastime and it certainly isn't my intention. But I can't but feel that we have a marked tendency to stress, so glibly, our empty preferences. The preference for 'Life' with a capital L, which is held up to be very different to life with a small l, I mean the life we in fact live. The preference for goodwill, for charity, for benevolence, how facile they've become, these deliverances.

If I were to state any moral precept it might be: Beware of the writer who puts forward his concern for you to embrace, who leaves you in no doubt of his worthiness, his usefulness, his altruism, who declares that his heart is in the right place, and ensures that it can be seen in full view, a pulsating mass where his characters ought to be. What is presented, so much of the time, as a body of active and positive thought is in fact a body lost in a prison of empty definition and cliché.

This kind of writer clearly trusts words absolutely. I have mixed feelings about words myself. Moving among them, sorting them out, watching them appear on the page, from this I derive a considerable pleasure. But at the same time I have another strong feeling about words which amounts to nothing less than nausea. Such a weight of words confronts us day in, day out, words spoken in a context such as this, words written by me and by others, the bulk of it a stale dead terminology; ideas endlessly repeated and permutated become platitudinous, trite,

meaningless. Given this nausea, it's very easy to be over-
come by it and step back into paralysis. I imagine most
writers know something of this kind of paralysis. But if it
is possible to confront this nausea, to follow it to its hilt,
to move through it and out of it, then it is possible to say
that something has occurred, that something has even
been achieved.

Language, under these conditions, is a highly ambig-
uous business. So often, below the word spoken, is the
thing known and unspoken. My characters tell me so
much and no more, with reference to their experience,
their aspirations, their motives, their history. Between
my lack of biographical data about them and the am-
biguity of what they say lies a territory which is not only
worthy of exploration but which it is compulsory to
explore. You and I, the characters which grow on a page,
most of the time we're inexpressive, giving little away,
unreliable, elusive, evasive, obstructive, unwilling. But
it's out of these attributes that a language arises. A language, I repeat, where under what is said, another thing
is being said.

Given characters who possess a momentum of their
own, my job is not to impose upon them, not to subject
them to a false articulation, by which I mean forcing a
character to speak where he could not speak, making him
speak in a way he could not speak, or making him speak
of what he could never speak. The relationship between
author and characters should be a highly respectful one,
both ways. And if it's possible to talk of gaining a kind of
freedom from writing, it doesn't come by leading one's
characters into fixed and calculated postures, but by
allowing them to carry their own can, by giving them a
legitimate elbowroom. This can be extremely painful. It's
much easier, much less pain, not to let them live.

I'd like to make quite clear at the same time that I

don't regard my own characters as uncontrolled, or anarchic. They're not. The function of selection and arrangement is mine. I do all the donkeywork, in fact, and I think I can say I pay meticulous attention to the shape of things, from the shape of a sentence to the overall structure of the play. This shaping, to put it mildly, is of the first importance. But I think a double thing happens. You arrange *and* you listen, following the clues you leave for yourself, through the characters. And sometimes a balance is found, where image can freely engender image and where at the same time you are able to keep your sights on the place where the characters are silent and in hiding. It is in the silence that they are most evident to me.

There are two silences. One when no word is spoken. The other when perhaps a torrent of language is being employed. This speech is speaking of a language locked beneath it. That is its continual reference. The speech we hear is an indication of that which we don't hear. It is a necessary avoidance, a violent, sly, anguished or mocking smoke screen which keeps the other in its place. When true silence falls we are still left with echo but are nearer nakedness. One way of looking at speech is to say that it is a constant stratagem to cover nakedness.

We have heard many times that tired, grimy phrase: 'Failure of communication' . . . and this phrase has been fixed to my work quite consistently. I believe the contrary. I think that we communicate only too well, in our silence, in what is unsaid, and that what takes place is a continual evasion, desperate rearguard attempts to keep ourselves to ourselves. Communication is too alarming. To enter into someone else's life is too frightening. To disclose to others the poverty within us is too fearsome a possibility.

I am not suggesting that no character in a play can ever

say what he in fact means. Not at all. I have found that there invariably does come a moment when this happens, when he says something, perhaps, which he has never said before. And where this happens, what he says is irrevocable, and can never be taken back.

A blank page is both an exciting and a frightening thing. It's what you start from. There follow two further periods in the progress of a play. The rehearsal period and the performance. A dramatist will absorb a great many things of value from an active and intense experience in the theatre, throughout these two periods. But finally he is again left looking at the blank page. In that page is something or nothing. You don't know until you've cornered it. And there's no guarantee that you will know then. But it always remains a chance worth taking.

I've written nine plays, for various mediums, and at the moment I haven't the slightest idea how I've managed to do it. Each play was, for me, 'a different kind of failure'. And that fact, I suppose, sent me on to write the next one.

And if I find writing plays an extremely difficult task, while still understanding it as a kind of celebration, how much more difficult it is to attempt to rationalise the process, and how much more abortive, as I think I've clearly demonstrated to you this morning.

Samuel Beckett says, at the beginning of his novel *The Unnamable*, 'The fact would seem to be, if in my situation one may speak of facts, not only that I shall have to speak of things of which I cannot speak, but also, which is even more interesting, but also that I, which is if possible even more interesting, that I shall have to, I forget, no matter.'

THE BIRTHDAY PARTY

The Birthday Party was first presented by Michael Codron and David Hall at the Arts Theatre, Cambridge, on 28 April 1958, and subsequently at the Lyric Opera House, Hammersmith, with the following cast:

PETEY, *a man in his sixties*		Willoughby Gray
MEG, *a woman in her sixties*		Beatrix Lehmann
STANLEY, *a man in his late thirties*		Richard Pearson
LULU, *a girl in her twenties*		Wendy Hutchinson
GOLDBERG, *a man in his fifties*		John Slater
MCCANN, *a man of thirty*		John Stratton

Directed by Peter Wood

The Birthday Party was revived by the Royal Shakespeare Company at the Aldwych Theatre, London, on 18 June 1964, with the following cast:

PETEY	Newton Blick
MEG	Doris Hare
STANLEY	Bryan Pringle
LULU	Janet Suzman
GOLDBERG	Brewster Mason
MCCANN	Patrick Magee

Directed by Harold Pinter

The Birthday Party was broadcast on BBC Television on 28 June 1987, with the following cast:

PETEY	Robert Lang
MEG	Joan Plowright
STANLEY	Kenneth Cranham
LULU	Julie Walters
GOLDBERG	Harold Pinter
MCCANN	Colin Blakely

Directed by Kenneth Ives

ACT I A morning in summer
ACT II Evening of the same day
ACT III The next morning

Act One

The living-room of a house in a seaside town. A door leading to the hall down left. Back door and small window up left. Kitchen hatch, centre back. Kitchen door up right. Table and chairs, centre.

PETEY enters from the door on the left with a paper and sits at the table. He begins to read. MEG'S voice comes through the kitchen hatch.

MEG. Is that you, Petey?

Pause.

Petey, is that you?

Pause.

Petey?

PETEY. What?

MEG. Is that you?

PETEY. Yes, it's me.

MEG. What? (*Her face appears at the hatch.*) Are you back?

PETEY. Yes.

MEG. I've got your cornflakes ready. (*She disappears and re-appears.*) Here's your cornflakes.

He rises and takes the plate from her, sits at the table, props up the paper and begins to eat. MEG enters by the kitchen door.

Are they nice?

PETEY. Very nice.

MEG. I thought they'd be nice. (*She sits at the table.*) You got your paper?

PETEY. Yes.

MEG. Is it good?

PETEY. Not bad.

MEG. What does it say?

PETEY. Nothing much.

MEG. You read me out some nice bits yesterday.

PETEY. Yes, well, I haven't finished this one yet.

MEG. Will you tell me when you come to something good?

PETEY. Yes.

    Pause.

MEG. Have you been working hard this morning?

PETEY. No. Just stacked a few of the old chairs. Cleaned up a bit.

MEG. Is it nice out?

PETEY. Very nice.

    Pause.

MEG. Is Stanley up yet?

PETEY. I don't know. Is he?

MEG. I don't know. I haven't seen him down yet.

PETEY. Well then, he can't be up.

MEG. Haven't you seen him down?

PETEY. I've only just come in.

MEG. He must be still asleep.

> *She looks round the room, stands, goes to the sideboard and takes a pair of socks from a drawer, collects wool and a needle and goes back to the table.*

What time did you go out this morning, Petey?

PETEY. Same time as usual.

MEG. Was it dark?

PETEY. No, it was light.

MEG (*beginning to darn*). But sometimes you go out in the morning and it's dark.

PETEY. That's in the winter.

MEG. Oh, in winter.

PETEY. Yes, it gets light later in winter.

MEG. Oh.

Pause.

What are you reading?

PETEY. Someone's just had a baby.

MEG. Oh, they haven't! Who?

PETEY. Some girl.

MEG. Who, Petey, who?

PETEY. I don't think you'd know her.

MEG. What's her name?

PETEY. Lady Mary Splatt.

MEG. I don't know her.

PETEY. No.

MEG. What is it?

PETEY (*studying the paper*). Er—a girl.

MEG. Not a boy?

PETEY. No.

MEG. Oh, what a shame. I'd be sorry. I'd much rather have a little boy.

PETEY. A little girl's all right.

MEG. I'd much rather have a little boy.

Pause.

PETEY. I've finished my cornflakes.

MEG. Were they nice?

PETEY. Very nice.

MEG. I've got something else for you.

PETEY. Good.

She rises, takes his plate and exits into the kitchen. She then appears at the hatch with two pieces of fried bread on a plate.

MEG. Here you are, Petey.

He rises, collects the plate, looks at it, sits at the table. MEG *re-enters.*

Is it nice?

PETEY. I haven't tasted it yet.

MEG. I bet you don't know what it is.

PETEY. Yes, I do.

MEG. What is it, then?

PETEY. Fried bread.

MEG. That's right.

> *He begins to eat.*
> *She watches him eat.*

PETEY. Very nice.

MEG. I knew it was.

PETEY (*turning to her*). Oh, Meg, two men came up to me on the beach last night.

MEG. Two men?

PETEY. Yes. They wanted to know if we could put them up for a couple of nights.

MEG. Put them up? Here?

PETEY. Yes.

MEG. How many men?

PETEY. Two.

MEG. What did you say?

PETEY. Well, I said I didn't know. So they said they'd come round to find out.

MEG. Are they coming?

PETEY. Well, they said they would.

MEG. Had they heard about us, Petey?

PETEY. They must have done.

MEG. Yes, they must have done. They must have heard this was a very good boarding house. It is. This house is on the list.

PETEY. It is.

MEG. I know it is.

PETEY. They might turn up today. Can you do it?

MEG. Oh, I've got that lovely room they can have.

PETEY. You've got a room ready?

MEG. I've got the room with the armchair all ready for visitors.

PETEY. You're sure?

MEG. Yes, that'll be all right then, if they come today.

PETEY. Good.

She takes the socks etc. back to the sideboard drawer.

MEG. I'm going to wake that boy.

PETEY. There's a new show coming to the Palace.

MEG. On the pier?

PETEY. No. The Palace, in the town.

MEG. Stanley could have been in it, if it was on the pier.

PETEY. This is a straight show.

MEG. What do you mean?

PETEY. No dancing or singing.

MEG. What do they do then?

PETEY. They just talk.

Pause.

MEG. Oh.

PETEY. You like a song eh, Meg?

MEG. I like listening to the piano. I used to like watching Stanley play the piano. Of course, he didn't sing. (*Looking at the door.*) I'm going to call that boy.

PETEY. Didn't you take him up his cup of tea?

MEG. I always take him up his cup of tea. But that was a long time ago.

PETEY. Did he drink it?

MEG. I made him. I stood there till he did. I'm going to call him. (*She goes to the door.*) Stan! Stanny! (*She listens.*) Stan! I'm coming up to fetch you if you don't come down! I'm coming up! I'm going to count three! One! Two! Three! I'm coming to get you! (*She exits and goes upstairs. In a moment, shouts from* STANLEY, *wild laughter from* MEG. PETEY *takes his plate to the hatch. Shouts. Laughter.*

PETEY *sits at the table. Silence. She returns.*) He's coming down. (*She is panting and arranges her hair.*) I told him if he didn't hurry up he'd get no breakfast.

PETEY. That did it, eh?

MEG. I'll get his cornflakes.

> MEG *exits to the kitchen.* PETEY *reads the paper.* STANLEY *enters. He is unshaven, in his pyjama jacket and wears glasses. He sits at the table.*

PETEY. Morning, Stanley.

STANLEY. Morning.

> *Silence.* MEG *enters with the bowl of cornflakes, which she sets on the table.*

MEG. So he's come down at last, has he? He's come down at last for his breakfast. But he doesn't deserve any, does he, Petey? (STANLEY *stares at the cornflakes.*) Did you sleep well?

STANLEY. I didn't sleep at all.

MEG. You didn't sleep at all? Did you hear that, Petey? Too tired to eat your breakfast, I suppose? Now you eat up those cornflakes like a good boy. Go on.

> *He begins to eat.*

STANLEY. What's it like out today?

PETEY. Very nice.

STANLEY. Warm?

PETEY. Well, there's a good breeze blowing.

STANLEY. Cold?

PETEY. No, no, I wouldn't say it was cold.

MEG. What are the cornflakes like, Stan?

STANLEY. Horrible.

MEG. Those flakes? Those lovely flakes? You're a liar, a little liar. They're refreshing. It says so. For people when they get up late.

STANLEY. The milk's off.

MEG. It's not. Petey ate his, didn't you, Petey?

PETEY. That's right.

MEG. There you are then.

STANLEY. All right, I'll go on to the second course.

MEG. He hasn't finished the first course and he wants to go on to the second course!

STANLEY. I feel like something cooked.

MEG. Well, I'm not going to give it to you.

PETEY. Give it to him.

MEG (*sitting at the table, right*). I'm not going to.

Pause.

STANLEY. No breakfast.

Pause.

All night long I've been dreaming about this breakfast.

MEG. I thought you said you didn't sleep.

STANLEY. Day-dreaming. All night long. And now she won't give me any. Not even a crust of bread on the table.

Pause.

Well, I can see I'll have to go down to one of those smart hotels on the front.

MEG (*rising quickly*). You won't get a better breakfast there than here.

She exits to the kitchen. STANLEY *yawns broadly.* MEG *appears at the hatch with a plate.*

Here you are. You'll like this.

PETEY rises, collects the plate, brings it to the table, puts it in front of STANLEY, *and sits.*

STANLEY. What's this?

PETEY. Fried bread.

MEG (*entering*). Well, I bet you don't know what it is.

STANLEY. Oh yes I do.

MEG. What?

STANLEY. Fried bread.

MEG. He knew.

STANLEY. What a wonderful surprise.

MEG. You didn't expect that, did you?

STANLEY. I bloody well didn't.

PETEY (*rising*). Well, I'm off.

MEG. You going back to work?

PETEY. Yes.

MEG. Your tea! You haven't had your tea!

PETEY. That's all right. No time now.

MEG. I've got it made inside.

PETEY. No, never mind. See you later. Ta-ta, Stan.

STANLEY. Ta-ta.

> PETEY *exits, left.*

Tch, tch, tch, tch.

MEG (*defensively*). What do you mean?

STANLEY. You're a bad wife.

MEG. I'm not. Who said I am?

STANLEY. Not to make your husband a cup of tea. Terrible.

MEG. He knows I'm not a bad wife.

STANLEY. Giving him sour milk instead.

MEG. It wasn't sour.

STANLEY. Disgraceful.

MEG. You mind your own business, anyway. (STANLEY *eats.*) You won't find many better wives than me, I can tell you. I keep a very nice house and I keep it clean.

STANLEY. Whoo!

MEG. Yes! And this house is very well known, for a very good boarding house for visitors.

STANLEY. Visitors? Do you know how many visitors you've had since I've been here?

MEG. How many?

STANLEY. One.

MEG. Who?

STANLEY. Me! I'm your visitor.

MEG. You're a liar. This house is on the list.

STANLEY. I bet it is.

MEG. I know it is.

He pushes his plate away and picks up the paper.

Was it nice?

STANLEY. What?

MEG. The fried bread.

STANLEY. Succulent.

MEG. You shouldn't say that word.

STANLEY. What word?

MEG. That word you said.

STANLEY. What, succulent—?

MEG. Don't say it!

STANLEY. What's the matter with it?

MEG. You shouldn't say that word to a married woman.

STANLEY. Is that a fact?

MEG. Yes.

STANLEY. Well, I never knew that.

MEG. Well, it's true.

STANLEY. Who told you that?

MEG. Never you mind.

STANLEY. Well, if I can't say it to a married woman who can I say it to?

MEG. You're bad.

STANLEY. What about some tea?

MEG. Do you want some tea? (STANLEY *reads the paper*.) Say please.

STANLEY. Please.

MEG. Say sorry first.

STANLEY. Sorry first.

MEG. No. Just sorry.

STANLEY. Just sorry!

MEG. You deserve the strap.

STANLEY. Don't do that!

> *She takes his plate and ruffles his hair as she passes.*
> STANLEY *exclaims and throws her arm away. She goes into*
> *the kitchen. He rubs his eyes under his glasses and picks up*
> *the paper. She enters.*

I brought the pot in.

STANLEY (*absently*). I don't know what I'd do without you.

MEG. You don't deserve it though.

STANLEY. Why not?

MEG (*pouring the tea, coyly*). Go on. Calling me that.

STANLEY. How long has that tea been in the pot?

MEG. It's good tea. Good strong tea.

STANLEY. This isn't tea. It's gravy!

MEG. It's not.

STANLEY. Get out of it. You succulent old washing bag.

MEG. I am not! And it isn't your place to tell me if I am!

STANLEY. And it isn't your place to come into a man's bed-room and—wake him up.

MEG. Stanny! Don't you like your cup of tea of a morning—the one I bring you?

STANLEY. I can't drink this muck. Didn't anyone ever tell you to warm the pot, at least?

MEG. That's good strong tea, that's all.

STANLEY (*putting his head in his hands*). Oh God, I'm tired.

> *Silence.* MEG *goes to the sideboard, collects a duster, and*
> *vaguely dusts the room, watching him. She comes to the*
> *table and dusts it.*

Not the bloody table!

> *Pause.*

MEG. Stan?

STANLEY. What?

MEG (*shyly*). Am I really succulent?

STANLEY. Oh, you are. I'd rather have you than a cold in the nose any day.

MEG. You're just saying that.

STANLEY (*violently*). Look, why don't you get this place cleared up! It's a pigsty. And another thing, what about my room? It needs sweeping. It needs papering. I need a new room!

MEG (*sensual, stroking his arm*). Oh, Stan, that's a lovely room. I've had some lovely afternoons in that room.

> *He recoils from her hand in disgust, stands and exits quickly by the door on the left. She collects his cup and the teapot and takes them to the hatch shelf. The street door slams.* STANLEY *returns.*

MEG. Is the sun shining? (*He crosses to the window, takes a cigarette and matches from his pyjama jacket, and lights his cigarette.*) What are you smoking?

STANLEY. A cigarette.

MEG. Are you going to give me one?

STANLEY. No.

MEG. I like cigarettes. (*He stands at the window, smoking. She crosses behind him and tickles the back of his neck.*) Tickle, tickle.

STANLEY (*pushing her*). Get away from me.

MEG. Are you going out?

STANLEY. Not with you.

MEG. But I'm going shopping in a minute.

STANLEY. Go.

MEG. You'll be lonely, all by yourself.

STANLEY. Will I?

MEG. Without your old Meg. I've got to get things in for the two gentlemen.

A pause. STANLEY *slowly raises his head. He speaks without turning.*

STANLEY. What two gentlemen?

MEG. I'm expecting visitors.

He turns.

STANLEY. What?

MEG. You didn't know that, did you?

STANLEY. What are you talking about?

MEG. Two gentlemen asked Petey if they could come and stay for a couple of nights. I'm expecting them. (*She picks up the duster and begins to wipe the cloth on the table.*)

STANLEY. I don't believe it.

MEG. It's true.

STANLEY (*moving to her*). You're saying it on purpose.

MEG. Petey told me this morning.

STANLEY (*grinding his cigarette*). When was this? When did he see them?

MEG. Last night.

STANLEY. Who are they?

MEG. I don't know.

STANLEY. Didn't he tell you their names?

MEG. No.

STANLEY (*pacing the room*). Here? They wanted to come here?

MEG. Yes, they did. (*She takes the curlers out of her hair.*)

STANLEY. Why?

MEG. This house is on the list.

STANLEY. But who are they?

MEG. You'll see when they come.

STANLEY (*decisively*). They won't come.

MEG. Why not?

STANLEY (*quickly*). I tell you they won't come. Why didn't they come last night, if they were coming?

MEG. Perhaps they couldn't find the place in the dark. It's not easy to find in the dark.

STANLEY. They won't come. Someone's taking the Michael. Forget all about it. It's a false alarm. A false alarm. (*He sits at the table.*) Where's my tea?

MEG. I took it away. You didn't want it.

STANLEY. What do you mean, you took it away?

MEG. I took it away.

STANLEY. What did you take it away for?

MEG. You didn't want it!

STANLEY. Who said I didn't want it?

MEG. You did!

STANLEY. Who gave you the right to take away my tea?

MEG. You wouldn't drink it.

> STANLEY *stares at her.*

STANLEY (*quietly*). Who do you think you're talking to?

MEG (*uncertainly*). What?

STANLEY. Come here.

MEG. What do you mean?

STANLEY. Come over here.

MEG. No.

STANLEY. I want to ask you something. (MEG *fidgets nervously. She does not go to him.*) Come on. (*Pause.*) All right. I can ask it from here just as well. (*Deliberately.*) Tell me, Mrs Boles, when you address yourself to me, do you ever ask yourself who exactly you are talking to? Eh?

> Silence. He groans, his trunk falls forward, his head falls into his hands.

MEG (*in a small voice*). Didn't you enjoy your breakfast, Stan? (*She approaches the table.*) Stan? When are you going to play the piano again? (STANLEY *grunts.*) Like you used to? (STANLEY *grunts.*) I used to like watching you play the piano. When are you going to play it again?

STANLEY. I can't, can I?

MEG. Why not?

STANLEY. I haven't got a piano, have I?

MEG. No, I meant like when you were working. That piano.

STANLEY. Go and do your shopping.

MEG. But you wouldn't have to go away if you got a job, would you? You could play the piano on the pier.

He looks at her, then speaks airily.

STANLEY. I've ... er ... I've been offered a job, as a matter of fact.

MEG. What?

STANLEY. Yes. I'm considering a job at the moment.

MEG. You're not.

STANLEY. A good one, too. A night club. In Berlin.

MEG. Berlin?

STANLEY. Berlin. A night club. Playing the piano. A fabulous salary. And all found.

MEG. How long for?

STANLEY. We don't stay in Berlin. Then we go to Athens.

MEG. How long for?

STANLEY. Yes. Then we pay a flying visit to ... er ... whatsisname. ...

MEG. Where?

STANLEY. Constantinople. Zagreb. Vladivostock. It's a round the world tour.

MEG (*sitting at the table*). Have you played the piano in those places before?

STANLEY. Played the piano? I've played the piano all over the world. All over the country. (*Pause.*) I once gave a concert.

MEG. A concert?

STANLEY (*reflectively*). Yes. It was a good one, too. They were all there that night. Every single one of them. It was a great success. Yes. A concert. At Lower Edmonton.

MEG. What did you wear?

STANLEY (*to himself*). I had a unique touch. Absolutely unique. They came up to me. They came up to me and said they were grateful. Champagne we had that night, the lot. (*Pause.*) My father nearly came down to hear me. Well, I dropped him a card anyway. But I don't think he could make it. No, I—I lost the address, that was it. (*Pause.*) Yes. Lower Edmonton. Then after that, you know what they did? They carved me up. Carved me up. It was all arranged, it was all worked out. My next concert. Somewhere else it was. In winter. I went down there to play. Then, when I got there, the hall was closed, the place was shuttered up, not even a caretaker. They'd locked it up. (*Takes off his glasses and wipes them on his pyjama jacket.*) A fast one. They pulled a fast one. I'd like to know who was responsible for that. (*Bitterly.*) All right, Jack, I can take a tip. They want me to crawl down on my bended knees. Well I can take a tip . . . any day of the week. (*He replaces his glasses, then looks at* MEG.) Look at her. You're just an old piece of rock cake, aren't you? (*He rises and leans across the table to her.*) That's what you are, aren't you?

MEG. Don't you go away again, Stan. You stay here. You'll be better off. You stay with your old Meg. (*He groans and lies across the table.*) Aren't you feeling well this morning, Stan. Did you pay a visit this morning?

> *He stiffens, then lifts himself slowly, turns to face her and speaks lightly, casually.*

STANLEY. Meg. Do you know what?

MEG. What?

STANLEY. Have you heard the latest?

MEG. No.

STANLEY. I'll bet you have.

MEG. I haven't.

STANLEY. Shall I tell you?

MEG. What latest?

STANLEY. You haven't heard it?

MEG. No.

STANLEY (*advancing*). They're coming today. They're coming in a van.

MEG. Who?

STANLEY. And do you know what they've got in that van?

MEG. What?

STANLEY. They've got a wheelbarrow in that van.

MEG (*breathlessly*). They haven't.

STANLEY. Oh yes they have.

MEG. You're a liar.

STANLEY (*advancing upon her*). A big wheelbarrow. And when the van stops they wheel it out, and they wheel it up the garden path, and then they knock at the front door.

MEG. They don't.

STANLEY. They're looking for someone.

MEG. They're not.

STANLEY. They're looking for someone. A certain person.

MEG (*hoarsely*). No, they're not!

STANLEY. Shall I tell you who they're looking for?

MEG. No!

STANLEY. You don't want me to tell you?

MEG. You're a liar!

A sudden knock on the front door. LULU'S *voice: Ooh-ooh!* MEG *edges past* STANLEY *and collects her shopping bag.* MEG *goes out.* STANLEY *sidles to the door and listens.*

VOICE (*through letter box*). Hullo, Mrs Boles . . .

MEG. Oh, has it come?

VOICE. Yes, it's just come.

MEG. What, is that it?

VOICE. Yes. I thought I'd bring it round.

MEG. Is it nice?

VOICE. Very nice. What shall I do with it?

MEG. Well, I don't . . . (*Whispers.*)

VOICE. No, of course not . . .(*Whispers.*)

MEG. All right, but . . . (*Whispers.*)

VOICE. I won't . . . (*Whispers.*) Ta-ta, Mrs Boles.

STANLEY *quickly sits at the table. Enter* LULU.

LULU. Oh, hullo.

STANLEY. Ay-ay.

LULU. I just want to leave this in here.

STANLEY. Do. (LULU *crosses to the sideboard and puts a solid, round parcel upon it.*) That's a bulky object.

LULU. You're not to touch it.

STANLEY. Why would I want to touch it?

LULU. Well, you're not to, anyway.

LULU *walks upstage.*

LULU. Why don't you open the door? It's all stuffy in here.

She opens the back door.

STANLEY (*rising*): Stuffy? I disinfected the place this morning.

LULU (*at the door*). Oh, that's better.

STANLEY. I think it's going to rain to-day. What do you think?

LULU. I hope so. You could do with it.

STANLEY. Me! I was in the sea at half past six.

LULU. Were you?

STANLEY. I went right out to the headland and back before breakfast. Don't you believe me!

She sits, takes out a compact and powders her nose.

LULU (*offering him the compact*). Do you want to have a look at your face? (STANLEY *withdraws from the table.*) You could do with a shave, do you know that? (STANLEY *sits, right at the table.*) Don't you ever go out? (*He does not answer.*) I mean, what do you do, just sit around the house like this all day long? (*Pause.*) Hasn't Mrs Boles got enough to do without having you under her feet all day long?

STANLEY. I always stand on the table when she sweeps the
   floor.

LULU. Why don't you have a wash? You look terrible.

STANLEY. A wash wouldn't make any difference.

LULU (*rising*). Come out and get a bit of air. You depress me,
   looking like that.

STANLEY. Air? Oh, I don't know about that.

LULU. It's lovely out. And I've got a few sandwiches.

STANLEY. What sort of sandwiches?

LULU. Cheese.

STANLEY. I'm a big eater, you know.

LULU. That's all right. I'm not hungry.

STANLEY (*abruptly*). How would you like to go away with
   me?

LULU. Where.

STANLEY. Nowhere. Still, we could go.

LULU. But where could we go?

STANLEY. Nowhere. There's nowhere to go. So we could just
   go. It wouldn't matter.

LULU. We might as well stay here.

STANLEY. No. It's no good here.

LULU. Well, where else is there?

STANLEY. Nowhere.

LULU. Well, that's a charming proposal. (*He gets up.*) Do you
   have to wear those glasses?

STANLEY. Yes.

LULU. So you're not coming out for a walk?

STANLEY. I can't at the moment.

LULU. You're a bit of a washout, aren't you?

> She exits, left. STANLEY *stands. He then goes to the mirror
> and looks in it. He goes into the kitchen, takes off his glasses
> and begins to wash his face. A pause. Enter, by the back door,*
> GOLDBERG *and* MCCANN. MCCANN *carries two suitcases,*
> GOLDBERG *a briefcase. They halt inside the door, then*

walk downstage. STANLEY, *wiping his face, glimpses their backs through the hatch.* GOLDBERG *and* MCCANN *look round the room.* STANLEY *slips on his glasses, sidles through the kitchen door and out of the back door.*

MCCANN. Is this it?

GOLDBERG. This is it.

MCCANN. Are you sure?

GOLDBERG. Sure I'm sure.

   Pause.

MCCANN. What now?

GOLDBERG. Don't worry yourself, McCann. Take a seat.

MCCANN. What about you?

GOLDBERG. What about me?

MCCANN. Are you going to take a seat?

GOLDBERG. We'll both take a seat. (MCCANN *puts down the suitcase and sits at the table, left.*) Sit back, McCann. Relax. What's the matter with you? I bring you down for a few days to the seaside. Take a holiday. Do yourself a favour. Learn to relax, McCann, or you'll never get anywhere.

MCCANN. Ah sure, I do try, Nat.

GOLDBERG (*sitting at the table, right*). The secret is breathing. Take my tip. It's a well-known fact. Breathe in, breathe out, take a chance, let yourself go, what can you lose? Look at me. When I was an apprentice yet, McCann, every second Friday of the month my Uncle Barney used to take me to the seaside, regular as clockwork. Brighton, Canvey Island, Rottingdean—Uncle Barney wasn't particular. After lunch on Shabbuss we'd go and sit in a couple of deck chairs—you know, the ones with canopies—we'd have a little paddle, we'd watch the tide coming in, going out, the sun coming down—golden days, believe me, McCann. (*Reminiscent.*) Uncle Barney. Of course, he was an impeccable dresser. One of the old school. He had a house just outside Basingstoke at the time. Respected by the whole community.

Culture? Don't talk to me about culture. He was an all-round man, what do you mean? He was a cosmopolitan.

MCCANN. Hey, Nat. . . .

GOLDBERG (*reflectively*). Yes. One of the old school.

MCCANN. Nat. How do we know this is the right house?

GOLDBERG. What?

MCCANN. How do we know this is the right house?

GOLDBERG. What makes you think it's the wrong house?

MCCANN. I didn't see a number on the gate.

GOLDBERG. I wasn't looking for a number.

MCCANN. No?

GOLDBERG (*settling in the armchair*). You know one thing Uncle Barney taught me? Uncle Barney taught me that the word of a gentleman is enough. That's why, when I had to go away on business I never carried any money. One of my sons used to come with me. He used to carry a few coppers. For a paper, perhaps, to see how the M.C.C. was getting on overseas. Otherwise my name was good. Besides, I was a very busy man.

MCCANN. What about this, Nat? Isn't it about time someone came in?

GOLDBERG. McCann, what are you so nervous about? Pull yourself together. Everywhere you go these days it's like a funeral.

MCCANN. That's true.

GOLDBERG. True? Of course it's true. It's more than true. It's a fact.

MCCANN. You may be right.

GOLDBERG. What is it, McCann? You don't trust me like you did in the old days?

MCCANN. Sure I trust you, Nat.

GOLDBERG. But why is it that before you do a job you're all over the place, and when you're doing the job you're as cool as a whistle?

MCCANN. I don't know, Nat. I'm just all right once I know what I'm doing. When I know what I'm doing, I'm all right.

GOLDBERG. Well, you do it very well.

MCCANN. Thank you, Nat.

GOLDBERG. You know what I said when this job came up. I mean naturally they approached me to take care of it. And you know who I asked for?

MCCANN. Who?

GOLDBERG. You.

MCCANN. That was very good of you, Nat.

GOLDBERG. No, it was nothing. You're a capable man, McCann.

MCCANN. That's a great compliment, Nat, coming from a man in your position.

GOLDBERG. Well, I've got a position, I won't deny it.

MCCANN. You certainly have.

GOLDBERG. I would never deny that I had a position.

MCCANN. And what a position!

GOLDBERG. It's not a thing I would deny.

MCCANN. Yes, it's true, you've done a lot for me. I appreciate it.

GOLDBERG. Say no more.

MCCANN. You've always been a true Christian.

GOLDBERG. In a way.

MCCANN. No, I just thought I'd tell you that I appreciate it.

GOLDBERG. It's unnecessary to recapitulate.

MCCANN. You're right there.

GOLDBERG. Quite unnecessary.

Pause. MCCANN *leans forward.*

MCCANN. Hey Nat, just one thing. . . .

GOLDBERG. What now?

MCCANN. This job—no, listen—this job, is it going to be like anything we've ever done before?

GOLDBERG. Tch, tch, tch.

MCCANN. No, just tell me that. Just that, and I won't ask any more.

> GOLDBERG *sighs, stands, goes behind the table, ponders, looks at* MCCANN, *and then speaks in a quiet, fluent, official tone.*

GOLDBERG. The main issue is a singular issue and quite distinct from your previous work. Certain elements, however, might well approximate in points of procedure to some of your other activities. All is dependent on the attitude of our subject. At all events, McCann, I can assure you that the assignment will be carried out and the mission accomplished with no excessive aggravation to you or myself. Satisfied?

MCCANN. Sure. Thank you, Nat.

> MEG *enters, left.*

GOLDBERG. Ah, Mrs Boles?

MEG. Yes?

GOLDBERG. We spoke to your husband last night. Perhaps he mentioned us? We heard that you kindly let rooms for gentlemen. So I brought my friend along with me. We were after a nice place, you understand. So we came to you. I'm Mr Goldberg and this is Mr McCann.

MEG. Very pleased to meet you.

> *They shake hands.*

GOLDBERG. We're pleased to meet you, too.

MEG. That's very nice.

GOLDBERG. You're right. How often do you meet someone it's a pleasure to meet?

MCCANN. Never.

GOLDBERG. But today it's different. How are you keeping, Mrs Boles?

MEG. Oh, very well, thank you.

GOLDBERG. Yes? Really?

MEG. Oh yes, really.

GOLDBERG. I'm glad.

GOLDBERG *sits at the table, right.*

GOLDBERG. Well, so what do you say? You can manage to put us up, eh, Mrs Boles?

MEG. Well, it would have been easier last week.

GOLDBERG. It would, eh?

MEG. Yes.

GOLDBERG. Why? How many have you got here at the moment?

MEG. Just one at the moment.

GOLDBERG. Just one?

MEG. Yes. Just one. Until you came.

GOLDBERG. And your husband, of course?

MEG. Yes, but he sleeps with me.

GOLDBERG. What does he do, your husband?

MEG. He's a deck-chair attendant.

GOLDBERG. Oh, very nice.

MEG. Yes, he's out in all weathers.

She begins to take her purchases from her bag.

GOLDBERG. Of course. And your guest? Is he a man?

MEG. A man?

GOLDBERG. Or a woman?

MEG. No. A man.

GOLDBERG. Been here long?

MEG. He's been here about a year now.

GOLDBERG. Oh yes. A resident. What's his name?

MEG. Stanley Webber.

GOLDBERG. Oh yes? Does he work here?

MEG. He used to work. He used to be a pianist. In a concert party on the pier.

GOLDBERG. Oh yes? On the pier, eh? Does he play a nice piano?

MEG. Oh, lovely. (*She sits at the table.*) He once gave a concert.

GOLDBERG. Oh? Where?

MEG (*falteringly*). In . . . a big hall. His father gave him champagne. But then they locked the place up and he couldn't get out. The caretaker had gone home. So he had to wait until the morning before he could get out. (*With confidence.*) They were very grateful. (*Pause.*) And then they all wanted to give him a tip. And so he took the tip. And then he got a fast train and he came down here.

GOLDBERG. Really?

MEG. Oh yes. Straight down.

Pause.

MEG. I wish he could have played tonight.

GOLDBERG. Why tonight?

MEG. It's his birthday today.

GOLDBERG. His birthday?

MEG. Yes. Today. But I'm not going to tell him until tonight.

GOLDBERG. Doesn't he know it's his birthday?

MEG. He hasn't mentioned it.

GOLDBERG (*thoughtfully*). Ah! Tell me. Are you going to have a party?

MEG. A party?

GOLDBERG. Weren't you going to have one?

MEG (*her eyes wide*). No.

GOLDBERG. Well, of course, you must have one. (*He stands.*) We'll have a party, eh? What do you say?

MEG. Oh yes!

GOLDBERG. Sure. We'll give him a party. Leave it to me.

MEG. Oh, that's wonderful, Mr Gold—

GOLDBERG. Berg.

MEG. Berg.

GOLDBERG. You like the idea?

MEG. Oh, I'm so glad you came today.

GOLDBERG. If we hadn't come today we'd have come to-morrow. Still, I'm glad we came today. Just in time for his birthday.

MEG. I wanted to have a party But you must have people for a party.

GOLDBERG. And now you've got McCann and me. McCann's the life and soul of any party.

MCCANN. What?

GOLDBERG. What do you think of that, McCann? There's a gentleman living here. He's got a birthday today, and he's forgotten all about it. So we're going to remind him. We're going to give him a party.

MCCANN. Oh, is that a fact?

MEG. Tonight.

GOLDBERG. Tonight.

MEG. I'll put on my party dress.

GOLDBERG. And I'll get some bottles.

MEG. And I'll invite Lulu this afternoon. Oh, this is going to cheer Stanley up. It will. He's been down in the dumps lately.

GOLDBERG. We'll bring him out of himself.

MEG. I hope I look nice in my dress.

GOLDBERG. Madam, you'll look like a tulip.

MEG. What colour?

GOLDBERG. Er—well, I'll have to see the dress first.

MCCANN. Could I go up to my room?

MEG. Oh, I've put you both together. Do you mind being both together?

GOLDBERG. I don't mind. Do you mind, McCann?

MCCANN. No.

MEG. What time shall we have the party?

GOLDBERG. Nine o'clock.

MCCANN (*at the door*). Is this the way?

MEG (*rising*). I'll show you. If you don't mind coming upstairs.

GOLDBERG. With a tulip? It's a pleasure.

MEG *and* GOLDBERG *exit laughing, followed by* MCCANN. STANLEY *appears at the window. He enters by the back door. He goes to the door on the left, opens it and listens. Silence, He walks to the table. He stands. He sits, as* MEG *enters. She crosses and hangs her shopping bag on a hook. He lights a match and watches it burn.*

STANLEY. Who is it?

MEG. The two gentlemen.

STANLEY. What two gentlemen?

MEG. The ones that were coming. I just took them to their room. They were thrilled with their room.

STANLEY. They've come?

MEG. They're very nice, Stan.

STANLEY. Why didn't they come last night?

MEG. They said the beds were wonderful.

STANLEY. Who are they?

MEG (*sitting*). They're very nice, Stanley.

STANLEY. I said, who are they?

MEG. I've told you, the two gentlemen.

STANLEY. I didn't think they'd come.

He rises and walks to the window.

MEG. They have. They were here when I came in.

STANLEY. What do they want here?

MEG. They want to stay.

STANLEY. How long for?

MEG. They didn't say.

STANLEY (*turning*). But why here? Why not somewhere else?

MEG. This house is on the list.

STANLEY (*coming down*). What are they called? What are their names?

MEG. Oh, Stanley, I can't remember.

STANLEY. They told you, didn't they? Or didn't they tell you?

MEG. Yes, they. . . .

STANLEY. Then what are they? Come on. Try to remember.

MEG. Why, Stan? Do you know them?

STANLEY. How do I know if I know them until I know their names?

MEG. Well . . . he told me, I remember.

STANLEY. Well?

She thinks.

MEG. Gold—something.

STANLEY. Goldsomething?

MEG. Yes. Gold. . . .

STANLEY. Yes?

MEG. Goldberg.

STANLEY. Goldberg?

MEG. That's right. That was one of them.

STANLEY *slowly sits at the table, left.*

Do you know them?

STANLEY *does not answer.*

Stan, they won't wake you up, I promise. I'll tell them they must be quiet.

STANLEY *sits still.*

They won't be here long, Stan. I'll still bring you up your early morning tea.

STANLEY *sits still.*

You mustn't be sad today. It's your birthday.

A pause.

STANLEY (*dumbly*). Uh?

MEG. It's your birthday, Stan. I was going to keep it a secret until tonight.

STANLEY. No.

MEG. It is. I've brought you a present. (*She goes to the sideboard, picks up the parcel, and places it on the table in front of him.*) Here. Go on. Open it.

STANLEY. What's this?

MEG. It's your present.

STANLEY. This isn't my birthday, Meg.

MEG. Of course it is. Open your present.

He stares at the parcel, slowly stands, and opens it. He takes out a boy's drum.

STANLEY (*flatly*). It's a drum. A boy's drum.

MEG (*tenderly*). It's because you haven't got a piano. (*He stares at her, then turns and walks towards the door, left.*) Aren't you going to give me a kiss? (*He turns sharply, and stops. He walks back towards her slowly. He stops at her chair, looking down upon her. Pause. His shoulders sag, he bends and kisses her on the cheek.*) There are some sticks in there. (STANLEY *looks into the parcel. He takes out two drumsticks. He taps them together. He looks at her.*)

STANLEY. Shall I put it round my neck?

She watches him, uncertainly. He hangs the drum around his neck, taps it gently with the sticks, then marches round the table, beating it regularly. MEG, *pleased, watches him. Still beating it regularly, he begins to go round the table a second time. Halfway round the beat becomes erratic, uncontrolled.* MEG *expresses dismay. He arrives at her chair, banging the drum, his face and the drumbeat now savage and possessed.*

Curtain

Act Two

MCCANN *is sitting at the table tearing a sheet of newspaper into five equal strips. It is evening. After a few moments* STANLEY *enters from the left. He stops upon seeing* MCCANN, *and watches him. He then walks towards the kitchen, stops, and speaks.*

STANLEY. Evening.
MCCANN. Evening.

> *Chuckles are heard from outside the back door, which is open.*

STANLEY. Very warm tonight. (*He turns towards the back door, and back.*) Someone out there?

> MCCANN *tears another length of paper.* STANLEY *goes into the kitchen and pours a glass of water. He drinks it looking through the hatch. He puts the glass down, comes out of the kitchen and walks quickly towards the door, left.* MCCANN *rises and intercepts him.*

MCCANN. I don't think we've met.
STANLEY. No, we haven't.
MCCANN. My name's McCann.
STANLEY. Staying here long?
MCCANN. Not long. What's your name?
STANLEY. Webber.
MCCANN. I'm glad to meet you, sir. (*He offers his hand.* STANLEY *takes it, and* MCCANN *holds the grip.*) Many happy returns of the day. (STANLEY *withdraws his hand. They face each other.*) Were you going out?
STANLEY. Yes.
MCCANN. On your birthday?
STANLEY. Yes. Why not?

MCCANN. But they're holding a party here for you tonight.
STANLEY. Oh really? That's unfortunate.
MCCANN. Ah no. It's very nice.

Voices from outside the back door.

STANLEY. I'm sorry. I'm not in the mood for a party tonight.
MCCANN. Oh, is that so? I'm sorry.
STANLEY. Yes, I'm going out to celebrate quietly, on my own.
MCCANN. That's a shame.

They stand.

STANLEY. Well, if you'd move out of my way—
MCCANN. But everything's laid on. The guests are expected.
STANLEY. Guests? What guests?
MCCANN. Myself for one. I had the honour of an invitation.

MCCANN *begins to whistle "The Mountains of Morne".*

STANLEY (*moving away*). I wouldn't call it an honour, would
you? It'll just be another booze-up.

STANLEY *joins* MCCANN *in whistling "The Mountains of
Morne". During the next five lines the whistling is continuous,
one whistling while the other speaks, and both whistling
together.*

MCCANN. But it is an honour.
STANLEY. I'd say you were exaggerating.
MCCANN. Oh no. I'd say it was an honour.
STANLEY. I'd say that was plain stupid.
MCCANN. Ah no.

They stare at each other.

STANLEY. Who are the other guests?
MCCANN. A young lady.
STANLEY. Oh yes? And. . . .?
MCCANN. My friend.
STANLEY. Your friend?

MCCANN. That's right. It's all laid on.

STANLEY *walks round the table towards the door.* MCCANN *meets him.*

STANLEY. Excuse me.

MCCANN. Where are you going?

STANLEY. I want to go out.

MCCANN. Why don't you stay here?

STANLEY *moves away, to the right of the table.*

STANLEY. So you're down here on holiday?

MCCANN. A short one. (STANLEY *picks up a strip of paper.* MCCANN *moves in.*) Mind that.

STANLEY. What is it?

MCCANN. Mind it. Leave it.

STANLEY. I've got a feeling we've met before.

MCCANN. No we haven't.

STANLEY. Ever been anywhere near Maidenhead?

MCCANN. No.

STANLEY. There's a Fuller's teashop. I used to have my tea there.

MCCANN. I don't know it.

STANLEY. And a Boots Library. I seem to connect you with the High Street.

MCCANN. Yes?

STANLEY. A charming town, don't you think?

MCCANN. I don't know it.

STANLEY. Oh no. A quiet, thriving community. I was born and brought up there. I lived well away from the main road.

MCCANN. Yes?

Pause.

STANLEY. You're here on a short stay?

MCCANN. That's right.

STANLEY. You'll find it very bracing.

MCCANN. Do you find it bracing?

STANLEY. Me? No. But you will. (*He sits at the table.*) I like it here, but I'll be moving soon. Back home. I'll stay there too, this time. No place like home. (*He laughs.*) I wouldn't have left, but business calls. Business called, and I had to leave for a bit. You know how it is.

MCCANN (*sitting at the table, left*). You in business?

STANLEY. No. I think I'll give it up. I've got a small private income, you see. I think I'll give it up. Don't like being away from home. I used to live very quietly—played records, that's about all. Everything delivered to the door. Then I started a little private business, in a small way, and it compelled me to come down here—kept me longer than I expected. You never get used to living in someone else's house. Don't you agree? I lived so quietly. You can only appreciate what you've had when things change. That's what they say, isn't it? Cigarette?

MCCANN. I don't smoke.

STANLEY *lights a cigarette. Voices from the back.*

STANLEY. Who's out there?

MCCANN. My friend and the man of the house.

STANLEY. You know what? To look at me, I bet you wouldn't think I'd led such a quiet life. The lines on my face, eh? It's the drink. Been drinking a bit down here. But what I mean is . . . you know how it is . . . away from your own . . . all wrong, of course . . . I'll be all right when I get back . . . but what I mean is, the way some people look at me you'd think I was a different person. I suppose I have changed, but I'm still the same man that I always was. I mean, you wouldn't think, to look at me, really . . . I mean, not really, that I was the sort of bloke to—to cause any trouble, would you? (MCCANN *looks at him.*) Do you know what I mean?

MCCANN. No. (*As STANLEY picks up a strip of paper.*) Mind that.

STANLEY (*quickly*). Why are you down here?

MCCANN. A short holiday.

STANLEY. This is a ridiculous house to pick on. (*He rises.*)

MCCANN. Why?

STANLEY. Because it's not a boarding house. It never was.

MCCANN. Sure it is.

STANLEY. Why did you choose this house?

MCCANN. You know, sir, you're a bit depressed for a man on his birthday.

STANLEY (*sharply*). Why do you call me sir?

MCCANN. You don't like it?

STANLEY (*to the table.*) Listen. Don't call me sir.

MCCANN. I won't, if you don't like it.

STANLEY (*moving away*). No. Anyway, this isn't my birthday.

MCCANN. No?

STANLEY. No. It's not till next month.

MCCANN. Not according to the lady.

STANLEY. Her? She's crazy. Round the bend.

MCCANN. That's a terrible thing to say.

STANLEY (*to the table*). Haven't you found that out yet? There's a lot you don't know. I think someone's leading you up the garden path.

MCCANN. Who would do that?

STANLEY (*leaning across the table*). That woman is mad!

MCCANN. That's slander.

STANLEY. And you don't know what you're doing.

MCCANN. Your cigarette is near that paper.

Voices from the back.

STANLEY. Where the hell are they? (*Stubbing his cigarette.*) Why don't they come in? What are they doing out there?

MCCANN. You want to steady yourself.

STANLEY *crosses to him and grips his arm.*

STANLEY (*urgently*). Look—

MCCANN. Don't touch me.

STANLEY. Look. Listen a minute.

MCCANN. Let go my arm.

STANLEY. Look. Sit down a minute.

MCCANN (*savagely, hitting his arm*). Don't do that!

STANLEY *backs across the stage, holding his arm.*

STANLEY. Listen. You knew what I was talking about before, didn't you?

MCCANN. I don't know what you're at at all.

STANLEY. It's a mistake! Do you understand?

MCCANN. You're in a bad state, man.

STANLEY (*whispering, advancing*). Has he told you anything? Do you know what you're here for? Tell me. You needn't be frightened of me. Or hasn't he told you?

MCCANN. Told me what?

STANLEY (*hissing*). I've explained to you, damn you, that all those years I lived in Basingstoke I never stepped outside the door.

MCCANN. You know, I'm flabbergasted with you.

STANLEY (*reasonably*). Look. You look an honest man. You're being made a fool of, that's all. You understand? Where do you come from?

MCCANN. Where do you think?

STANLEY. I know Ireland very well. I've many friends there. I love that country and I admire and trust its people. I trust them. They respect the truth and they have a sense of humour. I think their policemen are wonderful. I've been there. I've never seen such sunsets. What about coming out to have a drink with me? There's a pub down the road serves draught Guinness. Very difficult to get in these parts —(*He breaks off. The voices draw nearer.* GOLDBERG *and* PETEY *enter from the back door.*)

GOLDBERG (*as he enters*). A mother in a million. (*He sees* STANLEY.) Ah.

PETEY. Oh hullo, Stan. You haven't met Stanley, have you, Mr Goldberg?

GOLDBERG. I haven't had the pleasure.

PETEY. Oh well, this is Mr Goldberg, this is Mr Webber.

GOLDBERG. Pleased to meet you.

PETEY. We were just getting a bit of air in the garden.

GOLDBERG. I was telling Mr Boles about my old mum. What days. (*He sits at the table, right.*) Yes. When I was a youngster, of a Friday, I used to go for a walk down the canal with a girl who lived down my road. A beautiful girl. What a voice that bird had! A nightingale, my word of honour. Good? Pure? She wasn't a Sunday school teacher for nothing. Anyway, I'd leave her with a little kiss on the cheek —I never took liberties—we weren't like the young men these days in those days. We knew the meaning of respect. So I'd give her a peck and I'd bowl back home. Humming away I'd be, past the children's playground. I'd tip my hat to the toddlers, I'd give a helping hand to a couple of stray dogs, everything came natural. I can see it like yesterday. The sun falling behind the dog stadium. Ah! (*He leans back contentedly.*)

MCCANN. Like behind the town hall.

GOLDBERG. What town hall?

MCCANN. In Carrikmacross.

GOLDBERG. There's no comparison. Up the street, into my gate, inside the door, home. "Simey!" my old mum used to shout, "quick before it gets cold." And there on the table what would I see? The nicest piece of gefilte fish you could wish to find on a plate.

MCCANN. I thought your name was Nat.

GOLDBERG. She called me Simey.

PETEY. Yes, we all remember our childhood.

GOLDBERG. Too true. Eh, Mr Webber, what do you say? Childhood. Hot water bottles. Hot milk. Pancakes. Soap suds. What a life.

Pause.

PETEY (*rising from the table*). Well, I'll have to be off.

GOLDBERG. Off?

PETEY. It's my chess night.

GOLDBERG. You're not staying for the party?

PETEY. No, I'm sorry, Stan. I didn't know about it till just
now. And we've got a game on. I'll try and get back early.

GOLDBERG. We'll save some drink for you, all right? Oh, that
reminds me. You'd better go and collect the bottles.

MCCANN. Now?

GOLDBERG. Of course, now. Time's getting on. Round the
corner, remember? Mention my name.

PETEY. I'm coming your way.

GOLDBERG. Beat him quick and come back, Mr Boles.

PETEY. Do my best. See you later, Stan.

> PETEY *and* MCCANN *go out, left.* STANLEY *moves to the
> centre.*

GOLDBERG. A warm night.

STANLEY (*turning*). Don't mess me about!

GOLDBERG. I beg your pardon?

STANLEY (*moving downstage*). I'm afraid there's been a mistake. We're booked out. Your room is taken. Mrs Boles
forgot to tell you. You'll have to find somewhere else.

GOLDBERG. Are you the manager here?

STANLEY. That's right.

GOLDBERG. Is it a good game?

STANLEY. I run the house. I'm afraid you and your friend will
have to find other accommodation.

GOLDBERG (*rising*). Oh, I forgot, I must congratulate you on
your birthday. (*Offering his hand.*) Congratulations.

STANLEY (*ignoring hand*). Perhaps you're deaf.

GOLDBERG. No, what makes you think that? As a matter of
fact, every single one of my senses is at its peak. Not bad
going, eh? For a man past fifty. But a birthday, I always feel,

is a great occasion, taken too much for granted these days. What a thing to celebrate—birth! Like getting up in the morning. Marvellous! Some people don't like the idea of getting up in the morning. I've heard them. Getting up in the morning, they say, what is it? Your skin's crabby, you need a shave, your eyes are full of muck, your mouth is like a boghouse, the palms of your hands are full of sweat, your nose is clogged up, your feet stink, what are you but a corpse waiting to be washed? Whenever I hear that point of view I feel cheerful. Because I know what it is to wake up with the sun shining, to the sound of the lawnmower, all the little birds, the smell of the grass, church bells, tomato juice—

STANLEY. Get out.

Enter MCCANN, *with bottles.*

Get that drink out. These are unlicensed premises.

GOLDBERG. You're in a terrible humour today, Mr Webber. And on your birthday too, with the good lady getting her strength up to give you a party.

MCCANN *puts the bottles on the sideboard.*

STANLEY. I told you to get those bottles out.

GOLDBERG. Mr Webber, sit down a minute.

STANLEY. Let me—just make this clear. You don't bother me. To me, you're nothing but a dirty joke. But I have a responsibility towards the people in this house. They've been down here too long. They've lost their sense of smell. I haven't. And nobody's going to take advantage of them while I'm here. (*A little less forceful.*) Anyway, this house isn't your cup of tea. There's nothing here for you, from any angle, any angle. So why don't you just go, without any more fuss?

GOLDBERG. Mr Webber, sit down.

STANLEY. It's no good starting any kind of trouble.

GOLDBERG. Sit down.

STANLEY. Why should I?

GOLDBERG. If you want to know the truth, Webber, you're
beginning to get on my breasts.

STANLEY. Really? Well, that's—

GOLDBERG. Sit down.

STANLEY. No.

GOLDBERG *sighs, and sits at the table right.*

GOLDBERG. McCann.

MCCANN. Nat?

GOLDBERG. Ask him to sit down.

MCCANN. Yes, Nat. (MCCANN *moves to* STANLEY.) Do you
mind sitting down?

STANLEY. Yes, I do mind.

MCCANN. Yes now, but—it'd be better if you did.

STANLEY. Why don't you sit down?

MCCANN. No, not me—you.

STANLEY. No thanks.

Pause.

MCCANN. Nat.

GOLDBERG. What?

MCCANN. He won't sit down.

GOLDBERG. Well, ask him.

MCCANN. I've asked him.

GOLDBERG. Ask him again.

MCCANN (*to* STANLEY). Sit down.

STANLEY. Why?

MCCANN. You'd be more comfortable.

STANLEY. So would you.

Pause.

MCCANN. All right. If you will I will.

STANLEY. You first.

MCCANN *slowly sits at the table, left*

MCCANN. Well?

STANLEY. Right. Now you've both had a rest you can get out!

MCCANN (*rising*). That's a dirty trick! I'll kick the shite out of him!

GOLDBERG (*rising*). No! I have stood up.

MCCANN. Sit down again!

GOLDBERG. Once I'm up I'm up.

STANLEY. Same here.

MCCANN (*moving to* STANLEY). You've made Mr Goldberg stand up.

STANLEY (*his voice rising*). It'll do him good!

MCCANN. Get in that seat.

GOLDBERG. McCann.

MCCANN. Get down in that seat!

GOLDBERG (*crossing to him*). Webber. (*Quietly.*) SIT DOWN. (*Silence.* STANLEY *begins to whistle "The Mountains of Morne". He strolls casually to the chair at the table. They watch him. He stops whistling. Silence. He sits.*)

STANLEY. You'd better be careful.

GOLDBERG. Webber, what were you doing yesterday?

STANLEY. Yesterday?

GOLDBERG. And the day before. What did you do the day before that?

STANLEY. What do you mean?

GOLDBERG. Why are you wasting everybody's time, Webber? Why are you getting in everybody's way?

STANLEY. Me? What are you—

GOLDBERG. I'm telling you, Webber. You're a washout. Why are you getting on everybody's wick? Why are you driving that old lady off her conk?

MCCANN. He likes to do it!

GOLDBERG. Why do you behave so badly, Webber? Why do you force that old man out to play chess?

STANLEY. Me?

GOLDBERG. Why do you treat that young lady like a leper?

She's not the leper, Webber!

STANLEY. What the—

GOLDBERG. What did you wear last week, Webber? Where do you keep your suits?

MCCANN. Why did you leave the organization?

GOLDBERG. What would your old mum say, Webber?

MCCANN. Why did you betray us?

GOLDBERG. You hurt me, Webber. You're playing a dirty game.

MCCANN. That's a Black and Tan fact.

GOLDBERG. Who does he think he is?

MCCANN. Who do you think you are?

STANLEY. You're on the wrong horse.

GOLDBERG. When did you come to this place?

STANLEY. Last year.

GOLDBERG. Where did you come from?

STANLEY. Somewhere else.

GOLDBERG. Why did you come here?

STANLEY. My feet hurt!

GOLDBERG. Why did you stay?

STANLEY. I had a headache!

GOLDBERG. Did you take anything for it?

STANLEY. Yes.

GOLDBERG. What?

STANLEY. Fruit salts!

GOLDBERG. Enos or Andrews?

STANLEY. En— An—

GOLDBERG. Did you stir properly? Did they fizz?

STANLEY. Now, now, wait, you—

GOLDBERG. Did they fizz? Did they fizz or didn't they fizz?

MCCANN. He doesn't know!

GOLDBERG. You don't know. When did you last have a bath?

STANLEY. I have one every—

GOLDBERG. Don't lie.

MCCANN. You betrayed the organization. I know him!

STANLEY. You don't!

GOLDBERG. What can you see without your glasses?

STANLEY. Anything.

GOLDBERG. Take off his glasses.

> MCCANN *snatches his glasses and as* STANLEY *rises, reaching for them, takes his chair downstage centre, below the table,* STANLEY *stumbling as he follows.* STANLEY *clutches the chair and stays bent over it.*

Webber, you're a fake. (*They stand on each side of the chair.*) When did you last wash up a cup?

STANLEY. The Christmas before last.

GOLDBERG. Where?

STANLEY. Lyons Corner House.

GOLDBERG. Which one?

STANLEY. Marble Arch.

GOLDBERG. Where was your wife?

STANLEY. In—

GOLDBERG. Answer.

STANLEY (*turning, crouched*). What wife?

GOLDBERG. What have you done with your wife?

MCCANN. He's killed his wife!

GOLDBERG. Why did you kill your wife?

STANLEY (*sitting, his back to the audience*). What wife?

MCCANN. How did he kill her?

GOLDBERG. How did you kill her?

MCCANN. You throttled her.

GOLDBERG. With arsenic.

MCCANN. There's your man!

GOLDBERG. Where's your old mum?

STANLEY. In the sanatorium.

MCCANN. Yes!

GOLDBERG. Why did you never get married?

MCCANN. She was waiting at the porch.

GOLDBERG. You skeddadled from the wedding.

MCCANN. He left her in the lurch.

GOLDBERG. You left her in the pudding club.

MCCANN. She was waiting at the church.

GOLDBERG. Webber! Why did you change your name?

STANLEY. I forgot the other one.

GOLDBERG. What's your name now?

STANLEY. Joe Soap.

GOLDBERG. You stink of sin.

MCCANN. I can smell it.

GOLDBERG. Do you recognise an external force?

STANLEY. What?

GOLDBERG. Do you recognise an external force?

MCCANN. That's the question!

GOLDBERG. Do you recognise an external force, responsible for you, suffering for you?

STANLEY. It's late.

GOLDBERG. Late! Late enough! When did you last pray?

MCCANN. He's sweating!

GOLDBERG. When did you last pray?

MCCANN. He's sweating!

GOLDBERG. Is the number 846 possible or necessary?

STANLEY. Neither.

GOLDBERG. Wrong! Is the number 846 possible or necessary?

STANLEY. Both.

GOLDBERG. Wrong! It's necessary but not possible.

STANLEY. Both.

GOLDBERG. Wrong! Why do you think the number 846 is necessarily possible?

STANLEY. Must be.

GOLDBERG. Wrong! It's only necessarily necessary! We admit possibility only after we grant necessity. It is possible because necessary but by no means necessary through possibility. The possibility can only be assumed after the proof of necessity.

MCCANN. Right!

GOLDBERG. Right? Of course right! We're right and you're wrong, Webber, all along the line.

MCCANN. All along the line!

GOLDBERG. Where is your lechery leading you?

MCCANN. You'll pay for this.

GOLDBERG. You stuff yourself with dry toast.

MCCANN. You contaminate womankind.

GOLDBERG. Why don't you pay the rent?

MCCANN. Mother defiler!

GOLDBERG. Why do you pick your nose?

MCCANN. I demand justice!

GOLDBERG. What's your trade?

MCCANN. What about Ireland?

GOLDBERG. What's your trade?

STANLEY. I play the piano.

GOLDBERG. How many fingers do you use?

STANLEY. No hands!

GOLDBERG. No society would touch you. Not even a building society.

MCCANN. You're a traitor to the cloth.

GOLDBERG. What do you use for pyjamas?

STANLEY. Nothing.

GOLDBERG. You verminate the sheet of your birth.

MCCANN. What about the Albigensenist heresy?

GOLDBERG. Who watered the wicket in Melbourne?

MCCANN. What about the blessed Oliver Plunkett?

GOLDBERG. Speak up, Webber. Why did the chicken cross the road?

STANLEY. He wanted to—he wanted to—he wanted to. . . .

MCCANN. He doesn't know!

GOLDBERG. Why did the chicken cross the road?

STANLEY. He wanted to—he wanted to. . . .

GOLDBERG. Why did the chicken cross the road?

STANLEY. He wanted. . . .

MCCANN. He doesn't know. He doesn't know which came first!

GOLDBERG. Which came first?

MCCANN. Chicken? Egg? Which came first?

GOLDBERG and MCCANN. Which came first? Which came first? Which came first?

    STANLEY *screams.*

GOLDBERG. He doesn't know. Do you know your own face?

MCCANN. Wake him up. Stick a needle in his eye.

GOLDBERG. You're a plague, Webber. You're an overthrow.

MCCANN. You're what's left!

GOLDBERG. But we've got the answer to you. We can sterilise you.

MCCANN. What about Drogheda?

GOLDBERG. Your bite is dead. Only your pong is left.

MCCANN. You betrayed our land.

GOLDBERG. You betray our breed.

MCCANN. Who are you, Webber?

GOLDBERG. What makes you think you exist?

MCCANN. You're dead.

GOLDBERG. You're dead. You can't live, you can't think, you can't love. You're dead. You're a plague gone bad. There's no juice in you. You're nothing but an odour!

    Silence. They stand over him. He is crouched in the chair.
    He looks up slowly and kicks GOLDBERG *in the stomach.*
    GOLDBERG *falls.* STANLEY *stands.* MCCANN *seizes a chair*
    and lifts it above his head. STANLEY *seizes a chair and*
    covers his head with it. MCCANN *and* STANLEY *circle.*

GOLDBERG. Steady, McCann.

STANLEY (*circling*). Uuuuuhhhhh!

MCCANN. Right, Judas.

GOLDBERG (*rising*). Steady, McCann.

MCCANN. Come on!

STANLEY. Uuuuuuuhhhhh!

MCCANN. He's sweating.

STANLEY. Uuuuuhhhhh!

GOLDBERG. Easy, McCann.

MCCANN. The bastard sweatpig is sweating.

> *A loud drumbeat off left, descending the stairs.* GOLDBERG
> *takes the chair from* STANLEY. *They put the chairs down.*
> *They stop still. Enter* MEG, *in evening dress, holding sticks*
> *and drum.*

MEG. I brought the drum down. I'm dressed for the party.

GOLDBERG. Wonderful.

MEG. You like my dress?

GOLDBERG. Wonderful. Out of this world.

MEG. I know. My father gave it to me. (*Placing drum on table.*)
Doesn't it make a beautiful noise?

GOLDBERG. It's a fine piece of work. Maybe Stan'll play us a
little tune afterwards.

MEG. Oh yes. Will you, Stan?

STANLEY. Could I have my glasses?

GOLDBERG. Ah yes. (*He holds his hand out to* MCCANN.
MCCANN *passes him his glasses.*) Here they are. (*He holds
them out for* STANLEY, *who reaches for them.*) Here they are.
(STANLEY *takes them.*) Now. What have we got here?
Enough to scuttle a liner. We've got four bottles of Scotch
and one bottle of Irish.

MEG. Oh, Mr Goldberg, what should I drink?

GOLDBERG. Glasses, glasses first. Open the Scotch, McCann.

MEG (*at the sideboard*). Here's my very best glasses in here.

MCCANN. I don't drink Scotch.

GOLDBERG. You've got the Irish.

MEG (*bringing the glasses*). Here they are.

GOLDBERG. Good. Mrs Boles, I think Stanley should pour
the toast, don't you?

MEG. Oh yes. Come on, Stanley. (STANLEY *walks slowly to the
table.*) Do you like my dress, Mr Goldberg?

GOLDBERG. It's out on its own. Turn yourself round a minute.
I used to be in the business. Go on, walk up there.

MEG. Oh no.

GOLDBERG. Don't be shy. (*He slaps her bottom.*)

MEG. Oooh!

GOLDBERG. Walk up the boulevard. Let's have a look at you. What a carriage. What's your opinion, McCann? Like a Countess, nothing less. Madam, now turn about and promenade to the kitchen. What a deportment!

MCCANN (*to* STANLEY). You can pour my Irish too.

GOLDBERG. You look like a Gladiola.

MEG. Stan, what about my dress?

GOLDBERG. One for the lady, one for the lady. Now madam—your glass.

MEG. Thank you.

GOLDBERG. Lift your glasses, ladies and gentlemen. We'll drink a toast.

MEG. Lulu isn't here.

GOLDBERG. It's past the hour. Now—who's going to propose the toast? Mrs Boles, it can only be you.

MEG. Me?

GOLDBERG. Who else?

MEG. But what do I say?

GOLDBERG. Say what you feel. What you honestly feel. (MEG *looks uncertain.*) It's Stanley's birthday. Your Stanley. Look at him. Look at him and it'll come. Wait a minute, the light's too strong. Let's have proper lighting. McCann, have you got your torch?

MCCANN (*bringing a small torch from his pocket*). Here.

GOLDBERG. Switch out the light and put on your torch. (MCCANN *goes to the door, switches off the light, comes back, shines the torch on* MEG. *Outside the window there is still a faint light.*) Not on the lady, on the gentleman! You must shine it on the birthday boy. (MCCANN *shines the torch in* STANLEY'S *face.*) Now, Mrs Boles, it's all yours.

   Pause.

MEG. I don't know what to say.

GOLDBERG. Look at him. Just look at him.

MEG. Isn't the light in his eyes?

GOLDBERG. No, no. Go on.

MEG. Well—it's very, very nice to be here tonight, in my house, and I want to propose a toast to Stanley, because it's his birthday, and he's lived here for a long while now, and he's my Stanley now. And I think he's a good boy, although sometimes he's bad. (*An appreciative laugh from* GOLD-BERG.) And he's the only Stanley I know, and I know him better than all the world, although he doesn't think so. (*"Hear—hear" from* GOLDBERG.) Well, I could cry because I'm so happy, having him here and not gone away, on his birthday, and there isn't anything I wouldn't do for him, and all you good people here tonight. . . . (*She sobs.*)

GOLDBERG. Beautiful! A beautiful speech. Put the light on, McCann. (MCCANN *goes to the door.* STANLEY *remains still.*) That was a lovely toast. (*The light goes on.* LULU *enters from the door, left.* GOLDBERG *comforts* MEG.) Buck up now. Come on, smile at the birdy. That's better. Ah, look who's here.

MEG. Lulu.

GOLDBERG. How do you do, Lulu? I'm Nat Goldberg.

LULU. Hallo.

GOLDBERG. Stanley, a drink for your guest. You just missed the toast, my dear, and what a toast.

LULU. Did I?

GOLDBERG. Stanley, a drink for your guest. Stanley. (STAN-LEY *hands a glass to* LULU.) Right. Now raise your glasses. Everyone standing up? No, not you, Stanley. You must sit down.

MCCANN. Yes, that's right. He must sit down.

GOLDBERG. You don't mind sitting down a minute? We're going to drink to you.

MEG. Come on!

LULU. Come on!

STANLEY *sits in a chair at the table.*

GOLDBERG. Right. Now Stanley's sat down. (*Taking the
stage.*) Well, I want to say first that I've never been so
touched to the heart as by the toast we've just heard. How
often, in this day and age, do you come across real, true
warmth? Once in a lifetime. Until a few minutes ago, ladies
and gentlemen, I, like all of you, was asking the same question. What's happened to the love, the bonhomie, the unashamed expression of affection of the day before yesterday,
that our mums taught us in the nursery?

MCCANN. Gone with the wind.

GOLDBERG. That's what I thought, until today. I believe in a
good laugh, a day's fishing, a bit of gardening. I was very
proud of my old greenhouse, made out of my own spit and
faith. That's the sort of man I am. Not size but quality. A
little Austin, tea in Fullers, a library book from Boots, and
I'm satisfied. But just now, I say just now, the lady of the
house said her piece and I for one am knocked over by the
sentiments she expressed. Lucky is the man who's at the
receiving end, that's what I say. (*Pause.*) How can I put it
to you? We all wander on our tod through this world. It's
a lonely pillow to kip on. Right!

LULU (*admiringly*). Right!

GOLDBERG. Agreed. But tonight, Lulu, McCann, we've
known a great fortune. We've heard a lady extend the sum
total of her devotion, in all its pride, plume and peacock, to
a member of her own living race. Stanley, my heartfelt
congratulations. I wish you, on behalf of us all, a happy
birthday. I'm sure you've never been a prouder man than
you are today. Mazoltov! And may we only meet at Sim-
chahs! (LULU *and* MEG *applaud.*) Turn out the light, Mc-
Cann, while we drink the toast.

LULU. That was a wonderful speech.

MCCANN *switches out the light, comes back, and shines the torch in* STANLEY'S *face. The light outside the window is fainter.*

GOLDBERG. Lift your glasses. Stanley—happy birthday.

MCCANN. Happy birthday.

LULU. Happy birthday.

MEG. Many happy returns of the day, Stan.

GOLDBERG. And well over the fast.

They all drink.

MEG (*kissing him*). Oh, Stanny. . . .

GOLDBERG. Lights!

MCCANN. Right! (*He switches on the lights.*)

MEG. Clink my glass, Stan.

LULU. Mr Goldberg—

GOLDBERG. Call me Nat.

MEG (*to* MCCANN). You clink my glass.

LULU (*tp* GOLDBERG). You're empty. Let me fill you up.

GOLDBERG. It's a pleasure.

LULU. You're a marvellous speaker, Nat, you know that? Where did you learn to speak like that?

GOLDBERG. You liked it, eh?

LULU. Oh yes!

GOLDBERG. Well, my first chance to stand up and give a lecture was at the Ethical Hall, Bayswater. A wonderful opportunity. I'll never forget it. They were all there that night. Charlotte Street was empty. Of course, that's a good while ago.

LULU. What did you speak about?

GOLDBERG. The Necessary and the Possible. It went like a bomb. Since then I always speak at weddings.

STANLEY *is still.* GOLDBERG *sits left of the table.* MEG *joins* MCCANN *downstage, right,* LULU *is downstage, left.* MCCANN *pours more Irish from the bottle, which he carries, into his glass.*

MEG. Let's have some of yours.

MCCANN. In that?

MEG. Yes.

MCCANN. Are you used to mixing them?

MEG. No.

MCCANN. Give me your glass.

> MEG *sits on a shoe-box, downstage, right.* LULU, *at the table, pours more drink for* GOLDBERG *and herself, and gives* GOLDBERG *his glass.*

GOLDBERG. Thank you.

MEG (*to* MCCANN). Do you think I should?

GOLDBERG. Lulu, you're a big bouncy girl. Come and sit on my lap.

MCCANN. Why not?

LULU. Do you think I should?

GOLDBERG. Try it.

MEG (*sipping*). Very nice.

LULU. I'll bounce up to the ceiling.

MCCANN. I don't know how you can mix that stuff.

GOLDBERG. Take a chance.

MEG (*to* MCCANN). Sit down on this stool.

> LULU *sits on* GOLDBERG'S *lap.*

MCCANN. This?

GOLDBERG. Comfortable?

LULU. Yes thanks.

MCCANN (*sitting*). It's comfortable.

GOLDBERG. You know, there's a lot in your eyes.

LULU. And in yours, too.

GOLDBERG. Do you think so?

LULU (*giggling*). Go on!

MCCANN (*to* MEG). Where'd you get it?

MEG. My father gave it to me.

LULU. I didn't know I was going to meet you here tonight.

MCCANN (*to* MEG). Ever been to Carrikmacross?

MEG (*drinking*). I've been to King's Cross.

LULU. You came right out of the blue, you know that?

GOLDBERG (*as she moves*). Mind how you go. You're cracking a rib.

MEG (*standing*). I want to dance! (LULU *and* GOLDBERG *look into each other's eyes.* MCCANN *drinks.* MEG *crosses to* STANLEY). Stanley. Dance. (STANLEY *sits still.* MEG *dances round the room alone, then comes back to* MCCANN, *who fills her glass. She sits.*)

LULU (*to* GOLDBERG). Shall I tell you something?

GOLDBERG. What?

LULU. I trust you.

GOLDBERG (*lifting his glass*). Gesundheit.

LULU. Have you got a wife?

GOLDBERG. I had a wife. What a wife. Listen to this. Friday, of an afternoon, I'd take myself for a little constitutional, down over the park. Eh, do me a favour, just sit on the table a minute, will you? (LULU *sits on the table. He stretches and continues.*) A little constitutional. I'd say hullo to the little boys, the little girls—I never made distinctions—and then back I'd go, back to my bungalow with the flat roof. "Simey," my wife used to shout, "quick, before it gets cold!" And there on the table what would I see? The nicest piece of rollmop and pickled cucumber you could wish to find on a plate,

LULU. I thought your name was Nat.

GOLDBERG. She called me Simey.

LULU. I bet you were a good husband.

GOLDBERG. You should have seen her funeral.

LULU. Why?

GOLDBERG (*draws in his breath and wags head*). What a funeral.

MEG (*to* MCCANN). My father was going to take me to Ireland once. But then he went away by himself.

LULU (*to* GOLDBERG). Do you think you knew me when I was a little girl?

GOLDBERG. Were you a nice little girl?

LULU. I was.

MEG. I don't know if he went to Ireland.

GOLDBERG. Maybe I played piggy-back with you.

LULU. Maybe you did.

MEG. He didn't take me.

GOLDBERG. Or pop goes the weasel.

LULU. Is that a game?

GOLDBERG. Sure it's a game!

MCCANN. Why didn't he take you to Ireland?

LULU. You're tickling me!

GOLDBERG. You should worry.

LULU. I've always liked older men. They can soothe you.

They embrace.

MCCANN. I know a place. Roscrea. Mother Nolan's.

MEG. There was a night-light in my room, when I was a little girl.

MCCANN. One time I stayed there all night with the boys. Singing and drinking all night.

MEG. And my Nanny used to sit up with me, and sing songs to me.

MCCANN. And a plate of fry in the morning. Now where am I?

MEG. My little room was pink. I had a pink carpet and pink curtains, and I had musical boxes all over the room. And they played me to sleep. And my father was a very big doctor. That's why I never had any complaints. I was cared for, and I had little sisters and brothers in other rooms, all different colours.

MCCANN. Tullamore, where are you?

MEG (*to* MCCANN). Give us a drop more.

MCCANN (*filling her glass and singing*). Glorio, Glorio, to the bold Fenian men!

MEG. Oh, what a lovely voice.

GOLDBERG. Give us a song, McCann.

LULU. A love song!

MCCANN (*reciting*). The night that poor Paddy was stretched, the boys they all paid him a visit.

GOLDBERG. A love song!

MCCANN (*in a full voice, sings*)

> Oh, the Garden of Eden has vanished, they say,
> But I know the lie of it still.
> Just turn to the left at the foot of Ben Clay
> And stop when halfway to Coote Hill.
> It's there you will find it, I know sure enough,
> And it's whispering over to me:
> Come back, Paddy Reilly, to Bally-James-Duff,
> Come home, Paddy Reilly, to me!

LULU (*to* GOLDBERG). You're the dead image of the first man I ever loved.

GOLDBERG. It goes without saying.

MEG (*rising*). I want to play a game!

GOLDBERG. A game?

LULU. What game?

MEG. Any game.

LULU (*jumping up*). Yes, let's play a game.

GOLDBERG. What game?

MCCANN. Hide and seek.

LULU. Blind man's buff.

MEG. Yes!

GOLDBERG. You want to play blind man's buff?

LULU and MEG. Yes!

GOLDBERG. All right. Blind man's buff. Come on! Everyone up! (*Rising.*) McCann. Stanley—Stanley!

MEG. Stanley. Up.

GOLDBERG. What's the matter with him?

MEG (*bending over him*). Stanley, we're going to play a game. Oh, come on, don't be sulky, Stan.

LULU. Come on.

    STANLEY *rises*. MCCANN *rises*.

GOLDBERG. Right! Now—who's going to be blind first?

LULU. Mrs Boles.

MEG. Not me.

GOLDBERG. Of course you.

MEG. Who, me?

LULU (*taking her scarf from her neck*). Here you are.

MCCANN. How do you play this game?

LULU (*tying her scarf round* MEG'S *eyes*). Haven't you ever played blind man's buff? Keep still, Mrs Boles. You mustn't be touched. But you can't move after she's blind. You must stay where you are after she's blind. And if she touches you then you become blind. Turn round. How many fingers am I holding up?

MEG. I can't see.

LULU. Right.

GOLDBERG. Right! Everyone move about. McCann. Stanley. Now stop. Now still. Off you go!

    STANLEY *is downstage, right,* MEG *moves about the room.* GOLDBERG *fondles* LULU *at arm's length.* MEG *touches* MCCANN.

MEG. Caught you!

LULU. Take off your scarf.

MEG. What lovely hair!

LULU (*untying the scarf*). There.

MEG. It's you!

GOLDBERG. Put it on, McCann.

LULU (*tying it on* MCCANN). There. Turn round. How many fingers am I holding up?

MCCANN. I don't know.

GOLDBERG. Right! Everyone move about. Right. Stop! Still!

    MCCANN *begins to move.*

MEG. Oh, this is lovely!

GOLDBERG. Quiet! Tch, tch, tch. Now—all move again. Stop! Still!

> MCCANN *moves about.* GOLDBERG *fondles* LULU *at arm's length.* MCCANN *draws near* STANLEY. *He stretches his arm and touches* STANLEY'S *glasses.*

MEG. It's Stanley!

GOLDBERG (*to* LULU). Enjoying the game?

MEG. It's your turn, Stan.

> MCCANN *takes off the scarf.*

MCCANN (*to* STANLEY). I'll take your glasses.

> MCCANN *takes* STANLEY'S *glasses.*

MEG. Give me the scarf.

GOLDBERG (*holding* LULU). Tie his scarf, Mrs. Boles.

MEG. That's what I'm doing. (*To* STANLEY.) Can you see my nose?

GOLDBERG. He can't. Ready? Right! Everyone move. Stop! And still!

> STANLEY *stands blindfold.* MCCANN *backs slowly across the stage to the left. He breaks* STANLEY'S *glasses, snapping the frames.* MEG *is downstage, left,* LULU *and* GOLDBERG *upstage centre, close together.* STANLEY *begins to move, very slowly, across the stage to the left.* MCCANN *picks up the drum and places it sideways in* STANLEY'S *path.* STANLEY *walks into the drum and falls over with his foot caught in it.*

MEG. Ooh!

GOLDBERG. Sssh!

> STANLEY *rises. He begins to move towards* MEG, *dragging the drum on his foot. He reaches her and stops. His hands*

*move towards her and they reach her throat. He begins to
strangle her.* MCCANN *and* GOLDBERG *rush forward and
throw him off.*

BLACKOUT

*There is now no light at all through the window. The stage
is in darkness.*

LULU. The lights!

GOLDBERG. What's happened?

LULU. The lights!

MCCANN. Wait a minute.

GOLDBERG. Where is he?

MCCANN. Let go of me!

GOLDBERG. Who's this?

LULU. Someone's touching me!

MCCANN. Where is he?

MEG. Why has the light gone out?

GOLDBERG. Where's your torch? (MCCANN *shines the torch in*
GOLDBERG'S *face.*) Not on me! (MCCANN *shifts the torch.
It is knocked from his hand and falls. It goes out.*)

MCCANN. My torch!

LULU. Oh God!

GOLDBERG. Where's your torch? Pick up your torch!

MCCANN. I can't find it.

LULU. Hold me. Hold me.

GOLDBERG. Get down on your knees. Help him find the torch.

LULU. I can't.

MCCANN. It's gone.

MEG. Why has the light gone out?

GOLDBERG. Everyone quiet! Help him find the torch.

Silence. Grunts from MCCANN *and* GOLDBERG *on their
knees. Suddenly there is a sharp, sustained rat-a-tat with a
stick on the side of the drum from the back of the room.
Silence. Whimpers from* LULU.

GOLDBERG. Over here. McCann!

MCCANN. Here.

GOLDBERG. Come to me, come to me. Easy. Over there.

*GOLDBERG and MCCANN move up left of the table.
STANLEY moves down right of the table. LULU suddenly
perceives him moving towards her, screams and faints.
GOLDBERG and MCCANN turn and stumble against each
other.*

GOLDBERG. What is it?

MCCANN. Who's that?

GOLDBERG. What is it?

*In the darkness STANLEY picks up LULU and places her on
the table.*

MEG. It's Lulu!

GOLDBERG and MCCANN move downstage, right.

GOLDBERG. Where is she?

MCCANN. She fell.

GOLDBERG. Where?

MCCANN. About here.

GOLDBERG. Help me pick her up.

MCCANN (*moving downstage, left*). I can't find her.

GOLDBERG. She must be somewhere.

MCCANN. She's not here.

GOLDBERG (*moving downstage, left*). She must be.

MCCANN. She's gone.

*MCCANN finds the torch on the floor, shines it on the table
and STANLEY. LULU is lying spread-eagled on the table,
STANLEY bent over her. STANLEY, as soon as the torchlight
hits him, begins to giggle. GOLDBERG and MCCANN move
towards him. He backs, giggling, the torch on his face. They
follow him upstage, left. He backs against the hatch, giggling.
The torch draws closer. His giggle rises and grows as he*

flattens himself against the wall. Their figures converge upon him.

Curtain

Act Three

The next morning. PETEY *enters, left, with a newspaper and sits at the table. He begins to read.* MEG'S *voice comes through the kitchen hatch.*

MEG. Is that you, Stan? (*Pause.*) Stanny?

PETEY. Yes?

MEG. Is that you?

PETEY. It's me.

MEG (*appearing at the hatch*). Oh, it's you. I've run out of cornflakes.

PETEY. Well, what else have you got?

MEG. Nothing.

PETEY. Nothing?

MEG. Just a minute. (*She leaves the hatch and enters by the kitchen door.*) You got your paper?

PETEY. Yes.

MEG. Is it good?

PETEY. Not bad.

MEG. The two gentlemen had the last of the fry this morning.

PETEY. Oh, did they?

MEG. There's some tea in the pot though. (*She pours tea for him.*) I'm going out shopping in a minute. Get you something nice. I've got a splitting headache.

PETEY (*reading*). You slept like a log last night.

MEG. Did I?

PETEY. Dead out.

MEG. I must have been tired. (*She looks about the room and sees the broken drum in the fireplace.*) Oh, look. (*She rises and picks it up.*) The drum's broken. (PETEY *looks up.*) Why is it broken?

PETEY. I don't know.

She hits it with her hand.

MEG. It still makes a noise.

PETEY. You can always get another one.

MEG (*sadly*). It was probably broken in the party. I don't remember it being broken though, in the party. (*She puts it down.*) What a shame.

PETEY. You can always get another one, Meg.

MEG. Well, at least he did have it on his birthday, didn't he? Like I wanted him to.

PETEY (*reading*). Yes.

MEG. Have you seen him down yet? (PETEY *does not answer.*) Petey.

PETEY. What?

MEG. Have you seen him down?

PETEY. Who?

MEG. Stanley.

PETEY. No.

MEG. Nor have I. That boy should be up. He's late for his breakfast.

PETEY. There isn't any breakfast.

MEG. Yes, but he doesn't know that. I'm going to call him.

PETEY (*quickly*). No, don't do that, Meg. Let him sleep.

MEG. But you say he stays in bed too much.

PETEY. Let him sleep . . . this morning. Leave him.

MEG. I've been up once, with his cup of tea. But Mr McCann opened the door. He said they were talking. He said he'd made him one. He must have been up early. I don't know what they were talking about. I was surprised. Because Stanley's usually fast asleep when I wake him. But he wasn't this morning. I heard him talking. (*Pause.*) Do you think they know each other? I think they're old friends. Stanley had a lot of friends. I know he did. (*Pause.*) I didn't give him his tea. He'd already had one. I came down again and went on with my work. Then, after a bit, they came down to breakfast. Stanley must have gone to sleep again.

Pause.

PETEY. When are you going to do your shopping, Meg?

MEG. Yes, I must. (*Collecting the bag.*) I've got a rotten headache. (*She goes to the back door, stops suddenly and turns.*) Did you see what's outside this morning?

PETEY. What?

MEG. That big car.

PETEY. Yes.

MEG. It wasn't there yesterday. Did you . . . did you have a look inside it?

PETEY. I had a peep.

MEG (*coming down tensely, and whispering*). Is there anything in it?

PETEY. In it?

MEG. Yes.

PETEY. What do you mean, in it?

MEG. Inside it.

PETEY. What sort of thing?

MEG. Well . . . I mean . . . is there . . . is there a wheelbarrow in it?

PETEY. A wheelbarrow?

MEG. Yes.

PETEY. I didn't see one.

MEG. You didn't? Are you sure?

PETEY. What would Mr Goldberg want with a wheelbarrow?

MEG. Mr Goldberg?

PETEY. It's his car.

MEG (*relieved*). His car? Oh, I didn't know it was his car.

PETEY. Of course it's his car.

MEG. Oh, I feel better.

PETEY. What are you on about?

MEG. Oh, I do feel better.

PETEY. You go and get a bit of air.

MEG. Yes, I will. I will. I'll go and get the shopping. (*She goes towards the back door. A door slams upstairs. She turns.*) It's Stanley! He's coming down—what am I going to do about his breakfast? (*She rushes into the kitchen.*) Petey, what shall I give him? (*She looks through the hatch.*) There's no corn-flakes. (*They both gaze at the door. Enter* GOLDBERG. *He halts at the door, as he meets their gaze, then smiles.*)

GOLDBERG. A reception committee!

MEG. Oh, I thought it was Stanley.

GOLDBERG. You find a resemblance?

MEG. Oh no. You look quite different.

GOLDBERG (*coming into the room*). Different build, of course.

MEG (*entering from the kitchen*). I thought he was coming down for his breakfast. He hasn't had his breakfast yet.

GOLDBERG. Your wife makes a very nice cup of tea, Mr Boles, you know that?

PETEY. Yes, she does sometimes. Sometimes she forgets.

MEG. Is he coming down?

GOLDBERG. Down? Of course he's coming down. On a lovely sunny day like this he shouldn't come down? He'll be up and about in next to no time. (*He sits at the table.*) And what a breakfast he's going to get.

MEG. Mr Goldberg.

GOLDBERG. Yes?

MEG. I didn't know that was your car outside.

GOLDBERG. You like it?

MEG. Are you going to go for a ride?

GOLDBERG (*to* PETEY). A smart car, eh?

PETEY. Nice shine on it all right.

GOLDBERG. What is old is good, take my tip. There's room there. Room in the front, and room in the back. (*He strokes the teapot.*) The pot's hot. More tea, Mr Boles?

PETEY. No thanks.

GOLDBERG (*pouring tea*). That car? That car's never let me

down.

MEG. Are you going to go for a ride?

GOLDBERG *does not answer, drinks his tea.*

MEG. Well, I'd better be off now. (*She moves to the back door, and turns.*) Petey, when Stanley comes down. . . .

PETEY. Yes?

MEG. Tell him I won't be long.

PETEY. I'll tell him.

MEG (*vaguely*). I won't be long. (*She exits.*)

GOLDBERG (*sipping his tea*). A good woman. A charming woman. My mother was the same. My wife was identical.

PETEY. How is he this morning?

GOLDBERG. Who?

PETEY. Stanley. Is he any better?

GOLDBERG (*a little uncertainly*). Oh . . . a little better, I think, a little better. Of course, I'm not really qualified to say, Mr Boles. I mean, I haven't got the . . . the qualifications. The best thing would be if someone with the proper . . . mnn . . . qualifications . . . was to have a look at him. Someone with a few letters after his name. It makes all the difference.

PETEY. Yes.

GOLDBERG. Anyway, Dermot's with him at the moment. He's . . . keeping him company.

PETEY. Dermot?

GOLDBERG. Yes.

PETEY. It's a terrible thing.

GOLDBERG (*sighs*). Yes. The birthday celebration was too much for him.

PETEY. What came over him?

GOLDBERG (*sharply*). What came over him? Breakdown, Mr Boles. Pure and simple. Nervous breakdown.

PETEY. But what brought it on so suddenly?

GOLDBERG (*rising, and moving upstage*). Well, Mr Boles, it can happen in all sorts of ways. A friend of mine was telling me about it only the other day. We'd both been concerned with another case—not entirely similar, of course, but . . . quite alike, quite alike. (*He pauses.*) Anyway, he was telling me, you see, this friend of mine, that sometimes it happens gradual—day by day it grows and grows and grows . . . day by day. And then other times it happens all at once. Poof! Like that! The nerves break. There's no guarantee how it's going to happen, but with certain people . . . it's a foregone conclusion.

PETEY. Really?

GOLDBERG. Yes. This friend of mine—he was telling me about it—only the other day. (*He stands uneasily for a moment, then brings out a cigarette case and takes a cigarette.*) Have an Abdullah.

PETEY. No, no, I don't take them.

GOLDBERG. Once in a while I treat myself to a cigarette. An Abdullah, perhaps, or a . . . (*He snaps his fingers.*)

PETEY. What a night. (GOLDBERG *lights his cigarette with a lighter.*) Came in the front door and all the lights were out. Put a shilling in the slot, came in here and the party was over.

GOLDBERG (*coming downstage*). You put a shilling in the slot?

PETEY. Yes.

GOLDBERG. And the lights came on.

PETEY. Yes, then I came in here.

GOLDBERG (*with a short laugh*). I could have sworn it was a fuse.

PETEY (*continuing*). There was dead silence. Couldn't hear a thing. So I went upstairs and your friend—Dermot—met me on the landing. And he told me.

GOLDBERG (*sharply*). Who?

PETEY. Your friend—Dermot.

GOLDBERG (*heavily*). Dermot. Yes. (*He sits.*)

PETEY. They get over it sometimes though, don't they? I mean, they can recover from it, can't they?

GOLDBERG. Recover? Yes, sometimes they recover, in one way or another.

PETEY. I mean, he might have recovered by now, mightn't he?

GOLDBERG. It's conceivable. Conceivable.

PETEY *rises and picks up the teapot and cup.*

PETEY. Well, if he's no better by lunchtime I'll go and get hold of a doctor.

GOLDBERG (*briskly*). It's all taken care of, Mr Boles. Don't worry yourself.

PETEY (*dubiously*). What do you mean? (*Enter* MCCANN *with two suitcases.*) All packed up?

PETEY *takes the teapot and cups into the kitchen.* MCCANN *crosses left and puts down the suitcases. He goes up to the window and looks out.*

GOLDBERG. Well? (MCCANN *does not answer.*) McCann. I asked you well.

MCCANN (*without turning*). Well what?

GOLDBERG. What's what? (MCCANN *does not answer.*)

MCCANN (*turning to look at* GOLDBERG, *grimly*). I'm not going up there again.

GOLDBERG. Why not?

MCCANN. I'm not going up there again.

GOLDBERG. What's going on now?

MCCANN (*moving down*). He's quiet now. He stopped all that . . . talking a while ago.

PETEY *appears at the kitchen hatch, unnoticed.*

GOLDBERG. When will he be ready?

MCCANN (*sullenly*). You can go up yourself next time.

GOLDBERG. What's the matter with you?

MCCANN (*quietly*). I gave him. . . .

GOLDBERG. What?

MCCANN. I gave him his glasses.

GOLDBERG. Wasn't he glad to get them back?

MCCANN. The frames are bust.

GOLDBERG. How did that happen?

MCCANN. He tried to fit the eyeholes into his eyes. I left him doing it.

PETEY (*at the kitchen door*). There's some Sellotape somewhere. We can stick them together.

GOLDBERG *and* MCCANN *turn to see him. Pause.*

GOLDBERG. Sellotape? No, no, that's all right, Mr Boles. It'll keep him quiet for the time being, keep his mind off other things.

PETEY (*moving downstage*). What about a doctor?

GOLDBERG. It's all taken care of.

MCCANN *moves over right to the shoe-box, and takes out a brush and brushes his shoes.*

PETEY (*moves to the table*). I think he needs one.

GOLDBERG. I agree with you. It's all taken care of. We'll give him a bit of time to settle down, and then I'll take him to Monty.

PETEY. You're going to take him to a doctor?

GOLDBERG (*staring at him*). Sure. Monty.

Pause. MCCANN *brushes his shoes.*

So Mrs Boles has gone out to get us something nice for lunch?

PETEY. That's right.

GOLDBERG. Unfortunately we may be gone by then.

PETEY. Will you?

GOLDBERG. By then we may be gone.

Pause.

PETEY. Well, I think I'll see how my peas are getting on, in the meantime.

GOLDBERG. The meantime?

PETEY. While we're waiting.

GOLDBERG. Waiting for what? (PETEY *walks towards the back door*.) Aren't you going back to the beach?

PETEY. No, not yet. Give me a call when he comes down, will you, Mr Goldberg?

GOLDBERG (*earnestly*). You'll have a crowded beach today ... on a day like this. They'll be lying on their backs, swimming out to sea. My life. What about the deck-chairs? Are the deck-chairs ready?

PETEY. I put them all out this morning.

GOLDBERG. But what about the tickets? Who's going to take the tickets?

PETEY. That's all right. That'll be all right. Mr Goldberg. Don't you worry about that. I'll be back.

He exits. GOLDBERG *rises, goes to the window and looks after him.* MCCANN *crosses to the table, left, sits, picks up the paper and begins to tear it into strips.*

GOLDBERG. Is everything ready?

MCCANN. Sure.

GOLDBERG *walks heavily, brooding, to the table. He sits right of it noticing what* MCCANN *is doing.*

GOLDBERG. Stop doing that!

MCCANN. What?

GOLDBERG. Why do you do that all the time? It's childish, it's pointless. It's without a solitary point.

MCCANN. What's the matter with you today?

GOLDBERG. Questions, questions. Stop asking me so many questions. What do you think I am?

MCCANN *studies him. He then folds the paper, leaving the strips inside.*

MCCANN. Well?

Pause. GOLDBERG *leans back in the chair, his eyes closed.*

MCCANN. Well?

GOLDBERG (*with fatigue*). Well what?

MCCANN. Do we wait or do we go and get him?

GOLDBERG (*slowly*). You want to go and get him?

MCCANN. I want to get it over.

GOLDBERG. That's understandable.

MCCANN. So do we wait or do we go and get him?

GOLDBERG (*interrupting*). I don't know why, but I feel knocked out. I feel a bit . . . It's uncommon for me.

MCCANN. Is that so?

GOLDBERG. It's unusual.

MCCANN (*rising swiftly and going behind* GOLDBERG'S *chair. Hissing*). Let's finish and go. Let's get it over and go. Get the thing done. Let's finish the bloody thing. Let's get the thing done and go!

Pause.

Will I go up?

Pause.

Nat!

GOLDBERG *sits humped.* MCCANN *slips to his side.*

Simey!

GOLDBERG (*opening his eyes, regarding* MCCANN). What—did —you—call—me?

MCCANN. Who?

GOLDBERG (*murderously*). Don't call me that! (*He seizes* MCCANN *by the throat.*) NEVER CALL ME THAT!

MCCANN (*writhing*). Nat, Nat, Nat, NAT! I called you Nat. I was asking you, Nat. Honest to God. Just a question, that's all, just a question, do you see, do you follow me?

GOLDBERG (*jerking him away*). What question?

MCCANN. Will I go up?

GOLDBERG (*violently*). Up? I thought you weren't going to go up there again?

MCCANN. What do you mean? Why not?

GOLDBERG. You said so!

MCCANN. I never said that!

GOLDBERG. No?

MCCANN (*from the floor, to the room at large*). Who said that? I never said that! I'll go up now!

He jumps up and rushes to the door, left.

GOLDBERG. Wait!

He stretches his arms to the arms of the chair.

Come here.

MCCANN *approaches him very slowly.*

I want your opinion. Have a look in my mouth.

He opens his mouth wide.

Take a good look.

MCCANN *looks.*

You know what I mean?

MCCANN *peers.*

You know what? I've never lost a tooth. Not since the day I was born. Nothing's changed. (*He gets up.*) That's why I've reached my position, McCann. Because I've always been as fit as a fiddle. All my life I've said the same. Play up, play up, and play the game. Honour thy father and thy mother. All along the line. Follow the line, the line, McCann, and you can't go wrong. What do you think, I'm a self-made man? No! I sat where I was told to sit. I kept my eye on the ball. School? Don't talk to me about school. Top in all subjects. And for why? Because I'm telling you, I'm telling you, follow my line? Follow my mental? Learn by heart. Never write down a thing. And don't go too near the water.

And you'll find—that what I say is true.
Because I believe that the world . . . (*Vacant.*). . . .
Because I believe that the world . . . (*Desperate.*). . . .
BECAUSE I BELIEVE THAT THE WORLD . . . (*Lost.*). . . .

He sits in chair.

Sit down, McCann, sit here where I can look at you.

MCCANN *kneels in front of the table.*

(*Intensely, with growing certainty.*) My father said to me,
Benny, Benny, he said, come here. He was dying. I knelt
down. By him day and night. Who else was there? Forgive,
Benny, he said, and let live. Yes, Dad. Go home to your wife.
I will, Dad. Keep an eye open for low-lives, for schnorrers
and for layabouts. He didn't mention names. I lost my life
in the service of others, he said, I'm not ashamed. Do your
duty and keep your observations. Always bid good morning
to the neighbours. Never, never forget your family, for they
are the rock, the constitution and the core! If you're ever in
any difficulties Uncle Barney will see you in the clear. I knelt
down. (*He kneels, facing* MCCANN.) I swore on the good
book. And I knew the word I had to remember—Respect!
Because McCann— (*Gently.*) Seamus—who came before
your father? His father. And who came before him? Before
him? . . . (*Vacant—triumphant.*) Who came before your
father's father but your father's father's mother! Your
great-gran-granny.

Silence. He slowly rises.

And that's why I've reached my position, McCann. Because
I've always been as fit as a fiddle. My motto. Work hard and
play hard. Not a day's illness.

GOLDBERG *sits.*

GOLDBERG. All the same, give me a blow. (*Pause.*) Blow in my mouth.

> MCCANN *stands, puts his hands on his knees, bends, and blows in* GOLDBERG'S *mouth.*

One for the road.

> MCCANN *blows again in his mouth.* GOLDBERG *breathes deeply, smiles.*

GOLDBERG. Right!

> *Enter* LULU. MCCANN *looks at them, and goes to the door.*

MCCANN (*at the door*). I'll give you five minutes. (*He exits.*)

GOLDBERG. Come over here.

LULU. What's going to happen?

GOLDBERG. Come over here.

LULU. No, thank you.

GOLDBERG. What's the matter? You got the needle to Uncle Natey?

LULU. I'm going.

GOLDBERG. Have a game of pontoon first, for old time's sake.

LULU. I've had enough games.

GOLDBERG. A girl like you, at your age, at your time of health, and you don't take to games?

LULU. You're very smart.

GOLDBERG. Anyway, who says you don't take to them?

LULU. Do you think I'm like all the other girls?

GOLDBERG. Are all the other girls like that, too?

LULU. I don't know about any other girls.

GOLDBERG. Nor me. I've never touched another woman.

LULU (*distressed*). What would my father say, if he knew? And what would Eddie say?

GOLDBERG. Eddie?

LULU. He was my first love, Eddie was. And whatever happened, it was pure. With him! He didn't come into my room at night with a briefcase!

GOLDBERG. Who opened the briefcase, me or you? Lulu, schmulu, let bygones be bygones, do me a turn. Kiss and make up.

LULU. I wouldn't touch you.

GOLDBERG. And today I'm leaving.

LULU. You're leaving?

GOLDBERG. Today.

LULU (*with growing anger*). You used me for a night. A passing fancy.

GOLDBERG. Who used who?

LULU. You made use of me by cunning when my defences were down.

GOLDBERG. Who took them down?

LULU. That's what you did. You quenched your ugly thirst. You taught me things a girl shouldn't know before she's been married at least three times!

GOLDBERG. Now you're a jump ahead! What are you complaining about?

Enter MCCANN *quickly.*

LULU. You didn't appreciate me for myself. You took all those liberties only to satisfy your appetite. Oh Nat, why did you do it?

GOLDBERG. You wanted me to do it, Lulula, so I did it.

MCCANN. That's fair enough. (*Advancing.*) You had a long sleep, Miss.

LULU (*backing upstage left*). Me?

MCCANN. Your sort, you spend too much time in bed.

LULU. What do you mean?

MCCANN. Have you got anything to confess?

LULU. What?

MCCANN (*savagely*). Confess!

LULU. Confess what?

MCCANN. Down on your knees and confess!

LULU. What does he mean?

GOLDBERG. Confess. What can you lose?

LULU. What, to him?

GOLDBERG. He's only been unfrocked six months.

MCCANN. Kneel down, woman, and tell me the latest!

LULU (*retreating to the back door*). I've seen everything that's happened. I know what's going on. I've got a pretty shrewd idea.

MCCANN (*advancing*). I've seen you hanging about the Rock of Cashel, profaning the soil with your goings-on. Out of my sight!

LULU. I'm going.

> *She exits.* MCCANN *goes to the door, left, and goes out. He ushers in* STANLEY, *who is dressed in a dark well cut suit and white collar. He holds his broken glasses in his hand. He is clean-shaven.* MCCANN *follows and closes the door.* GOLDBERG *meets* STANLEY, *seats him in a chair.*

GOLDBERG. How are you, Stan?

> *Pause.*

Are you feeling any better?

> *Pause.*

What's the matter with your glasses?

> GOLDBERG *bends to look.*

They're broken. A pity.

> STANLEY *stares blankly at the floor.*

MCCANN (*at the table*). He looks better, doesn't he?

GOLDBERG. Much better.

MCCANN. A new man.

GOLDBERG. You know what we'll do?

MCCANN. What?

GOLDBERG. We'll buy him another pair.

They begin to woo him, gently and with relish. During the following sequence STANLEY *shows no reaction. He remains, with no movement, where he sits.*

MCCANN. Out of our own pockets.

GOLDBERG. It goes without saying. Between you and me, Stan, it's about time you had a new pair of glasses.

MCCANN. You can't see straight.

GOLDBERG. It's true. You've been cockeyed for years.

MCCANN. Now you're even more cockeyed.

GOLDBERG. He's right. You've gone from bad to worse.

MCCANN. Worse than worse.

GOLDBERG. You need a long convalescence.

MCCANN. A change of air.

GOLDBERG. Somewhere over the rainbow.

MCCANN. Where angels fear to tread.

GOLDBERG. Exactly.

MCCANN. You're in a rut.

GOLDBERG. You look anaemic.

MCCANN. Rheumatic.

GOLDBERG. Myopic.

MCCANN. Epileptic.

GOLDBERG. You're on the verge.

MCCANN. You're a dead duck.

GOLDBERG. But we can save you.

MCCANN. From a worse fate.

GOLDBERG. True.

MCCANN. Undeniable.

GOLDBERG. From now on, we'll be the hub of your wheel.

MCCANN. We'll renew your season ticket.

GOLDBERG. We'll take tuppence off your morning tea.

MCCANN. We'll give you a discount on all inflammable goods.

GOLDBERG. We'll watch over you.

MCCANN. Advise you.

GOLDBERG. Give you proper care and treatment.

MCCANN. Let you use the club bar.

GOLDBERG. Keep a table reserved.

MCCANN. Help you acknowledge the fast days.

GOLDBERG. Bake you cakes.

MCCANN. Help you kneel on kneeling days.

GOLDBERG. Give you a free pass.

MCCANN. Take you for constitutionals.

GOLDBERG. Give you hot tips.

MCCANN. We'll provide the skipping rope.

GOLDBERG. The vest and pants.

MCCANN. The ointment.

GOLDBERG. The hot poultice.

MCCANN. The fingerstall.

GOLDBERG. The abdomen belt.

MCCANN. The ear plugs.

GOLDBERG. The baby powder.

MCCANN. The back scratcher.

GOLDBERG. The spare tyre.

MCCANN. The stomach pump.

GOLDBERG. The oxygen tent.

MCCANN. The prayer wheel.

GOLDBERG. The plaster of Paris.

MCCANN. The crash helmet.

GOLDBERG. The crutches.

MCCANN. A day and night service.

GOLDBERG. All on the house.

MCCANN. That's it.

GOLDBERG. We'll make a man of you.

MCCANN. And a woman.

GOLDBERG. You'll be re-orientated.

MCCANN. You'll be rich.

GOLDBERG. You'll be adjusted.

MCCANN. You'll be our pride and joy.

GOLDBERG. You'll be a mensch.

MCCANN. You'll be a success.

GOLDBERG. You'll be integrated.

MCCANN. You'll give orders.

GOLDBERG. You'll make decisions.

MCCANN. You'll be a magnate.

GOLDBERG. A statesman.

MCCANN. You'll own yachts.

GOLDBERG. Animals.

MCCANN. Animals.

> GOLDBERG *looks at* MCCANN.

GOLDBERG. I said animals. (*He turns back to* STANLEY.) You'll be able to make or break, Stan. By my life. (*Silence.* STANLEY *is still.*) Well? What do you say?

> STANLEY'S *head lifts very slowly and turns in* GOLD- BERG'S *direction.*

GOLDBERG. What do you think? Eh, boy?

> STANLEY *begins to clench and unclench his eyes.*

MCCANN. What's your opinion, sir? Of this prospect, sir?

GOLDBERG. Prospect. Sure. Sure it's a prospect.

> STANLEY'S *hands clutching his glasses begin to tremble.*

What's your opinion of such a prospect? Eh, Stanley?

> STANLEY *concentrates, his mouth opens, he attempts to speak, fails and emits sounds from his throat.*

STANLEY. Uh-gug . . . uh-gug . . . eeehhh-gag . . . (*On the breath.*) Caahh . . . caahh. . . .

> They watch him. He draws a long breath which shudders down his body. He concentrates.

GOLDBERG. Well, Stanny boy, what do you say, eh?

> They watch. He concentrates. His head lowers, his chin draws into his chest, he crouches.

STANLEY. Ug-gughh . . . uh-gughhh. . . .

MCCANN. What's your opinion, sir?

STANLEY. Caaahhh . . . caaahhh. . . .

MCCANN. Mr Webber! What's your opinion?

GOLDBERG. What do you say, Stan? What do you think of the prospect?

MCCANN. What's your opinion of the prospect?

> STANLEY'S *body shudders, relaxes, his head drops, he becomes still again, stooped.* PETEY *enters from door, downstage, left.*

GOLDBERG. Still the same old Stan. Come with us. Come on, boy.

MCCANN. Come along with us.

PETEY. Where are you taking him?

> *They turn. Silence.*

GOLDBERG. We're taking him to Monty.

PETEY. He can stay here.

GOLDBERG. Don't be silly.

PETEY. We can look after him here.

GOLDBERG. Why do you want to look after him?

PETEY. He's my guest.

GOLDBERG. He needs special treatment.

PETEY. We'll find someone.

GOLDBERG. No. Monty's the best there is. Bring him, McCann.

> *They help* STANLEY *out of the chair. They all three move towards the door, left.*

PETEY. Leave him alone!

> *They stop.* GOLDBERG *studies him.*

GOLDBERG (*insidiously*). Why don't you come with us, Mr Boles?

MCCANN. Yes, why don't you come with us?

GOLDBERG. Come with us to Monty. There's plenty of room in the car.

PETEY makes no move. They pass him and reach the door. MCCANN opens the door and picks up the suitcases.

PETEY (*broken*). Stan, don't let them tell you what to do!

They exit.

Silence. PETEY stands. The front door slams. Sound of a car starting. Sound of a car going away. Silence. PETEY slowly goes to the table. He sits on a chair, left. He picks up the paper and opens it. The strips fall to the floor. He looks down at them. MEG comes past the window and enters by the back door. PETEY studies the front page of the paper.

MEG (*coming downstage*). The car's gone.

PETEY. Yes.

MEG. Have they gone?

PETEY. Yes.

MEG. Won't they be in for lunch?

PETEY. No.

MEG. Oh, what a shame. (*She puts her bag on the table.*) It's hot out. (*She hangs her coat on a hook.*) What are you doing?

PETEY. Reading.

MEG. Is it good?

PETEY. All right.

She sits by the table.

MEG. Where's Stan?

Pause.

Is Stan down yet, Petey?

PETEY. No . . . he's. . . .

MEG. Is he still in bed?

PETEY. Yes, he's . . . still asleep.

MEG. Still? He'll be late for his breakfast.

PETEY. Let him . . . sleep.

Pause.

MEG. Wasn't it a lovely party last night?

PETEY. I wasn't there.

MEG. Weren't you?

PETEY. I came in afterwards.

MEG. Oh.

Pause.

It was a lovely party. I haven't laughed so much for years. We had dancing and singing. And games. You should have been there.

PETEY. It was good, eh?

Pause.

MEG. I was the belle of the ball.

PETEY. Were you?

MEG. Oh yes. They all said I was.

PETEY. I bet you were, too.

MEG. Oh, it's true. I was.

Pause.

I know I was.

Curtain

THE ROOM

The Room was first presented at the Hampstead Theatre Club on 21st January, 1960, with the following cast:

BERT HUDD, *a man of fifty* — Howard Lang
ROSE, *a woman of sixty* — Vivien Merchant
MR KIDD, *an old man* — Henry Woolf
MR SANDS ⎱ *a young couple* — John Rees
MRS SANDS ⎰ — Auriol Smith
RILEY — Thomas Baptiste

Directed by Harold Pinter

The Room was subsequently presented at the Royal Court Theatre on 8th March, 1960, with four changes in the cast:

BERT HUDD — Michael Brennan
MR KIDD — John Cater
MR SANDS — Michael Caine
MRS SANDS — Anne Bishop

Directed by Anthony Page

THE ROOM

Scene: A room in a large house. A door down right. A gas-fire down left. A gas-stove and sink, up left. A window up centre. A table and chairs, centre. A rocking-chair, left centre. The foot of a double-bed protrudes from alcove, up right.

BERT *is at the table, wearing a cap, a magazine propped in front of him.* ROSE *is at the stove.*

ROSE. Here you are. This'll keep the cold out.

She places bacon and eggs on a plate, turns off the gas and takes the plate to the table.

It's very cold out, I can tell you. It's murder.

She returns to the stove and pours water from the kettle into the teapot, turns off the gas and brings the teapot to the table, pours salt and sauce on the plate and cuts two slices of bread. BERT *begins to eat.*

That's right. You eat that. You'll need it. You can feel it in here. Still, the room keeps warm. It's better than the basement, anyway.

She butters the bread.

I don't know how they live down there. It's asking for trouble. Go on. Eat it up. It'll do you good.

She goes to the sink, wipes a cup and saucer and brings them to the table.

If you want to go out you might as well have something inside you. Because you'll feel it when you get out.

She pours milk into the cup.

Just now I looked out of the window. It was enough for me. There wasn't a soul about. Can you hear the wind?

She sits in the rocking-chair.

I've never seen who it is. Who is it? Who lives down there? I'll have to ask. I mean, you might as well know, Bert. But whoever it is, it can't be too cosy.

Pause.

I think it's changed hands since I was last there. I didn't see who moved in then. I mean the first time it was taken.

Pause.

Anyway, I think they've gone now.

Pause.

But I think someone else has gone in now. I wouldn't like to live in that basement. Did you ever see the walls? They were running. This is all right for me. Go on, Bert. Have a bit more bread.

She goes to the table and cuts a slice of bread.

I'll have some cocoa on when you come back.

She goes to the window and settles the curtain.

No, this room's all right for me. I mean, you know where you are. When it's cold, for instance.

She goes to the table.

What about the rasher? Was it all right? It was a good one, I know, but not as good as the last lot I got in. It's the weather.

She goes to the rocking-chair, and sits.

Anyway, I haven't been out. I haven't been so well. I didn't feel up to it. Still, I'm much better today. I don't know about you though. I don't know whether you ought to go out. I mean, you shouldn't, straight after you've been laid up. Still. Don't worry, Bert. You go. You won't be long.

She rocks.

It's good you were up here, I can tell you. It's good you weren't down there, in the basement. That's no joke. Oh, I've left the tea. I've left the tea standing.

She goes to the table and pours tea into the cup.

No, it's not bad. Nice weak tea. Lovely weak tea. Here you are. Drink it down. I'll wait for mine. Anyway, I'll have it a bit stronger.

She takes a plate to the sink and leaves it.

Those walls would have finished you off. I don't know who lives down there now. Whoever it is, they're taking a big chance. Maybe they're foreigners.

She goes to the rocking-chair and sits.

I'd have pulled you through.

Pause.

There isn't room for two down there, anyway. I think there was one first, before he moved out. Maybe they've got two now.

She rocks.

If they ever ask you, Bert, I'm quite happy where I am. We're quiet, we're all right. You're happy up here. It's not far up either, when you come in from outside. And we're not bothered. And nobody bothers us.

Pause.

I don't know why you have to go out. Couldn't you run it down tomorrow? I could put the fire in later. You could sit by the fire. That's what you like, Bert, of an evening. It'll be dark in a minute as well, soon.

She rocks.

It gets dark now.

She rises and pours out tea at the table.

I made plenty. Go on.

She sits at table.

You looked out today? It's got ice on the roads. Oh, I know you can drive. I'm not saying you can't drive. I mentioned to Mr Kidd this morning that you'd be doing a run today. I told him you hadn't been too grand, but I said, still, he's a marvellous driver. I wouldn't mind what time, where, nothing, Bert. You know how to drive. I told him.

She wraps her cardigan about her.

But it's cold. It's really cold today, chilly. I'll have you some nice cocoa on for when you get back.

She rises, goes to the window, and looks out.

It's quiet. Be coming on for dark. There's no one about.

She stands, looking.

Wait a minute.

Pause.

I wonder who that is.

Pause.

No. I thought I saw someone.

Pause.

No.

She drops the curtain.

You know what though? It looks a bit better. It's not so windy. You'd better put on your thick jersey.

She goes to the rocking-chair, sits and rocks.

This is a good room. You've got a chance in a place like this. I look after you, don't I, Bert? Like when they offered us the basement here I said no straight off. I knew that'd be no good. The ceiling right on top of you. No, you've got a window here, you can move yourself, you can come home at night, if you have to go out, you can do your job, you can come home, you're all right. And I'm here. You stand a chance.

Pause.

I wonder who has got it now. I've never seen them, or heard of them. But I think someone's down there. Whoever's got it can keep it. That looked a good rasher, Bert. I'll have a cup of tea later. I like mine a bit stronger. You like yours weak.

A knock at the door. She stands.

Who is it?

Pause.

Hallo!

Knock repeated.

Come in then.

Knock repeated.

Who is it?

Pause. The door opens and MR KIDD *comes in.*

MR KIDD. I knocked.
ROSE. I heard you.
MR KIDD. Eh?
ROSE. We heard you.
MR KIDD. Hallo, Mr Hudd, how are you, all right? I've been looking at the pipes.
ROSE. Are they all right?

MR KIDD. Eh?

ROSE. Sit down, Mr Kidd.

MR KIDD. No, that's all right. I just popped in, like, to see how things were going. Well, it's cosy in here, isn't it?

ROSE. Oh, thank you, Mr Kidd.

MR KIDD. You going out today, Mr Hudd? I went out. I came straight in again. Only to the corner, of course.

ROSE. Not many people about today, Mr Kidd.

MR KIDD. So I thought to myself, I'd better have a look at those pipes. In the circumstances. I only went to the corner, for a few necessary items. It's likely to snow. Very likely, in my opinion.

ROSE. Why don't you sit down, Mr Kidd?

MR KIDD. No, no, that's all right.

ROSE. Well, it's a shame you have to go out in this weather, Mr Kidd. Don't you have a help?

MR KIDD. Eh?

ROSE. I thought you had a woman to help.

MR KIDD. I haven't got any woman.

ROSE. I thought you had one when we first came.

MR KIDD. No women here.

ROSE. Maybe I was thinking of somewhere else.

MR KIDD. Plenty of women round the corner. Not here though. Oh no. Eh, have I seen that before?

ROSE. What?

MR KIDD. That.

ROSE. I don't know. Have you?

MR KIDD. I seem to have some remembrance.

ROSE. It's just an old rocking-chair.

MR KIDD. Was it here when you came?

ROSE. No, I brought it myself.

MR KIDD. I could swear blind I've seen that before.

ROSE. Perhaps you have.

MR KIDD. What?

ROSE. I say, perhaps you have.

MR KIDD. Yes, maybe I have.

ROSE. Take a seat, Mr Kidd.

MR KIDD. I wouldn't take an oath on it though.

BERT *yawns and stretches, and continues looking at his magazine.*

No; I won't sit down, with Mr Hudd just having a bit of a rest after his tea. I've got to go and get mine going in a minute. You're going out then, Mr Hudd? I was just looking at your van. She's a very nice little van, that. I notice you wrap her up well for the cold. I don't blame you. Yes, I was hearing you go off, when was it, the other morning, yes. Very smooth. I can tell a good gear-change.

ROSE. I thought your bedroom was at the back, Mr Kidd.

MR KIDD. My bedroom?

ROSE. Wasn't it at the back? Not that I ever knew.

MR KIDD. I wasn't in my bedroom.

ROSE. Oh, well.

MR KIDD. I was up and about.

ROSE. I don't get up early in this weather. I can take my time. I take my time.

Pause.

MR KIDD. This was my bedroom.

ROSE. This? When?

MR KIDD. When I lived here.

ROSE. I didn't know that.

MR KIDD. I will sit down for a few ticks. (*He sits in the armchair.*)

ROSE. Well, I never knew that.

MR KIDD. Was this chair here when you came?

ROSE. Yes.

MR KIDD. I can't recollect this one.

Pause.

ROSE. When was that then?

MR KIDD. Eh?

ROSE. When was this your bedroom?

MR KIDD. A good while back.

Pause.

ROSE. I was telling Bert I was telling you how he could drive.

MR KIDD. Mr Hudd? Oh, Mr Hudd can drive all right. I've seen him bowl down the road all right. Oh yes.

ROSE. Well, Mr Kidd, I must say this is a very nice room. It's a very comfortable room.

MR KIDD. Best room in the house.

ROSE. It must get a bit damp downstairs.

MR KIDD. Not as bad as upstairs.

ROSE. What about downstairs?

MR KIDD. Eh?

ROSE. What about downstairs?

MR KIDD. What about it?

ROSE. Must get a bit damp.

MR KIDD. A bit. Not as bad as upstairs though.

ROSE. Why's that?

MR KIDD. The rain comes in.

Pause.

ROSE. Anyone live up there?

MR KIDD. Up there? There was. Gone now.

ROSE. How many floors you got in this house?

MR KIDD. Floors. (*He laughs.*) Ah, we had a good few of them in the old days.

ROSE. How many have you got now?

MR KIDD. Well, to tell you the truth, I don't count them now.

ROSE. Oh.

MR KIDD. No, not now.

ROSE. It must be a bit of a job.

MR KIDD. Oh, I used to count them, once. Never got tired of it. I used to keep a tack on everything in this house. I had a lot to keep my eye on, then. I was able for it too. That was when my sister was alive. But I lost track a bit, after she died. She's been dead some time now, my sister. It was a good house then. She was a capable woman. Yes. Fine size of a woman too. I think she took after my mum. Yes, I think she took after my old mum, from what I can recollect. I think my mum was a Jewess. Yes, I wouldn't be surprised to learn that she was a Jewess. She didn't have many babies.

ROSE. What about your sister, Mr Kidd?

MR KIDD. What about her?

ROSE. Did she have any babies?

MR KIDD. Yes, she had a resemblance to my old mum, I think. Taller, of course.

ROSE. When did she die then, your sister?

MR KIDD. Yes, that's right, it was after she died that I must have stopped counting. She used to keep things in very good trim. And I gave her a helping hand. She was very grateful, right until her last. She always used to tell me how much she appreciated all the – little things – that I used to do for her. Then she copped it. I was her senior. Yes, I was her senior. She had a lovely boudoir. A beautiful boudoir.

ROSE. What did she die of?

MR KIDD. Who?

ROSE. Your sister.

Pause.

MR KIDD. I've made ends meet.

Pause.

ROSE. You full at the moment, Mr Kidd?

MR KIDD. Packed out.

ROSE. All sorts, I suppose?

MR KIDD. Oh yes, I make ends meet.

ROSE. We do, too, don't we, Bert?

Pause.

Where's your bedroom now then, Mr Kidd?

MR KIDD. Me? I can take my pick. (*Rising.*) You'll be going out soon then, Mr Hudd? Well, be careful how you go. Those roads'll be no joke. Still, you know how to manipulate your van all right, don't you? Where you going? Far? Be long?

ROSE. He won't be long.

MR KIDD. No, of course not. Shouldn't take him long.

ROSE. No.

MR KIDD. Well then, I'll pop off. Have a good run, Mr Hudd. Mind how you go. It'll be dark soon too. But not for a good while yet. Arivederci.

> *He exits.*

ROSE. I don't believe he had a sister, ever.

> *She takes the plate and cup to the sink.* BERT *pushes his chair back and rises.*

All right. Wait a minute. Where's your jersey?

> *She brings the jersey from the bed.*

Here you are. Take your coat off. Get into it.

> *She helps him into his jersey.*

Right. Where's your muffler?

> *She brings a muffler from the bed.*

Here you are. Wrap it round. That's it. Don't go too fast, Bert, will you? I'll have some cocoa on when you get back. You won't be long. Wait a minute. Where's your overcoat? You'd better put on your overcoat.

> *He fixes his muffler, goes to the door and exits. She stands, watching the door, then turns slowly to the table, picks up the magazine, and puts it down. She stands and listens, goes to the fire, bends, lights the fire and warms her hands. She stands and looks about the room. She looks at the window*

*and listens, goes quickly to the window, stops and straightens
the curtain. She comes to the centre of the room, and looks
towards the door. She goes to the bed, puts on a shawl, goes to
the sink, takes a bin from under the sink, goes to the door and
opens it.*

ROSE. Oh!

MR *and* MRS SANDS *are disclosed on the landing.*

MRS SANDS. So sorry. We didn't mean to be standing here,
like. Didn't mean to give you a fright. We've just come up
the stairs.

ROSE. That's all right.

MRS SANDS. This is Mr Sands. I'm Mrs Sands.

ROSE. How do you do?

MR SANDS *grunts acknowledgement.*

MRS SANDS. We were just going up the stairs. But you can't
see a thing in this place. Can you, Toddy?

MR SANDS. Not a thing.

ROSE. What were you looking for?

MRS SANDS. The man who runs the house.

MR SANDS. The landlord. We're trying to get hold of the
landlord.

MRS SANDS. What's his name, Toddy?

ROSE. His name's Mr Kidd.

MRS SANDS. Kidd. Was that the name, Toddy?

MR SANDS. Kidd? No, that's not it.

ROSE. Mr Kidd. That's his name.

MR SANDS. Well, that's not the bloke we're looking for.

ROSE. Well, you must be looking for someone else.

Pause.

MR SANDS. I suppose we must be.

ROSE. You look cold.

MRS SANDS. It's murder out. Have you been out?

ROSE. No.

MRS SANDS. We've not long come in.

ROSE. Well, come inside, if you like, and have a warm.

>*They come into the centre of the room.*

>(*Bringing the chair from the table to the fire*). Sit down here.
You can get a good warm.

MRS SANDS. Thanks. (*She sits.*)

ROSE. Come over by the fire, Mr. Sands.

MR SANDS. No, it's all right. I'll just stretch my legs.

MRS SANDS. Why? You haven't been sitting down.

MR SANDS. What about it?

MRS SANDS. Well, why don't you sit down?

MR SANDS. Why should I?

MRS SANDS. You must be cold.

MR SANDS. I'm not.

MRS SANDS. You must be. Bring over a chair and sit down.

MR SANDS. I'm all right standing up, thanks.

MRS SANDS. You don't look one thing or the other standing
up.

MR SANDS. I'm quite all right, Clarissa.

ROSE. Clarissa? What a pretty name.

MRS SANDS. Yes, it is nice, isn't it? My father and mother
gave it to me.

>*Pause.*

>You know, this is a room you can sit down and feel cosy in.

MR SANDS (*looking at the room*). It's a fair size, all right.

MRS SANDS. Why don't you sit down, Mrs –

ROSE. Hudd. No thanks.

MR SANDS. What did you say?

ROSE. When?

MR SANDS. What did you say the name was?

ROSE. Hudd.

MR SANDS. That's it. You're the wife of the bloke you
mentioned then?

MRS SANDS. No, she isn't. That was Mr Kidd.

MR SANDS. Was it? I thought it was Hudd.

MRS SANDS. No, it was Kidd. Wasn't it, Mrs Hudd?

ROSE. That's right. The landlord.

MRS SANDS. No, not the landlord. The other man.

ROSE. Well, that's his name. He's the landlord.

MR SANDS. Who?

ROSE. Mr Kidd.

Pause.

MR SANDS. Is he?

MRS SANDS. Maybe there are two landlords.

Pause.

MR SANDS. That'll be the day.

MRS SANDS. What did you say?

MR SANDS. I said that'll be the day.

Pause.

ROSE. What's it like out?

MRS SANDS. It's very dark out.

MR SANDS. No darker than in.

MRS SANDS. He's right there.

MR SANDS. It's darker in than out, for my money.

MRS SANDS. There's not much light in this place, is there, Mrs Hudd? Do you know, this is the first bit of light we've seen since we came in?

MR SANDS. The first crack.

ROSE. I never go out at night. We stay in.

MRS SANDS. Now I come to think of it, I saw a star.

MR SANDS. You saw what?

MRS SANDS. Well, I think I did.

MR SANDS. You think you saw what?

MRS SANDS. A star.

MR SANDS. Where?

MRS SANDS. In the sky.

MR SANDS. When?

MRS SANDS. As we were coming along.

MR SANDS. Go home.

MRS SANDS. What do you mean?

MR SANDS. You didn't see a star.

MRS SANDS. Why not?

MR SANDS. Because I'm telling you. I'm telling you you didn't see a star.

Pause.

ROSE. I hope it's not too dark out. I hope it's not too icy. My husband's in his van. He doesn't drive slow either. He never drives slow.

MR SANDS (*guffawing*). Well, he's taking a big chance tonight then.

ROSE. What?

MR SANDS. No – I mean, it'd be a bit dodgy driving tonight.

ROSE. He's a very good driver.

Pause.

How long have you been here?

MRS SANDS. I don't know. How long have we been here, Toddy?

MR SANDS. About half an hour.

MRS SANDS. Longer than that, much longer.

MRS SANDS. About thirty-five minutes.

ROSE. Well, I think you'll find Mr Kidd about somewhere. He's not long gone to make his tea.

MR SANDS. He lives here, does he?

ROSE. Of course he lives here.

MR SANDS. And you say he's the landlord, is he?

ROSE. Of course he is.

MR SANDS. Well, say I wanted to get hold of him, where would I find him?

ROSE. Well – I'm not sure.

MR SANDS. He lives here, does he?

ROSE. Yes, but I don't know –

MR SANDS. You don't know exactly where he hangs out?

ROSE. No, not exactly.

MR SANDS. But he does live here, doesn't he?

Pause.

MRS SANDS. This is a very big house, Toddy.

MR SANDS. Yes, I know it is. But Mrs Hudd seems to know Mr Kidd very well.

ROSE. No, I wouldn't say that. As a matter of fact, I don't know him at all. We're very quiet. We keep ourselves to ourselves. I never interfere. I mean, why should I? We've got our room. We don't bother anyone else. That's the way it should be.

MRS SANDS. It's a nice house, isn't it? Roomy.

ROSE. I don't know about the house. We're all right, but I wouldn't mind betting there's a lot wrong with this house. (*She sits in the rocking-chair.*) I think there's a lot of damp.

MRS SANDS. Yes, I felt a bit of damp when we were in the basement just now.

ROSE. You were in the basement?

MRS SANDS. Yes, we went down there when we came in.

ROSE. Why?

MRS SANDS. We were looking for the landlord.

ROSE. What was it like down there?

MR SANDS. Couldn't see a thing.

ROSE. Why not?

MR SANDS. There wasn't any light.

ROSE. But what was – you said it was damp?

MRS SANDS. I felt a bit, didn't you, Tod?

MR SANDS. Why? Haven't you ever been down there, Mrs Hudd?

ROSE. Oh yes, once, a long time ago.

MR SANDS. Well, you know what it's like then, don't you?

ROSE It was a long time ago

MR SANDS. You haven't been here all that long, have you?

ROSE. I was just wondering whether anyone was living down there now.

MRS SANDS. Yes. A man.

ROSE. A man?

MRS SANDS. Yes.

ROSE. One man?

MR SANDS. Yes, there was a bloke down there, all right.

He perches on the table.

MRS SANDS. You're sitting down!

MR SANDS (*jumping up*). Who is?

MRS SANDS. You were.

MR SANDS. Don't be silly. I perched.

MRS SANDS. I saw you sit down.

MR SANDS. You did not see me sit down because I did not sit bloody well down. I perched!

MRS SANDS. Do you think I can't perceive when someone's sitting down?

MR SANDS. Perceive! That's all you do. Perceive.

MRS SANDS. You could do with a bit more of that instead of all that tripe you get up to.

MR SANDS. You don't mind some of that tripe!

MRS SANDS. You take after your uncle, that's who you take after!

MR SANDS. And who do you take after?

MRS SANDS (*rising*). I didn't bring you into the world.

MR SANDS. You didn't what?

MRS SANDS. I said, I didn't bring you into the world.

MR SANDS. Well, who did then? That's what I want to know. Who did? Who did bring me into the world?

She sits, muttering. He stands, muttering.

ROSE. You say you saw a man downstairs, in the basement?

MRS SANDS. Yes, Mrs Hudd, you see, the thing is, Mrs

Hudd, we'd heard they'd got a room to let here, so we thought we'd come along and have a look. Because we're looking for a place, you see, somewhere quiet, and we knew this district was quiet, and we passed the house a few months ago and we thought it looked very nice, but we thought we'd call of an evening, to catch the landlord, so we came along this evening. Well, when we got here we walked in the front door and it was very dark in the hall and there wasn't anyone about. So we went down to the basement. Well, we got down there only due to Toddy having such good eyesight really. Between you and me, I didn't like the look of it much, I mean the feel, we couldn't make much out, it smelt damp to me. Anyway, we went through a kind of partition, then there was another partition, and we couldn't see where we were going, well, it seemed to me it got darker the more we went, the further we went in, I thought we must have come to the wrong house. So I stopped. And Toddy stopped. And then this voice said, this voice came – it said – well, it gave me a bit of a fright, I don't know about Tod, but someone asked if he could do anything for us. So Tod said we were looking for the landlord and this man said the landlord would be upstairs. Then Tod asked was there a room vacant. And this man, this voice really, I think he was behind the partition, said yes there was a room vacant. He was very polite, I thought, but we never saw him, I don't know why they never put a light on. Anyway, we got out then and we came up and we went to the top of the house. I don't know whether it was the top. There was a door locked on the stairs, so there might have been another floor, but we didn't see anyone, and it was dark, and we were just coming down again when you opened your door.

ROSE. You said you were going up.

MRS SANDS. What?

ROSE. You said you were going up before.

MRS SANDS. No, we were coming down.

ROSE. You didn't say that before.

MRS SANDS. We'd been up.

MR SANDS. We'd been up. We were coming down.

Pause.

ROSE. This man, what was he like, was he old?

MRS SANDS. We didn't see him.

ROSE. Was he old?

Pause.

MR SANDS. Well, we'd better try to get hold of this landlord,
if he's about.

ROSE. You won't find any rooms vacant in this house.

MR SANDS. Why not?

ROSE. Mr Kidd·told me. He told me.

MR SANDS. Mr Kidd?

ROSE. He told me he was full up.

MR SANDS. The man in the basement said there was one. One
room. Number seven he said.

Pause.

ROSE. That's this room.

MR SANDS. We'd better go and get hold of the landlord.

MRS SANDS (*rising*). Well, thank you for the warm-up, Mrs
Hudd. I feel better now.

ROSE. This room is occupied.

MR SANDS. Come on.

MRS SANDS. Goodnight, Mrs Hudd. I hope your husband
won't be too long. Must be lonely for you, being all alone
here.

MR SANDS. Come on.

> *They go out.* ROSE *watches the door close, starts towards it,
> and stops. She takes the chair back to the table, picks
> up the magazine, looks at it, and puts it down. She goes to the
> rocking-chair, sits, rocks, stops, and sits still. There is a sharp
> knock at the door, which opens. Enter* MR KIDD.

MR KIDD. I came straight in.

ROSE (*rising*). Mr Kidd! I was just going to find you. I've got to speak to you.

MR KIDD. Look here, Mrs Hudd, I've got to speak to you. I came up specially.

ROSE. There were two people in here just now. They said this room was going vacant. What were they talking about?

MR KIDD. As soon as I heard the van go I got ready to come and see you. I'm knocked out.

ROSE. What was it all about? Did you see those people? How can this room be going? It's occupied. Did they get hold of you, Mr Kidd?

MR KIDD. Get hold of me? Who?

ROSE. I told you. Two people. They were looking for the landlord.

MR KIDD. I'm just telling you. I've been getting ready to come and see you, as soon as I heard the van go.

ROSE. Well then, who were they?

MR KIDD. That's why I came up before. But he hadn't gone yet. I've been waiting for him to go the whole week-end.

ROSE. Mr Kidd, what did they mean about this room?

MR KIDD. What room?

ROSE. Is this room vacant?

MR KIDD. Vacant?

ROSE. They were looking for the landlord.

MR KIDD. Who were?

ROSE. Listen, Mr Kidd, you are the landlord, aren't you? There isn't any other landlord?

MR KIDD. What? What's that got to do with it? I don't know what you're talking about. I've got to tell you, that's all. I've got to tell you. I've had a terrible week-end. You'll have to see him. I can't take it any more. You've got to see him.

Pause.

ROSE. Who?

MR KIDD. The man. He's been waiting to see you. He wants to see you. I can't get rid of him. I'm not a young man, Mrs Hudd, that's apparent. It's apparent. You've got to see him.

ROSE. See who?

MR KIDD. The man. He's downstairs now. He's been there the whole week-end. He said that when Mr Hudd went out I was to tell him. That's why I came up before. But he hadn't gone yet. So I told him. I said he hasn't gone yet. I said, well when he goes, I said, you can go up, go up, have done with it. No, he says, you must ask her if she'll see me. So I came up again, to ask you if you'll see him.

ROSE. Who is he?

MR KIDD. How do I know who he is? All I know is he won't say a word, he won't indulge in any conversation, just – has he gone? that and nothing else. He wouldn't even play a game of chess. All right, I said, the other night, while we're waiting I'll play you a game of chess. You play chess, don't you? I tell you, Mrs Hudd, I don't know if he even heard what I was saying. He just lies there. It's not good for me. He just lies there, that's all, waiting.

ROSE. He lies there, in the basement?

MR KIDD. Shall I tell him it's all right, Mrs Hudd?

ROSE. But it's damp down there.

MR KIDD. Shall I tell him it's all right?

ROSE. That what's all right?

MR KIDD. That you'll see him.

ROSE. See him? I beg your pardon, Mr Kidd. I don't know him. Why should I see him?

MR KIDD. You won't see him?

ROSE. Do you expect me to see someone I don't know? With my husband not here too?

MR KIDD. But he knows you, Mrs Hudd, he knows you.

ROSE. How could he, Mr Kidd, when I don't know him?

MR KIDD. You must know him.

ROSE. But I don't know anybody. We're quiet here. We've just moved into this district.

MR KIDD. But he doesn't come from this district. Perhaps you knew him in another district.

ROSE. Mr Kidd, do you think I go around knowing men in one district after another? What do you think I am?

MR KIDD. I don't know what I think.

He sits.

I think I'm going off my squiff.

ROSE. You need rest. An old man like you. What you need is rest.

MR KIDD. He hasn't given me any rest. Just lying there. In the black dark. Hour after hour. Why don't you leave me be, both of you? Mrs Hudd, have a bit of pity. Please see him. Why don't you see him?

ROSE. I don't know him.

MR KIDD. You can never tell. You might know him.

ROSE. I don't know him.

MR KIDD (*rising*). I don't know what'll happen if you don't see him.

ROSE. I've told you I don't know this man!

MR KIDD. I know what he'll do. I know what he'll do. If you don't see him now, there'll be nothing else for it, he'll come up on his own bat, when your husband's here, that's what he'll do. He'll come up when Mr Hudd's here, when your husband's here.

ROSE. He'd never do that.

MR KIDD. He would do that. That's exactly what he'll do. You don't think he's going to go away without seeing you, after he's come all this way, do you? You don't think that, do you?

ROSE. All this way?

MR KIDD. You don't think he's going to do that, do you?

Pause.

ROSE. He wouldn't do that.

MR KIDD. Oh yes. I know it.

Pause.

ROSE. What's the time?

MR KIDD. I don't know.

Pause.

ROSE. Fetch him. Quick. Quick!

> MR KIDD *goes out. She sits in the rocking-chair.*
> *After a few moments the door opens. Enter a blind Negro.*
> *He closes the door behind him, walks further, and feels with*
> *a stick till he reaches the armchair. He stops.*

RILEY. Mrs Hudd?

ROSE. You just touched a chair. Why don't you sit in it?

> *He sits.*

RILEY. Thank you.

ROSE. Don't thank me for anything. I don't want you up here. I don't know who you are. And the sooner you get out the better.

> *Pause.*

(*Rising.*) Well, come on. Enough's enough. You can take a liberty too far, you know. What do you want? You force your way up here. You disturb my evening. You come in and sit down here. What do you want?

> *He looks about the room.*

What are you looking at? You're blind, aren't you? So what are you looking at? What do you think you've got here, a little girl? I can keep up with you. I'm one ahead of people like you. Tell me what you want and get out.

RILEY. My name is Riley.

ROSE. I don't care if it's – What? That's not your name. That's not your name. You've got a grown-up woman in this room, do you hear? Or are you deaf too? You're not deaf too, are

you? You're all deaf and dumb and blind, the lot of you.
A bunch of cripples.

Pause.

RILEY. This is a large room.

ROSE. Never mind about the room. What do you know about
this room? You know nothing about it. And you won't be
staying in it long either. My luck. I get these creeps come in,
smelling up my room. What do you want?

RILEY. I want to see you.

ROSE. Well you can't see me, can you? You're a blind man. An
old, poor blind man. Aren't you? Can't see a dickeybird.

Pause.

They say I know you. That's an insult, for a start. Because I
can tell you, I wouldn't know you to spit on, not from a mile
off.

Pause.

Oh, these customers. They come in here and stink the place
out. After a handout. I know all about it. And as for you saying you know me, what liberty is that? Telling my landlord
too. Upsetting my landlord. What do you think you're up
to? We're settled down here, cosy, quiet, and our landlord
thinks the world of us, we're his favourite tenants, and you
come in and drive him up the wall, and drag my name into
it! What did you mean by dragging my name into it, and my
husband's name? How did you know what our name was?

Pause.

You've led him a dance, have you, this week-end? You've
got him going, have you? A poor, weak old man, who lets a
respectable house. Finished. Done for. You push your way
in and shove him about. And you drag my name into it.

Pause.

Come on, then. You say you wanted to see me. Well, I'm
here. Spit it out or out you go. What do you want?

RILEY. I have a message for you.

ROSE. You've got what? How could you have a message for me, Mister Riley, when I don't know you and nobody knows I'm here and I don't know anybody anyway. You think I'm an easy touch, don't you? Well, why don't you give it up as a bad job? Get off out of it. I've had enough of this. You're not only a nut, you're a blind nut and you can get out the way you came.

   Pause.

What message? Who have you got a message from? Who?

RILEY. Your father wants you to come home.

   Pause.

ROSE. Home?

RILEY. Yes.

ROSE. Home? Go now. Come on. It's late. It's late.

RILEY. To come home.

ROSE. Stop it. I can't take it. What do you want? What do you want?

RILEY. Come home, Sal.

   Pause.

ROSE. What did you call me?

RILEY. Come home, Sal.

ROSE. Don't call me that.

RILEY. Come, now.

ROSE. Don't call me that.

RILEY. So now you're here.

ROSE. Not Sal.

RILEY. Now I touch you.

ROSE. Don't touch me.

RILEY. Sal.

ROSE. I can't.

RILEY. I want you to come home.

ROSE. No.

RILEY. With me.

ROSE. I can't.

RILEY. I waited to see you.

ROSE. Yes.

RILEY. Now I see you.

ROSE. Yes.

RILEY. Sal.

ROSE. Not that.

RILEY. So, now.

Pause.

So, now.

ROSE. I've been here.

RILEY. Yes.

ROSE. Long.

RILEY. Yes.

ROSE. The day is a hump. I never go out.

RILEY. No.

ROSE. I've been here.

RILEY. Come home now, Sal.

She touches his eyes, the back of his head and his temples with her hands. Enter BERT.
He stops at the door, then goes to the window and draws the curtains. It is dark. He comes to the centre of the room and regards the woman.

BERT. I got back all right.

ROSE (*going towards him*). Yes.

BERT. I got back all right.

Pause.

ROSE. Is it late?

BERT. I had a good bowl down there.

Pause.

I drove her down, hard. They got it dark out.

ROSE. Yes.

BERT. Then I drove her back, hard. They got it very icy out.
ROSE. Yes.
BERT. But I drove her.

Pause.

I sped her.

Pause.

I caned her along. She was good. Then I got back. I could
see the road all right. There was no cars. One there was. He
wouldn't move. I bumped him. I got my road. I had all my
way. There again and back. They shoved out of it. I kept on
the straight. There was no mixing it. Not with her. She was
good. She went with me. She don't mix it with me. I use
my hand. Like that. I get hold of her. I go where I go. She
took me there. She brought me back.

Pause.

I got back all right.

He takes the chair from the table and sits to the left of the
NEGRO'S chair, close to it. He regards the NEGRO for some
moments. Then with his foot he lifts the armchair up. The
NEGRO falls on to the floor. He rises slowly.

RILEY. Mr Hudd, your wife—
BERT. Lice!

He strikes the NEGRO, knocking him down, and then kicks
his head against the gas-stove several times. The NEGRO
lies still. BERT walks away.
Silence.
ROSE stands clutching her eyes.

ROSE. Can't see. I can't see. I can't see.

Blackout

Curtain

THE DUMB WAITER

The Dumb Waiter was first presented at the Hampstead Theatre Club on 21 January 1960, with the following cast:

BEN   Nicholas Selby
GUS   George Tovey

Directed by James Roose-Evans

The Dumb Waiter was transferred to the Royal Court Theatre on 8 March 1960, with the same cast.

The Dumb Waiter was produced for televison by the BBC on 23 July 1985, with the following cast:

BEN   Colin Blakely
GUS   Kenneth Cranham

Directed by Kenneth Ives

THE DUMB WAITER

Scene: A basement room. Two beds, flat against the back wall. A serving hatch, closed, between the beds. A door to the kitchen and lavatory, left. A door to a passage, right.

BEN *is lying on a bed, left, reading a paper.* GUS *is sitting on a bed, right, tying his shoelaces, with difficulty. Both are dressed in shirts, trousers and braces.*

Silence.

GUS *ties his laces, rises, yawns and begins to walk slowly to the door, left. He stops, looks down, and shakes his foot.*

BEN *lowers his paper and watches him.* GUS *kneels and unties his shoe-lace and slowly takes off the shoe. He looks inside it and brings out a flattened matchbox. He shakes it and examines it. Their eyes meet.* BEN *rattles his paper and reads.* GUS *puts the matchbox in his pocket and bends down to put on his shoe. He ties his lace, with difficulty.* BEN *lowers his paper and watches him.* GUS *walks to the door, left, stops, and shakes the other foot. He kneels, unties his shoe-lace, and slowly takes off the shoe. He looks inside it and brings out a flattened cigarette packet. He shakes it and examines it. Their eyes meet.* BEN *rattles his paper and reads.* GUS *puts the packet in his pocket, bends down, puts on his shoe and ties the lace.*

He wanders off, left.

BEN *slams the paper down on the bed and glares after him. He picks up the paper and lies on his back, reading.*

Silence.

A lavatory chain is pulled twice off, left, but the lavatory does not flush.

Silence.

GUS *re-enters, left, and halts at the door, scratching his head.*
BEN *slams down the paper.*

BEN. Kaw!

He picks up the paper.

What about this? Listen to this!

He refers to the paper.

A man of eighty-seven wanted to cross the road. But there was a lot of traffic, see? He couldn't see how he was going to squeeze through. So he crawled under a lorry.

GUS. He what?

BEN. He crawled under a lorry. A stationary lorry.

GUS. No?

BEN. The lorry started and ran over him.

GUS. Go on!

BEN. That's what it says here.

GUS. Get away.

BEN. It's enough to make you want to puke, isn't it?

GUS. Who advised him to do a thing like that?

BEN. A man of eighty-seven crawling under a lorry!

GUS. It's unbelievable.

BEN. It's down here in black and white.

GUS. Incredible.

> *Silence.*
> GUS *shakes his head and exits.* BEN *lies back and reads.*
> *The lavatory chain is pulled once off left, but the lavatory does not flush.*
> BEN *whistles at an item in the paper.*
> GUS *re-enters.*

I want to ask you something.

BEN. What are you doing out there?

GUS. Well, I was just —

BEN. What about the tea?

GUS. I'm just going to make it.

BEN. Well, go on, make it.

GUS. Yes, I will. (*He sits in a chair. Ruminatively.*) He's laid on some very nice crockery this time, I'll say that. It's sort of striped. There's a white stripe.

BEN *reads.*

It's very nice. I'll say that.

BEN *turns the page.*

You know, sort of round the cup. Round the rim. All the rest of it's black, you see. Then the saucer's black, except for right in the middle, where the cup goes, where it's white.

BEN *reads.*

Then the plates are the same, you see. Only they've got a black stripe – the plates – right across the middle. Yes, I'm quite taken with the crockery.

BEN (*still reading*). What do you want plates for? You're not going to eat.

GUS. I've brought a few biscuits.

BEN. Well, you'd better eat them quick.

GUS. I always bring a few biscuits. Or a pie. You know I can't drink tea without anything to eat.

BEN. Well, make the tea then, will you? Time's getting on.

GUS *brings out the flattened cigarette packet and examines it.*

GUS. You got any cigarettes? I think I've run out.

He throws the packet high up and leans forward to catch it.

I hope it won't be a long job, this one.

Aiming carefully, he flips the packet under his bed.

Oh, I wanted to ask you something.

BEN (*slamming his paper down*). Kaw!

GUS. What's that?

BEN. A child of eight killed a cat!

GUS. Get away.

BEN. It's a fact. What about that, eh? A child of eight killing a
cat!

GUS. How did he do it?

BEN. It was a girl.

GUS. How did she do it?

BEN. She –

> *He picks up the paper and studies it.*

It doesn't say.

GUS. Why not?

BEN. Wait a minute. It just says – Her brother, aged eleven,
viewed the incident from the toolshed.

GUS. Go on!

BEN. That's bloody ridiculous.

> *Pause.*

GUS. I bet he did it.

BEN. Who?

GUS. The brother.

BEN. I think you're right.

> *Pause.*

(*Slamming down the paper.*) What about that, eh? A kid of
eleven killing a cat and blaming it on his little sister of eight!
It's enough to –

> *He breaks off in disgust and seizes the paper.* GUS *rises.*

GUS. What time is he getting in touch?

> BEN *reads.*

What time is he getting in touch?

BEN. What's the matter with you? It could be any time. Any
time.

GUS (*moves to the foot of* BEN'S *bed*). Well, I was going to ask
you something.

BEN. What?

GUS. Have you noticed the time that tank takes to fill?

BEN. What tank?

GUS. In the lavatory.

BEN. No. Does it?

GUS. Terrible.

BEN. Well, what about it?

GUS. What do you think's the matter with it?

BEN. Nothing.

GUS. Nothing?

BEN. It's got a deficient ballcock, that's all.

GUS. A deficient what?

BEN. Ballcock.

GUS. No? Really?

BEN. That's what I should say.

GUS. Go on! That didn't occur to me.

GUS *wanders to his bed and presses the mattress.*

I didn't have a very restful sleep today, did you? It's not much of a bed. I could have done with another blanket too. (*He catches sight of a picture on the wall.*) Hello, what's this? (*Peering at it.*) 'The First Eleven.' Cricketers. You seen this, Ben?

BEN (*reading*). What?

GUS. The first eleven.

BEN. What?

GUS. There's a photo here of the first eleven.

BEN. What first eleven?

GUS (*studying the photo*). It doesn't say.

BEN. What about that tea?

GUS. They all look a bit old to me.

GUS *wanders downstage, looks out front, then all about the room.*

I wouldn't like to live in this dump. I wouldn't mind if you had a window, you could see what it looked like outside.

BEN. What do you want a window for?

GUS. Well, I like to have a bit of a view, Ben. It whiles away the time.

He walks about the room.

I mean, you come into a place when it's still dark, you come into a room you've never seen before, you sleep all day, you do your job, and then you go away in the night again.

Pause.

I like to get a look at the scenery. You never get the chance in this job.

BEN. You get your holidays, don't you?

GUS. Only a fortnight.

BEN (*lowering the paper*). You kill me. Anyone would think you're working every day. How often do we do a job? Once a week? What are you complaining about?

GUS. Yes, but we've got to be on tap though, haven't we? You can't move out of the house in case a call comes.

BEN. You know what your trouble is?

GUS. What?

BEN. You haven't got any interests.

GUS. I've got interests.

BEN. What? Tell me one of your interests.

Pause.

GUS. I've got interests.

BEN. Look at me. What have I got?

GUS. I don't know. What?

BEN. I've got my woodwork. I've got my model boats. Have you ever seen me idle? I'm never idle. I know how to occupy my time, to its best advantage. Then when a call comes, I'm ready.

GUS. Don't you ever get a bit fed up?

BEN. Fed up? What with?

Silence.

BEN *reads.* GUS *feels in the pocket of his jacket, which hangs on the bed.*

GUS. You got any cigarettes? I've run out.

The lavatory flushes off left.

There she goes.

GUS *sits on his bed.*

No, I mean, I say the crockery's good. It is. It's very nice. But that's about all I can say for this place. It's worse than the last one. Remember that last place we were in? Last time, where was it? At least there was a wireless there. No, honest. He doesn't seem to bother much about our comfort these days.

BEN. When are you going to stop jabbering?

GUS. You'd get rheumatism in a place like this, if you stay long.

BEN. We're not staying long. Make the tea, will you? We'll be on the job in a minute.

GUS *picks up a small bag by his bed and brings out a packet of tea. He examines it and looks up.*

GUS. Eh, I've been meaning to ask you.

BEN. What the hell is it now?

GUS. Why did you stop the car this morning, in the middle of that road?

BEN (*lowering the paper*). I thought you were asleep.

GUS. I was, but I woke up when you stopped. You did stop, didn't you?

Pause.

In the middle of that road. It was still dark, don't you remember? I looked out. It was all misty. I thought perhaps you wanted to kip, but you were sitting up dead straight, like you were waiting for something.

BEN. I wasn't waiting for anything.

GUS. I must have fallen asleep again. What was all that about then? Why did you stop?

BEN (*picking up the paper*). We were too early.

GUS. Early? (*He rises.*) What do you mean? We got the call, didn't we, saying we were to start right away. We did. We shoved out on the dot. So how could we be too early?

BEN (*quietly*). Who took the call, me or you?

GUS. You.

BEN. We were too early.

GUS. Too early for what?

Pause.

You mean someone had to get out before we got in?

He examines the bedclothes.

I thought these sheets didn't look too bright. I thought they ponged a bit. I was too tired to notice when I got in this morning. Eh, that's taking a bit of a liberty, isn't it? I don't want to share my bed-sheets. I told you things were going down the drain. I mean, we've always had clean sheets laid on up till now. I've noticed it.

BEN. How do you know those sheets weren't clean?

GUS. What do you mean?

BEN. How do you know they weren't clean? You've spent the whole day in them, haven't you?

GUS. What, you mean it might be my pong? (*He sniffs sheets.*) Yes. (*He sits slowly on bed.*) It could be my pong, I suppose. It's difficult to tell. I don't really know what I pong like, that's the trouble.

BEN (*referring to the paper*). Kaw!

GUS. Eh, Ben.

BEN. Kaw!

GUS. Ben.

BEN. What?

GUS. What town are we in? I've forgotten.

BEN. I've told you. Birmingham.

GUS. Go on!

He looks with interest about the room.

That's in the Midlands. The second biggest city in Great Britain. I'd never have guessed.

He snaps his fingers.

Eh, it's Friday today, isn't it? It'll be Saturday tomorrow.

BEN. What about it?

GUS (*excited*). We could go and watch the Villa.

BEN. They're playing away.

GUS. No, are they? Caarr! What a pity.

BEN. Anyway, there's no time. We've got to get straight back.

GUS. Well, we have done in the past, haven't we? Stayed over and watched a game, haven't we? For a bit of relaxation.

BEN. Things have tightened up, mate. They've tightened up.

GUS *chuckles to himself.*

GUS. I saw the Villa get beat in a cup-tie once. Who was it against now? White shirts. It was one-all at half-time. I'll never forget it. Their opponents won by a penalty. Talk about drama. Yes, it was a disputed penalty. Disputed. They got beat two-one, anyway, because of it. You were there yourself.

BEN. Not me.

GUS. Yes, you were there. Don't you remember that disputed penalty?

BEN. No.

GUS. He went down just inside the area. Then they said he was just acting. I didn't think the other bloke touched him myself. But the referee had the ball on the spot.

BEN. Didn't touch him! What are you talking about? He laid him out flat!

GUS. Not the Villa. The Villa don't play that sort of game.
BEN. Get out of it.

Pause.

GUS. Eh, that must have been here, in Birmingham.
BEN. What must?
GUS. The Villa. That must have been here.
BEN. They were playing away.
GUS. Because you know who the other team was? It was the
Spurs. It was Tottenham Hotspur.
BEN. Well, what about it?
GUS. We've never done a job in Tottenham.
BEN. How do you know?
GUS. I'd remember Tottenham.

BEN *turns on his bed to look at him.*

BEN. Don't make me laugh, will you?

BEN *turns back and reads.* GUS *yawns and speaks through
his yawn.*

GUS. When's he going to get in touch?

Pause.

Yes, I'd like to see another football match. I've always been
an ardent football fan. Here, what about coming to see the
Spurs tomorrow?
BEN (*tonelessly*). They're playing away.
GUS. Who are?
BEN. The Spurs.
GUS. Then they might be playing here.
BEN. Don't be silly.
GUS. If they're playing away they might be playing here. They
might be playing the Villa.
BEN (*tonelessly*). But the Villa are playing away.

Pause. An envelope slides under the door, right. GUS *sees it.
He stands, looking at it.*

GUS. Ben.
BEN. Away. They're all playing away.
GUS. Ben, look here.
BEN. What?
GUS. Look.

BEN *turns his head and sees the envelope. He stands.*

BEN. What's that?
GUS. I don't know.
BEN. Where did it come from?
GUS. Under the door.
BEN. Well, what is it?
GUS. I don't know.

They stare at it.

BEN. Pick it up.
GUS. What do you mean?
BEN. Pick it up!

GUS *slowly moves towards it, bends and picks it up.*

What is it?
GUS. An envelope.
BEN. Is there anything on it?
GUS. No.
BEN. Is it sealed?
GUS. Yes.
BEN. Open it.
GUS. What?
BEN. Open it!

GUS *opens it and looks inside.*

What's in it?

GUS *empties twelve matches into his hand.*

GUS. Matches.

BEN. Matches?

GUS. Yes.

BEN. Show it to me.

GUS *passes the envelope.* BEN *examines it.*

Nothing on it. Not a word.

GUS. That's funny, isn't it?

BEN. It came under the door?

GUS. Must have done.

BEN. Well, go on.

GUS. Go on where?

BEN. Open the door and see if you can catch anyone outside.

GUS. Who, me?

BEN. Go on!

GUS *stares at him, puts the matches in his pocket, goes to his bed and brings a revolver from under the pillow. He goes to the door, opens it, looks out and shuts it.*

GUS. No one.

He replaces the revolver.

BEN. What did you see?

GUS. Nothing.

BEN. They must have been pretty quick.

GUS *takes the matches from his pocket and looks at them.*

GUS. Well, they'll come in handy.

BEN. Yes.

GUS. Won't they?

BEN. Yes, you're always running out, aren't you?

GUS. All the time.

BEN. Well, they'll come in handy then.

GUS. Yes.

BEN. Won't they?

GUS. Yes, I could do with them. I could do with them too.

BEN. You could, eh?

GUS. Yes.

BEN. Why?

GUS. We haven't got any.

BEN. Well, you've got some now, haven't you?

GUS. I can light the kettle now.

BEN. Yes, you're always cadging matches. How many have you got there?

GUS. About a dozen.

BEN. Well, don't lose them. Red too. You don't even need a box.

GUS *probes his ear with a match.*

(*Slapping his hand*). Don't waste them! Go on, go and light it.

GUS. Eh?

BEN. Go and light it.

GUS. Light what?

BEN. The kettle.

GUS. You mean the gas.

BEN. Who does?

GUS. You do.

BEN (*his eyes narrowing*). What do you mean, I mean the gas?

GUS. Well, that's what you mean, don't you? The gas.

BEN (*powerfully*). If I say go and light the kettle I mean go and light the kettle.

GUS. How can you light a kettle?

BEN. It's a figure of speech! Light the kettle. It's a figure of speech!

GUS. I've never heard it.

BEN. Light the kettle! It's common usage!

GUS. I think you've got it wrong.

BEN (*menacing*). What do you mean?

GUS. They say put on the kettle.

BEN (*taut*). Who says?

They stare at each other, breathing hard.

(*Deliberately.*) I have never in all my life heard anyone say put on the kettle.

GUS. I bet my mother used to say it.

BEN. Your mother? When did you last see your mother?

GUS. I don't know, about –

BEN. Well, what are you talking about your mother for?

They stare.

Gus, I'm not trying to be unreasonable. I'm just trying to point out something to you.

GUS. Yes, but –

BEN. Who's the senior partner here, me or you?

GUS. You.

BEN. I'm only looking after your interests, Gus. You've got to learn, mate.

GUS. Yes, but I've never heard –

BEN (*vehemently*). Nobody says light the gas! What does the gas light?

GUS. What does the gas –?

BEN (*grabbing him with two hands by the throat, at arm's length*). THE KETTLE, YOU FOOL!

GUS *takes the hands from his throat.*

GUS. All right, all right.

Pause.

BEN. Well, what are you waiting for?

GUS. I want to see if they light.

BEN. What?

GUS. The matches.

He takes out the flattened box and tries to strike.

No.

He throws the box under the bed.
BEN *stares at him.*

GUS *raises his foot.*

Shall I try it on here?

BEN *stares.* GUS *strikes a match on his shoe. It lights.*

Here we are.

BEN (*wearily*). Put on the bloody kettle, for Christ's sake.

BEN *goes to his bed, but, realising what he has said, stops and half turns. They look at each other.* GUS *slowly exits, left.* BEN *slams his paper down on the bed and sits on it, head in hands.*

GUS (*entering*). It's going.

BEN. What?

GUS. The stove.

GUS *goes to his bed and sits.*

I wonder who it'll be tonight.

Silence.

Eh, I've been wanting to ask you something.

BEN (*putting his legs on the bed*). Oh, for Christ's sake.

GUS. No. I was going to ask you something.

He rises and sits on BEN'S *bed.*

BEN. What are you sitting on my bed for?

GUS *sits.*

What's the matter with you? You're always asking me questions. What's the matter with you?

GUS. Nothing.

BEN. You never used to ask me so many damn questions. What's come over you?

GUS. No, I was just wondering.

BEN. Stop wondering. You've got a job to do . Why don't you just do it and shut up?

GUS. That's what I was wondering about.

BEN. What?

GUS. The job.

BEN. What job?

GUS (*tentatively*). I thought perhaps you might know something.

> BEN *looks at him.*

I thought perhaps you – I mean – have you got any idea – who it's going to be tonight?

BEN. Who what's going to be?

> *They look at each other.*

GUS (*at length*). Who it's going to be.

> *Silence.*

BEN. Are you feeling all right?

GUS. Sure.

BEN. Go and make the tea.

GUS. Yes, sure.

> GUS *exits, left,* BEN *looks after him. He then takes his revolver from under the pillow and checks it for ammunition.* GUS *re-enters.*

The gas has gone out.

BEN. Well, what about it?

GUS. There's a meter.

BEN. I haven't got any money.

GUS. Nor have I.

BEN. You'll have to wait.

GUS. What for?

BEN. For Wilson.

GUS. He might not come. He might just send a message. He doesn't always come.

BEN. Well, you'll have to do without it, won't you?

GUS. Blimey.

BEN. You'll have a cup of tea afterwards. What's the matter with you?

GUS. I like to have one before.

> BEN *holds the revolver up to the light and polishes it.*

BEN. You'd better get ready anyway.

GUS. Well, I don't know, that's a bit much, you know, for my money.

> *He picks up a packet of tea from the bed and throws it into the bag.*

I hope he's got a shilling, anyway, if he comes. He's entitled to have. After all, it's his place, he could have seen there was enough gas for a cup of tea.

BEN. What do you mean, it's his place?

GUS. Well, isn't it?

BEN. He's probably only rented it. It doesn't have to be his place.

GUS. I know it's his place. I bet the whole house is. He's not even laying on any gas now either.

> GUS *sits on his bed.*

It's his place all right. Look at all the other places. You go to this address, there's a key there, there's a teapot, there's never a soul in sight – (*He pauses.*) Eh, nobody ever hears a thing, have you ever thought of that? We never get any complaints, do we, too much noise or anything like that? You never see a soul, do you? – except the bloke who comes. You ever noticed that? I wonder if the walls are sound-proof. (*He touches the wall above his bed.*) Can't tell. All you do is wait, eh? Half the time he doesn't even bother to put in an appearance, Wilson.

BEN. Why should he? He's a busy man.

GUS (*thoughtfully*). I find him hard to talk to, Wilson. Do you know that, Ben?

BEN. Scrub round it, will you?

Pause.

GUS. There are a number of things I want to ask him. But I can never get round to it, when I see him.

Pause.

I've been thinking about the last one.
BEN. What last one?
GUS. That girl.

BEN *grabs the paper, which he reads.*

(*Rising, looking down at* BEN). How many times have you read that paper?

BEN *slams the paper down and rises.*

BEN (*angrily*). What do you mean?
GUS. I was just wondering how many times you'd –
BEN. What are you doing, criticizing me?
GUS. No, I was just –
BEN. You'll get a swipe round your earhole if you don't watch your step.
GUS. Now look here, Ben –
BEN. I'm not looking anywhere! (*He addresses the room.*) How many times have I – ! A bloody liberty!
GUS. I didn't mean that.
BEN. You just get on with it, mate. Get on with it, that's all.

BEN *gets back on the bed.*

GUS. I was just thinking about that girl, that's all.

GUS *sits on his bed.*

She wasn't much to look at, I know, but still. It was a mess though, wasn't it? What a mess. Honest, I can't remember a mess like that one. They don't seem to hold together like

men, women. A looser texture, like. Didn't she spread, eh?
She didn't half spread. Kaw! But I've been meaning to ask
you.

>   BEN *sits up and clenches his eyes.*

Who clears up after we've gone? I'm curious about that.
Who does the clearing up? Maybe they don't clear up.
Maybe they just leave them there, eh? What do you think?
How many jobs have we done? Blimey, I can't count them.
What if they never clear anything up after we've gone.

BEN (*pityingly*). You mutt. Do you think we're the only
branch of this organization? Have a bit of common. They
got departments for everything.

GUS. What cleaners and all?

BEN. You birk!

GUS. No, it was that girl made me start to think –

>   *There is a loud clatter and racket in the bulge of wall between
>   the beds, of something descending. They grab their revolvers,
>   jump up and face the wall. The noise comes to a stop. Silence.
>   They look at each other.* BEN *gestures sharply towards the
>   wall.* GUS *approaches the wall slowly. He bangs it with his
>   revolver. It is hollow.* BEN *moves to the head of his bed, his
>   revolver cocked.* GUS *puts his revolver on his bed and pats
>   along the bottom of the centre panel. He finds a rim. He lifts
>   the panel. Disclosed is a serving-hatch, a 'dumb waiter'. A
>   wide box is held by pulleys.* GUS *peers into the box. He brings
>   out a piece of paper.*

BEN. What is it?

GUS. You have a look at it.

BEN. Read it.

GUS (*reading*). Two braised steak and chips. Two sago pud-
dings. Two teas without sugar.

BEN. Let me see that. (*He takes the paper.*)

GUS (*to himself*). Two teas without sugar.

BEN. Mmnn.

GUS. What do you think of that?

BEN. Well –

The box goes up. BEN *levels his revolver.*

GUS. Give us a chance! They're in a hurry, aren't they?

BEN *re-reads the note.* GUS *looks over his shoulder.*

That's a bit – that's a bit funny, isn't it?

BEN (*quickly*). No. It's not funny. It probably used to be a café here, that's all. Upstairs. These places change hands very quickly.

GUS. A café?

BEN. Yes.

GUS. What, you mean this was the kitchen, down here?

BEN. Yes, they change hands overnight, these places. Go into liquidation. The people who run it, you know, they don't find it a going concern, they move out.

GUS. You mean the people who ran this place didn't find it a going concern and moved out?

BEN. Sure.

GUS. WELL, WHO'S GOT IT NOW?

Silence.

BEN. What do you mean, who's got it now?

GUS. Who's got it now? If they moved out, who moved in?

BEN. Well, that all depends –

The box descends with a clatter and bang. BEN *levels his revolver.* GUS *goes to the box and brings out a piece of paper.*

GUS (*reading*). Soup of the day. Liver and onions. Jam tart.
A pause. GUS *looks at* BEN. BEN *takes the note and reads it. He walks slowly to the hatch.* GUS *follows.* BEN *looks into the hatch but not up it.* GUS *puts his hand on* BEN'S *shoulder.* BEN *throws it off.* GUS *puts his finger to his mouth. He leans*

on the hatch and swiftly looks up it. BEN *flings him away in alarm.* BEN *looks at the note. He throws his revolver on the bed and speaks with decision.*

BEN. We'd better send something up.
GUS. Eh?
BEN. We'd better send something up.
GUS. Oh! Yes. Yes. Maybe you're right.

They are both relieved at the decision.

BEN (*purposefully*). Quick! What have you got in that bag?
GUS. Not much.

   GUS *goes to the hatch and shouts up it.*

Wait a minute!
BEN. Don't do that!

   GUS *examines the contents of the bag and brings them out, one by one.*

GUS. Biscuits. A bar of chocolate. Half a pint of milk.
BEN. That all?
GUS. Packet of tea.
BEN. Good.
GUS. We can't send the tea. That's all the tea we've got.
BEN. Well, there's no gas. You can't do anything with it, can you?
GUS. Maybe they can send us down a bob.
BEN. What else is there?
GUS (*reaching into bag*). One Eccles cake.
BEN. One Eccles cake?
GUS. Yes.
BEN. You never told me you had an Eccles cake.
GUS. Didn't I?
BEN. Why only one? Didn't you bring one for me?
GUS. I didn't think you'd be keen.
BEN. Well, you can't send up one Eccles cake, anyway.

GUS. Why not?
BEN. Fetch one of those plates.
GUS. All right.

   GUS *goes towards the door, left, and stops.*

   Do you mean I can keep the Eccles cake then?
BEN. Keep it?
GUS. Well, they don't know we've got it, do they?
BEN. That's not the point.
GUS. Can't I keep it?
BEN. No, you can't. Get the plate.

   GUS *exits, left.* BEN *looks in the bag. He brings out a packet of crisps. Enter* GUS *with a plate.*

   (*Accusingly, holding up the crisps*). Where did these come from?
GUS. What?
BEN. Where did these crisps come from?
GUS. Where did you find them?
BEN (*hitting him on the shoulder*). You're playing a dirty game, my lad!
GUS. I only eat those with beer!
BEN. Well, where were you going to get the beer?
GUS. I was saving them till I did.
BEN. I'll remember this. Put everything on the plate.

   They pile everything on to the plate. The box goes up without the plate.

   Wait a minute!

   They stand.

GUS. It's gone up.
BEN. It's all your stupid fault, playing about!
GUS. What do we do now?
BEN. We'll have to wait till it comes down.

BEN *puts the plate on the bed, puts on his shoulder holster, and starts to put on his tie.*

You'd better get ready.

GUS *goes to his bed, puts on his tie, and starts to fix his holster.*

GUS. Hey, Ben.
BEN. What?
GUS. What's going on here?

Pause.

BEN. What do you mean?
GUS. How can this be a café?
BEN. It used to be a café.
GUS. Have you seen the gas stove?
BEN. What about it?
GUS. It's only got three rings.
BEN. So what?
GUS. Well, you couldn't cook much on three rings, not for a busy place like this.
BEN (*irritably*). That's why the service is slow!

BEN *puts on his waistcoat.*

GUS. Yes, but what happens when we're not here? What do they do then? All these menus coming down and nothing going up. It might have been going on like this for years.

BEN *brushes his jacket.*

What happens when we go?

BEN *puts on his jacket.*

They can't do much business.

The box descends. They turn about. GUS *goes to the hatch and brings out a note.*

GUS (*reading*). Macaroni Pastitsio. Ormitha Macarounada.

BEN. What was that?

GUS. Macaroni Pastitsio. Ormitha Macarounada.

BEN. Greek dishes.

GUS. No.

BEN. That's right.

GUS. That's pretty high class.

BEN. Quick before it goes up.

GUS *puts the plate in the box.*

GUS (*calling up the hatch*). Three McVitie and Price! One Lyons Red Label! One Smith's Crisps! One Eccles cake! One Fruit and Nut!

BEN. Cadbury's.

GUS (*up the hatch*). Cadbury's!

BEN (*handing the milk*). One bottle of milk.

GUS (*up the hatch*). One bottle of milk! Half a pint! (*He looks at the label.*) Express Dairy! (*He puts the bottle in the box.*)

The box goes up.

Just did it.

BEN. You shouldn't shout like that.

GUS. Why not?

BEN. It isn't done.

BEN *goes to his bed.*

Well, that should be all right, anyway, for the time being.

GUS. You think so, eh?

BEN. Get dressed, will you? It'll be any minute now.

GUS *puts on his waistcoat.* BEN *lies down and looks up at the ceiling.*

GUS. This is some place. No tea and no biscuits.

BEN. Eating makes you lazy, mate. You're getting lazy, you know that? You don't want to get slack on your job.

GUS. Who me?

BEN. Slack, mate, slack.

GUS. Who me? Slack?

BEN. Have you checked your gun? You haven't even checked your gun. It looks disgraceful, anyway. Why don't you ever polish it?

> GUS *rubs his revolver on the sheet.* BEN *takes out a pocket mirror and straightens his tie.*

GUS. I wonder where the cook is. They must have had a few, to cope with that. Maybe they had a few more gas stoves. Eh! Maybe there's another kitchen along the passage.

BEN. Of course there is! Do you know what it takes to make an Ormitha Macarounada?

GUS. No, what?

BEN. An Ormitha –! Buck your ideas up, will you?

GUS. Takes a few cooks, eh?

> GUS *puts his revolver in its holster.*

The sooner we're out of this place the better.

> *He puts on his jacket.*

Why doesn't he get in touch? I feel like I've been here years. (*He takes his revolver out of its holster to check the ammunition.*) We've never let him down though, have we? We've never let him down. I was thinking only the other day, Ben. We're reliable, aren't we?

> *He puts his revolver back in its holster.*

Still, I'll be glad when it's over tonight.

> *He brushes his jacket.*

I hope the bloke's not going to get excited tonight, or anything. I'm feeling a bit off. I've got a splitting headache.

> *Silence.*

The box descends. BEN *jumps up.*
GUS *collects the note.*

(*Reading.*) One Bamboo Shoots, Water Chestnuts and Chicken. One Char Siu and Beansprouts.

BEN. Beansprouts?

GUS. Yes.

BEN. Blimey.

GUS. I wouldn't know where to begin.

He looks back at the box. The packet of tea is inside it. He picks it up.

They've sent back the tea.

BEN (*anxious*). What'd they do that for?

GUS. Maybe it isn't tea-time.

The box goes up. Silence.

BEN (*throwing the tea on the bed, and speaking urgently*). Look here. We'd better tell them.

GUS. Tell them what?

BEN. That we can't do it, we haven't got it.

GUS. All right then.

BEN. Lend us your pencil. We'll write a note.

GUS, *turning for a pencil, suddenly discovers the speaking-tube, which hangs on the right wall of the hatch facing his bed.*

GUS. What's this?

BEN. What?

GUS. This.

BEN (*examining it*). This? It's a speaking-tube.

GUS. How long has that been there?

BEN. Just the job. We should have used it before, instead of shouting up there.

GUS. Funny I never noticed it before.

BEN. Well, come on.

GUS. What do you do?

BEN. See that? That's a whistle.

GUS. What, this?

BEN. Yes, take it out. Pull it out.

   GUS *does so.*

That's it.

GUS. What do we do now?

BEN. Blow into it.

GUS. Blow?

BEN. It whistles up there if you blow. Then they know you
   want to speak. Blow.

   GUS *blows. Silence.*

GUS (*tube at mouth*). I can't hear a thing.

BEN. Now you speak! Speak into it!

   GUS *looks at* BEN, *then speaks into the tube.*

GUS. The larder's bare!

BEN. Give me that!

   He grabs the tube and puts it to his mouth.

(*Speaking with great deference.*) Good evening. I'm sorry to
– bother you, but we just thought we'd better let you know
that we haven't got anything left. We sent up all we had.
There's no more food down here.

   He brings the tube slowly to his ear.

What?

   To mouth.

What?

   To ear. He listens. To mouth.

No, all we had we sent up.

   To ear. He listens. To mouth.

Oh, I'm very sorry to hear that.

To ear. He listens. To GUS.

The Eccles cake was stale.

He listens. To GUS.

The chocolate was melted.

He listens. To GUS.

The milk was sour.

GUS. What about the crisps?

BEN (*listening*). The biscuits were mouldy.

He glares at GUS. *Tube to mouth.*

Well, we're very sorry about that.

Tube to ear.

What?

To mouth.

What?

To ear.

Yes. Yes.

To mouth.

Yes certainly. Certainly. Right away.

To ear. The voice has ceased. He hangs up the tube.

(*Excitedly*). Did you hear that?

GUS. What?

BEN. You know what he said? Light the kettle! Not put on the kettle! Not light the gas! But light the kettle!

GUS. How can we light the kettle?

BEN. What do you mean?

GUS. There's no gas.

BEN (*clapping hand to head*). Now what do we do?

GUS. What did he want us to light the kettle for?

BEN. For tea. He wanted a cup of tea.

GUS. *He* wanted a cup of tea! What about me? I've been wanting a cup of tea all night!

BEN (*despairingly*). What do we do now?

GUS. What are we supposed to drink?

BEN *sits on his bed, staring*.

What about us?

BEN *sits*.

I'm thirsty too. I'm starving. And he wants a cup of tea. That beats the band, that does.

BEN *lets his head sink on to his chest*.

I could do with a bit of sustenance myself. What about you? You look as if you could do with something too.

GUS *sits on his bed*.

We send him up all we've got and he's not satisfied. No, honest, it's enough to make the cat laugh. Why did you send him up all that stuff? (*Thoughtfully.*) Why did I send it up?

Pause.

Who knows what he's got upstairs? He's probably got a salad bowl. They must have something up there. They won't get much from down here. You notice they didn't ask for any salads? They've probably got a salad bowl up there. Cold meat, radishes, cucumbers. Watercress. Roll mops.

Pause.

Hardboiled eggs.

Pause.

The lot. They've probably got a crate of beer too. Probably eating my crisps with a pint of beer now. Didn't have anything to say about those crisps, did he? They do all right, don't worry about that. You don't think they're just going to sit there and wait for stuff to come up from down here, do you? That'll get them nowhere.

Pause.

They do all right.

Pause.

And he wants a cup of tea.

Pause.

That's past a joke, in my opinion.

He looks over at BEN, *rises, and goes to him.*

What's the matter with you? You don't look too bright. I feel like an Alka-Seltzer myself.

BEN *sits up.*

BEN (*in a low voice*). Time's getting on.

GUS. I know. I don't like doing a job on an empty stomach.

BEN (*wearily*). Be quiet a minute. Let me give you your instructions.

GUS. What for? We always do it the same way, don't we?

BEN. Let me give you your instructions.

GUS *sighs and sits next to* BEN *on the bed. The instructions are stated and repeated automatically.*

When we get the call, you go over and stand behind the door.

GUS. Stand behind the door.

BEN. If there's a knock on the door you don't answer it.

GUS. If there's a knock on the door I don't answer it.

BEN. But there won't be a knock on the door.

GUS. So I won't answer it.

BEN. When the bloke comes in –

GUS. When the bloke comes in –

BEN. Shut the door behind him.

GUS. Shut the door behind him.

BEN. Without divulging your presence.

GUS. Without divulging my presence.

BEN. He'll see me and come towards me.

GUS. He'll see you and come towards you.

BEN. He won't see you.

GUS (absently). Eh?

BEN. He won't see you.

GUS. He won't see me.

BEN. But he'll see me.

GUS. He'll see you.

BEN. He won't know you're there.

GUS. He won't know you're there.

BEN. He won't know *you're* there.

GUS. He won't know I'm there.

BEN. I take out my gun.

GUS. You take out your gun.

BEN. He stops in his tracks.

GUS. He stops in his tracks.

BEN. If he turns round –

GUS. If he turns round –

BEN. You're there.

GUS. I'm here.

BEN *frowns and presses his forehead.*

You've missed something out.

BEN. I know. What?

GUS. I haven't taken my gun out, according to you.

BEN. You take your gun out –

GUS. After I've closed the door.

BEN. After you've closed the door.

GUS. You've never missed that out before, you know that?

BEN. When he sees you behind him –

GUS. Me behind him –

BEN. And me in front of him –

GUS. And you in front of him –

BEN. He'll feel uncertain –

GUS. Uneasy.

BEN. He won't know what to do.

GUS. So what will he do?

BEN. He'll look at me and he'll look at you.

GUS. We won't say a word.

BEN. We'll look at him.

GUS. He won't say a word.

BEN. He'll look at us.

GUS. And we'll look at him.

BEN. Nobody says a word.

Pause.

GUS. What do we do if it's a girl?

BEN. We do the same.

GUS. Exactly the same?

BEN. Exactly.

Pause.

GUS. We don't do anything different?

BEN. We do exactly the same.

GUS. Oh.

GUS *rises, and shivers.*

Excuse me.

He exits through the door on the left. BEN *remains sitting on the bed, still.*
The lavatory chain is pulled once off left, but the lavatory does not flush.
Silence.

GUS *re-enters and stops inside the door, deep in thought. He looks at* BEN, *then walks slowly across to his own bed. He is troubled. He stands, thinking. He turns and looks at* BEN. *He moves a few paces towards him.*

(*Slowly in a low, tense voice.*) Why did he send us matches if he knew there was no gas?

Silence.
BEN *stares in front of him.* GUS *crosses to the left side of* BEN, *to the foot of his bed, to get to his other ear.*

Ben. Why did he send us matches if he knew there was no gas?

BEN *looks up.*

Why did he do that?
BEN. Who?
GUS. Who sent us those matches?
BEN. What are you talking about?

GUS *stares down at him.*

GUS (*thickly*). Who is it upstairs?
BEN (*nervously*). What's one thing to do with another?
GUS. Who is it, though?
BEN. What's one thing to do with another?

BEN *fumbles for his paper on the bed.*

GUS. I asked you a question.
BEN. Enough!
GUS (*with growing agitation*). I asked you before. Who moved in? I asked you. You said the people who had it before moved out. Well, who moved in?
BEN (*hunched*). Shut up.
GUS. I told you, didn't I?
BEN (*standing*). Shut up!

GUS (*feverishly*). I told you before who owned this place, didn't I? I told you.

   BEN *hits him viciously on the shoulder.*

I told you who ran this place, didn't I?

   BEN *hits him viciously on the shoulder.*

(*Violently.*) Well, what's he playing all these games for? That's what I want to know. What's he doing it for?

BEN. What games?

GUS (*passionately, advancing*). What's he doing it for? We've been through our tests, haven't we? We got right through our tests, years ago, didn't we? We took them together, don't you remember, didn't we? We've proved ourselves before now, haven't we? We've always done our job. What's he doing all this for? What's the idea? What's he playing these games for?

   The box in the shaft comes down behind them. The noise is this time accompanied by a shrill whistle, as it falls. GUS *rushes to the hatch and seizes the note.*

(*Reading.*) Scampi!

   He crumples the note, picks up the tube, takes out the whistle, blows and speaks.

WE'VE GOT NOTHING LEFT! NOTHING! DO YOU UNDERSTAND?

   BEN *seizes the tube and flings* GUS *away. He follows* GUS *and slaps him hard, back-handed, across the chest.*

BEN. Stop it! You maniac!

GUS. But you heard!

BEN (*savagely*). That's enough! I'm warning you!

   Silence.
   BEN *hangs the tube. He goes to his bed and lies down. He picks up his paper and reads.*

Silence.
The box goes up.
They turn quickly, their eyes meet. BEN *turns to his paper.*
Slowly GUS *goes back to his bed, and sits.*
Silence.
The hatch falls back into place.
They turn quickly, their eyes meet. BEN *turns back to his paper.*
Silence.
BEN *throws his paper down.*

BEN. Kaw!

He picks up the paper and looks at it.

Listen to this!

Pause.

What about that, eh?

Pause.

Kaw!

Pause.

Have you ever heard such a thing?
GUS (*dully*). Go on!
BEN. It's true.
GUS. Get away.
BEN. It's down here in black and white.
GUS (*very low*). Is that a fact?
BEN. Can you imagine it.
GUS. It's unbelievable.
BEN. It's enough to make you want to puke, isn't it?
GUS (*almost inaudible*). Incredible.

BEN *shakes his head. He puts the paper down and rises. He fixes the revolver in his holster.*

GUS stands up. He goes towards the door on the left.

BEN. Where are you going?
GUS. I'm going to have a glass of water.

He exits. BEN brushes dust off his clothes and shoes. The whistle in the speaking-tube blows. He goes to it, takes the whistle out and puts the tube to his ear. He listens. He puts it to his mouth.

BEN. Yes.

To ear. He listens. To mouth.

Straight away. Right.

To ear. He listens. To mouth.

Sure we're ready.

To ear. He listens. To mouth.

Understood. Repeat. He has arrived and will be coming in straight away. The normal method to be employed. Understood.

To ear. He listens. To mouth.

Sure we're ready.

To ear. He listens. To mouth.

Right.

He hangs the tube up.

Gus!

He takes out a comb and combs his hair, adjusts his jacket to diminish the bulge of the revolver. The lavatory flushes off left. BEN goes quickly to the door, left.

Gus!

The door right opens sharply. BEN *turns, his revolver levelled at the door.*
GUS *stumbles in.*
He is stripped of his jacket, waistcoat, tie, holster and revolver.
He stops, body stooping, his arms at his sides.
He raises his head and looks at BEN.
A long silence.
They stare at each other.

Curtain

A SLIGHT ACHE

A Slight Ache was first performed on the BBC Third Programme on 9th July 1959, with the following cast:

EDWARD	Maurice Denham
FLORA	Vivien Merchant

Directed by Donald McWhinnie

It was presented by Michael Codron at the Arts Theatre, London, on 18th January 1961, and subsequently at the Criterion Theatre, with the following cast:

EDWARD	Emlyn Williams
FLORA	Alison Leggat
MATCHSELLER	Richard Briers

Directed by Donald McWhinnie

It was produced at the Young Vic in June 1987 with the following cast:

EDWARD	Barry Foster
FLORA	Jill Johnson
MATCHSELLER	Malcolm Ward

Directed by Kevin Billington

A SLIGHT ACHE

*A country house, with two chairs and a table laid for breakfast
at the centre of the stage. These will later be removed and the
action will be focused on the scullery on the right and the study
on the left, both indicated with a minimum of scenery and
props. A large well kept garden is suggested at the back of the
stage with flower beds, trimmed hedges, etc. The garden gate,
which cannot be seen by the audience, is off right.*

FLORA *and* EDWARD *are discovered sitting at the breakfast table.*
EDWARD *is reading the paper.*

FLORA: Have you noticed the honeysuckle this morning?

EDWARD: The what?

FLORA: The honeysuckle.

EDWARD: Honeysuckle? Where?

FLORA: By the back gate, Edward.

EDWARD: Is that honeysuckle? I thought it was . . . convolvulus, or something.

FLORA: But you know it's honeysuckle.

EDWARD: I tell you I thought it was convolvulus.
[*Pause.*]

FLORA: It's in wonderful flower.

EDWARD: I must look.

FLORA: The whole garden's in flower this morning. The
clematis. The convolvulus. Everything. I was out at seven.
I stood by the pool.

EDWARD: Did you say—that the convolvulus was in flower?

FLORA: Yes.

EDWARD: But good God, you just denied there was any.

FLORA: I was talking about the honeysuckle.

EDWARD: About the what?

FLORA [*calmly*]: Edward—you know that shrub outside the toolshed . . .

EDWARD: Yes, yes.

FLORA: That's convolvulus.

EDWARD: That?

FLORA: Yes.

EDWARD: Oh.

   [*Pause.*]

   I thought it was japonica.

FLORA: Oh, good Lord no.

EDWARD: Pass the teapot, please.

   Pause. She pours tea for him.

   I don't see why I should be expected to distinguish between these plants. It's not my job.

FLORA: You know perfectly well what grows in your garden.

EDWARD: Quite the contrary. It is clear that I don't.

   [*Pause.*]

FLORA [*rising*]: I was up at seven. I stood by the pool. The peace. And everything in flower. The sun was up. You should work in the garden this morning. We could put up the canopy.

EDWARD: The canopy? What for?

FLORA: To shade you from the sun.

EDWARD: Is there a breeze?

FLORA: A light one.

EDWARD: It's very treacherous weather, you know.

   [*Pause.*]

FLORA: Do you know what today is?

EDWARD: Saturday.

FLORA: It's the longest day of the year.

EDWARD: Really?

FLORA: It's the height of summer today.

EDWARD: Cover the marmalade.

FLORA: What?

EDWARD: Cover the pot. There's a wasp. [*He puts the paper down on the table.*] Don't move. Keep still. What are you doing?

FLORA: Covering the pot.

EDWARD: Don't move. Leave it. Keep still.

[*Pause.*]

Give me the 'Telegraph'.

FLORA: Don't hit it. It'll bite.

EDWARD: Bite? What do you mean, bite? Keep still.

[*Pause.*]

It's landing.

FLORA: It's going in the pot.

EDWARD: Give me the lid.

FLORA: It's in.

EDWARD: Give me the lid.

FLORA: I'll do it.

EDWARD: Give it to me! Now . . . Slowly . . .

FLORA: What are you doing?

EDWARD: Be quiet. Slowly . . . carefully . . . on . . . the . . . pot! Ha-ha-ha. Very good.

He sits on a chair to the right of the table.

FLORA: Now he's in the marmalade.

EDWARD: Precisely.

Pause. She sits on a chair to the left of the table and reads the 'Telegraph'.

FLORA: Can you hear him?

EDWARD: Hear him?

FLORA: Buzzing.

EDWARD: Nonsense. How can you hear him? It's an earthenware lid.

FLORA: He's becoming frantic.

EDWARD: Rubbish. Take it away from the table.

FLORA: What shall I do with it?

EDWARD: Put it in the sink and drown it.

FLORA: It'll fly out and bite me.

EDWARD: It will not bite you! Wasps don't bite. Anyway, it won't fly out. It's stuck. It'll drown where it is, in the marmalade.

FLORA: What a horrible death.

EDWARD: On the contrary.

[*Pause.*]

FLORA: Have you got something in your eyes?

EDWARD: No. Why do you ask?

FLORA: You keep clenching them, blinking them.

EDWARD: I have a slight ache in them.

FLORA: Oh, dear.

EDWARD: Yes, a slight ache. As if I hadn't slept.

FLORA: Did you sleep, Edward?

EDWARD: Of course I slept. Uninterrupted. As always.

FLORA: And yet you feel tired.

EDWARD: I didn't say I felt tired. I merely said I had a slight ache in my eyes.

FLORA: Why is that, then?

EDWARD: I really don't know.

[*Pause.*]

FLORA: Oh goodness!

EDWARD: What is it?

FLORA: I can see it. It's trying to come out.

EDWARD: How can it?

FLORA: Through the hole. It's trying to crawl out, through the spoon-hole.

EDWARD: Mmmnn, yes. Can't do it, of course. [*Silent pause.*] Well, let's kill it, for goodness' sake.

FLORA: Yes, let's. But how?

EDWARD: Bring it out on the spoon and squash it on a plate.

FLORA: It'll fly away. It'll bite.

EDWARD: If you don't stop saying that word I shall leave this table.

FLORA: But wasps do bite.

EDWARD: They don't bite. They sting. It's snakes . . . that bite.

FLORA: What about horseflies?

[*Pause.*]

EDWARD [*to himself*]: Horseflies suck.

[*Pause.*]

FLORA [*tentatively*]: If we . . . if we wait long enough, I suppose it'll choke to death. It'll suffocate in the marmalade.

EDWARD [*briskly*]: You do know I've got work to do this morning, don't you? I can't spend the whole day worrying about a wasp.

FLORA: Well, kill it.

EDWARD: You want to kill it?

FLORA: Yes.

EDWARD: Very well. Pass me the hot water jug.

FLORA: What are you going to do?

EDWARD: Scald it. Give it to me.

She hands him the jug. Pause.

Now . . .

FLORA [*whispering*]: Do you want me to lift the lid?

EDWARD: No, no, no. I'll pour down the spoon hole. Right . . . down the spoon-hole.

FLORA: Listen!

EDWARD: What?

FLORA: It's buzzing.

EDWARD: Vicious creatures.

[*Pause.*]

Curious, but I don't remember seeing any wasps at all, all

summer, until now. I'm sure I don't know why. I mean, there must have been wasps.

FLORA: Please.

EDWARD: This couldn't be the first wasp, could it?

FLORA: Please.

EDWARD: The first wasp of summer? No. It's not possible.

FLORA: Edward.

EDWARD: Mmmmnnn?

FLORA: Kill it.

EDWARD: Ah, yes. Tilt the pot. Tilt. Aah . . . down here . . . right down . . . blinding him . . . that's . . . it.

FLORA: Is it?

EDWARD: Lift the lid. All right, I will. There he is! Dead. What a monster. [*He squashes it on a plate.*]

FLORA: What an awful experience.

EDWARD: What a beautiful day it is. Beautiful. I think I shall work in the garden this morning. Where's that canopy?

FLORA: It's in the shed.

EDWARD: Yes, we must get it out. My goodness, just look at that sky. Not a cloud. Did you say it was the longest day of the year today?

FLORA: Yes.

EDWARD: Ah, it's a good day. I feel it in my bones. In my muscles. I think I'll stretch my legs in a minute. Down to the pool. My God, look at that flowering shrub over there. Clematis. What a wonderful . . . [*He stops suddenly.*]

FLORA: What?

[*Pause.*]

Edward, what is it?

[*Pause.*]

Edward . . .

EDWARD [*thickly*]: He's there.

FLORA: Who?

EDWARD [*low, murmuring*]: Blast and damn it, he's there, he's there at the back gate.

FLORA: Let me see.

She moves over to him to look. Pause.

[*Lightly.*] Oh, it's the matchseller.

EDWARD: He's back again.

FLORA: But he's always there.

EDWARD: Why? What is he doing there?

FLORA: But he's never disturbed you, has he? The man's been standing there for weeks. You've never mentioned it.

EDWARD: What is he doing there?

FLORA: He's selling matches, of course.

EDWARD: It's ridiculous. What's the time?

FLORA: Half past nine.

EDWARD: What in God's name is he doing with a tray full of matches at half past nine in the morning?

FLORA: He arrives at seven o'clock.

EDWARD: Seven o'clock?

FLORA: He's always there at seven.

EDWARD: Yes, but you've never . . . actually seen him arrive?

FLORA: No, I . . .

EDWARD: Well, how do you know he's . . . not been standing there all night?

[*Pause.*]

FLORA: Do you find him interesting, Edward?

EDWARD [*casually*]: Interesting? No. No, I . . . don't find him interesting.

FLORA: He's a very nice old man, really.

EDWARD: You've spoken to him?

FLORA: No. No, I haven't spoken to him. I've nodded.

EDWARD [*pacing up and down*]: For two months he's been standing on that spot, do you realize that? Two months. I haven't been able to step outside the back gate.

FLORA: Why on earth not?

EDWARD [*to himself*]: It used to give me great pleasure, such pleasure, to stroll along through the long grass, out through the back gate, pass into the lane. That pleasure is now denied me. It's my own house, isn't it? It's my own gate.

FLORA: I really can't understand this, Edward.

EDWARD: Damn. And do you know I've never seen him sell one box? Not a box. It's hardly surprising. He's on the wrong road. It's not a road at all. What is it? It's a lane, leading to the monastery. Off everybody's route. Even the monks take a short cut to the village, when they want to go . . . to the village. No one goes up it. Why doesn't he stand on the main road if he wants to sell matches, by the *front* gate? The whole thing's preposterous.

FLORA [*going over to him*]: I don't know why you're getting so excited about it. He's a quiet, harmless old man, going about his business. He's quite harmless.

EDWARD: I didn't say he wasn't harmless. Of course he's harmless. How could he be other than harmless?

Fade out and silence.

FLORA'S *voice, far in the house, drawing nearer.*

FLORA [*off*]: Edward, where are you? Edward? Where are you, Edward?

She appears.

Edward?
Edward, what are you doing in the scullery?

EDWARD [*looking through the scullery window*]: Doing?

FLORA: I've been looking everywhere for you. I put up the canopy ages ago. I came back and you were nowhere to be seen. Have you been out?

EDWARD: No.

FLORA: Where have you been?

EDWARD: Here.

FLORA: I looked in your study. I even went into the attic.

EDWARD [*tonelessly*]: What would I be doing in the attic?

FLORA: I couldn't imagine what had happened to you. Do you know it's twelve o'clock?

EDWARD: Is it?

FLORA: I even went to the bottom of the garden, to see if you were in the toolshed.

EDWARD [*tonelessly*]: What would I be doing in the toolshed?

FLORA: You must have seen me in the garden. You can see through this window.

EDWARD: Only part of the garden.

FLORA: Yes.

EDWARD: Only a corner of the garden. A very small corner.

FLORA: What are you doing in here?

EDWARD: Nothing. I was digging out some notes, that's all.

FLORA: Notes?

EDWARD: For my essay.

FLORA: Which essay?

EDWARD: My essay on space and time.

FLORA: But . . . I've never . . . I don't know that one.

EDWARD: You don't know it?

FLORA: I thought you were writing one about the Belgian Congo.

EDWARD: I've been engaged on the dimensionality and continuity of space . . . and time . . . for years.

FLORA: And the Belgian Congo?

EDWARD [*shortly*]: Never mind about the Belgian Congo.
[*Pause.*]

FLORA: But you don't keep notes in the scullery.

EDWARD: You'd be surprised. You'd be highly surprised.

FLORA: Good Lord, what's that? Is that a bullock let loose? No. It's the matchseller! My goodness, you can see him . . . through the hedge. He looks bigger. Have you been watching him? He looks . . . like a bullock.
[*Pause.*]
Edward?
[*Pause.*]

[*Moving over to him.*] Are you coming outside? I've put up the canopy. You'll miss the best of the day. You can have an hour before lunch.

EDWARD: I've no work to do this morning.

FLORA: What about your essay? You don't intend to stay in the scullery all day, do you?

EDWARD: Get out. Leave me alone.

[*A slight pause.*]

FLORA: Really Edward. You've never spoken to me like that in all your life.

EDWARD: Yes, I have.

FLORA: Oh, Weddie. Beddie-Weddie . . .

EDWARD: Do not call me that!

FLORA: Your eyes are bloodshot.

EDWARD: Damn it.

FLORA: It's too dark in here to peer . . .

EDWARD: Damn.

FLORA: It's so bright outside.

EDWARD: Damn.

FLORA: And it's dark in here.

[*Pause.*]

EDWARD: Christ blast it!

FLORA: You're frightened of him.

EDWARD: I'm not.

FLORA: You're frightened of a poor old man. Why?

EDWARD: I am not!

FLORA: He's a poor, harmless old man.

EDWARD: Aaah my eyes.

FLORA: Let me bathe them.

EDWARD: Keep away.

[*Pause.*]

[*Slowly.*] I want to speak to that man. I want to have a word with him.

[*Pause.*]

It's quite absurd, of course. I really can't tolerate something

so . . . absurd, right on my doorstep. I shall not tolerate
it. He's sold nothing all morning. No one passed. Yes. A
monk passed. A non-smoker. In a loose garment. It's
quite obvious he was a non-smoker but still, the man made
no effort. He made no effort to clinch a sale, to rid himself
of one of his cursed boxes. His one chance, all morning,
and he made no effort.

[*Pause.*]

I haven't wasted my time. I've hit, in fact, upon the truth.
He's not a matchseller at all. The bastard isn't a matchseller
at all. Curious I never realized that before. He's an impostor.
I watched him very closely. He made no move towards the
monk. As for the monk, the monk made no move towards
him. The monk was moving along the lane. He didn't
pause, or halt, or in any way alter his step. As for the matchseller—how ridiculous to go on calling him by that title.
What a farce. No, there is something very false about that man.
I intend to get to the bottom of it. I'll soon get rid of him
He can go and ply his trade somewhere else. Instead of
standing like a bullock . . . a bullock, outside my back gate.

FLORA: But if he isn't a matchseller, what is his trade?

EDWARD: We'll soon find out.

FLORA: You're going out to speak to him?

EDWARD: Certainly not! Go out to *him*? Certainly . . . not.
I'll invite him in here. Into my study. Then we'll . . . get
to the bottom of it.

FLORA: Why don't you call the police and have him removed?

He laughs. Pause.

Why don't you call the police, Edward? You could say
he was a public nuisance. Although I . . . I can't say I
find him a nuisance.

EDWARD: Call him in.

FLORA: Me?

EDWARD: Go out and call him in.

FLORA: Are you serious?

[*Pause.*]

Edward, I could call the police. Or even the vicar.

EDWARD: Go and get him.

She goes out. Silence.

EDWARD *waits.*

FLORA [*in the garden*]: Good morning.

[*Pause.*]

We haven't met. I live in this house here. My husband and I.

[*Pause.*]

I wonder if you could . . . would you care for a cup of tea?

[*Pause.*]

Or a glass of lemon? It must be so dry, standing here.

[*Pause.*]

Would you like to come inside for a little while? It's much cooler. There's something we'd very much like to . . . tell you, that will benefit you. Could you spare a few moments? We won't keep you long.

[*Pause.*]

Might I buy your tray of matches, do you think? We've run out, completely, and we always keep a very large stock. It happens that way, doesn't it? Well, we can discuss it inside. Do come. This way. Ah now, do come. Our house is full of curios, you know. My husband's been rather a collector. We have goose for lunch. Do you care for goose?

She moves to the gate.

Come and have lunch with us. This way. That's . . . right. May I take your arm? There's a good deal of *nettle* inside the gate. [*The* MATCHSELLER *appears.*] Here. This way. Mind now. Isn't it beautiful weather? It's the longest day of the year today.

[*Pause.*]

That's honeysuckle. And that's convolvulus. There's clematis. And do you see that plant by the conservatory? That's japonica.

Silence. She enters the study.

FLORA: He's here.

EDWARD: I know.

FLORA: He's in the hall.

EDWARD: I know he's here. I can smell him.

FLORA: Smell him?

EDWARD: I smelt him when he came under my window. Can't you smell the house now?

FLORA: What are you going to do with him, Edward? You won't be rough with him in any way? He's very old. I'm not sure if he can hear, or even see. And he's wearing the oldest—

EDWARD: I don't want to know what he's wearing.

FLORA: But you'll see for yourself in a minute, if you speak to him.

EDWARD: I shall.

[*Slight pause.*]

FLORA: He's an old man. You won't ... be rough with him?

EDWARD: If he's so old, why doesn't he seek shelter ... from the storm?

FLORA: But there's no storm. It's summer, the longest day ...

EDWARD: There was a storm, last week. A summer storm. He stood without moving, while it raged about him.

FLORA: When was this?

EDWARD: He remained quite still, while it thundered all about him.

[*Pause.*]

FLORA: Edward ... are you sure it's wise to bother about all this?

EDWARD: Tell him to come in.

FLORA: I . . .

EDWARD: Now.

She goes and collects the MATCHSELLER.

FLORA: Hullo. Would you like to go in? I won't be long.
Up these stairs here.
[*Pause.*]
You can have some sherry before lunch.
[*Pause.*]
Shall I take your tray? No. Very well, take it with you.
Just . . . up those stairs. The door at the . . .
[*She watches him move.*]
the door . . .
[*Pause.*]
the door at the top. I'll join you . . . later. [*She goes out.*]

The MATCHSELLER *stands on the threshold of the study.*

EDWARD [*cheerfully*]: Here I am. Where are you?
[*Pause.*]
Don't stand out there, old chap. Come into my study.
[*He rises.*] Come in.

The MATCHSELLER *enters.*

That's right. Mind how you go. That's . . . it. Now.
make yourself comfortable. Thought you might like some
refreshment, on a day like this. Sit down, old man. What
will you have? Sherry? Or what about a double scotch? Eh?
[*Pause.*]
I entertain the villagers annually, as a matter of fact. I'm
not the squire, but they look upon me with some regard.
Don't believe we've got a squire here any more, actually.
Don't know what became of him. Nice old man he was.
Great chess-player, as I remember. Three daughters. The
pride of the county. Flaming red hair. Alice was the eldest.
Sit yourself down, old chap. Eunice I think was number

two. The youngest one was the best of the bunch. Sally. No, no, wait a minute, no, it wasn't Sally, it was . . . Fanny. Fanny. A flower. You must be a stranger here. Unless you lived here once, went on a long voyage and have lately returned. Do you know the district?

[*Pause.*]

Now, now, you mustn't . . . stand about like that. Take a seat. Which one would you prefer? We have a great variety, as you see. Can't stand uniformity. Like different seats, different backs. Often when I'm working, you know, I draw up one chair, scribble a few lines, put it by, draw up another, sit back, ponder, put it by . . . [*absently*] . . . sit back . . . put it by . . .

[*Pause.*]

I write theological and philosophical essays . . .

[*Pause.*]

Now and again I jot down a few observations on certain tropical phenomena—not from the same standpoint, of course. [*Silent pause.*] Yes. Africa, now. Africa's always been my happy hunting ground. Fascinating country. Do you know it? I get the impression that you've . . . been around a bit. Do you by any chance know the Membunza Mountains? Great range south of Katambaloo. French Equatorial Africa, if my memory serves me right. Most extraordinary diversity of flora and fauna. Especially fauna. I understand in the Gobi Desert you can come across some very strange sights. Never been there myself. Studied the maps though. Fascinating things, maps.

[*Pause.*]

Do you live in the village? I don't often go down, of course. Or are you passing through? On your way to another part of the country? Well, I can tell you, in my opinion you won't find many prettier parts than here. We win the first prize regularly, you know, the best kept village in the area. Sit down.

[*Pause.*]

I say, can you hear me?

[*Pause.*]

I said, I say, can you hear me?

[*Pause.*]

You possess most extraordinary repose, for a man of your age, don't you? Well, perhaps that's not quite the right word . . . repose. Do you find it chilly in here? I'm sure it's chillier in here than out. I haven't been out yet, today, though I shall probably spend the whole afternoon working, in the garden, under my canopy, at my table, by the pool.

[*Pause.*]

Oh, I understand you met my *wife*? Charming woman, don't you think? Plenty of grit there, too. Stood by me through thick and thin, that woman. In season and out of season. Fine figure of a woman she was, too, in her youth. Wonderful carriage, flaming red hair. [*He stops abruptly.*]

[*Pause.*]

Yes, I . . . I was in much the same position myself then as you are now, you understand. Struggling to make my way in the world. I was in commerce too. [*With a chuckle.*] Oh, yes, I know what it's like—the weather, the rain, beaten from pillar to post, up hill and down dale . . . the rewards were few . . . winters in hovels . . . up till all hours working at your thesis . . . yes, I've done it all. Let me advise you. Get a good woman to stick by you. Never mind what the world says. Keep at it. Keep your shoulder to the wheel. It'll pay dividends.

Pause.

[*With a laugh.*] You must excuse my chatting away like this. We have few visitors this time of the year. All our friends summer abroad. I'm a home bird myself. Wouldn't mind taking a trip to Asia Minor, mind you, or to certain lower regions of the Congo, but Europe? Out of the question. Much too noisy. I'm sure you agree. Now look, what will you have to drink? A glass of ale? Curaçao Fockink Orange? Ginger beer? Tia Maria? A Wachenheimer Fuchsmantel Reisling Beeren Auslese? Gin and it? Chateauneuf-du-Pape? A little Asti Spumante? Or what do you say to a straightforward Piesporter Goldtropfschen Feine Auslese (Reichsgraf von Kesselstaff)? Any preference?

[*Pause.*]

You look a trifle warm. Why don't you take off your balaclava? I'd find that a little itchy myself. But then I've always been one for freedom of movement. Even in the depth of winter I wear next to nothing.

[*Pause.*]

I say, can I ask you a personal question? I don't want to seem inquisitive but aren't you rather on the wrong road for matchselling? Not terribly busy, is it? Of course you may not care for petrol fumes or the noise of traffic. I can quite understand that.

[*Pause.*]

Do forgive me peering but is that a glass eye you're wearing?

[*Pause.*]

Do take off your balaclava, there's a good chap, put your tray down and take your ease, as they say in this part of the world. [*He moves towards him.*] I must say you keep quite a good stock, don't you? Tell me, between ourselves, are those boxes full, or are there just a few half-empty ones among them? Oh yes, I used to be in commerce. Well now, before the good lady sounds the gong for petit déjeuner will you join me in an apéritif? I recommend a glass of cider. Now . . . just a minute . . . I know I've got some—Look out! Mind your tray!

The tray falls, and the matchboxes.

Good God, what . . . ?

[*Pause.*]
You've dropped your tray.

Pause. He picks the matchboxes up.

[*Grunts.*] Eh, these boxes are all wet. You've no right to sell wet matches, you know. Uuuuugggh. This feels suspiciously like fungus. You won't get very far in this trade if you don't take care of your goods. [*Grunts, rising.*] Well, here you are.
[*Pause.*]
Here's your tray.

He puts the tray into the MATCHSELLER'S *hands, and sits. Pause.*

Now listen, let me be quite frank with you, shall I? I really cannot understand why you don't sit down. There are four chairs at your disposal. Not to mention the hassock. I can't possibly talk to you unless you're settled. Then and only then can I speak to you. Do you follow me? You're not being terribly helpful. [*Slight pause.*] You're sweating. The sweat's pouring out of you. Take off that balaclava.
[*Pause.*]
Go into the corner then. Into the corner. Go on. Get into the shade of the corner. Back. Backward.
[*Pause.*]
Get back!
[*Pause.*]
Ah, you understand me. Forgive me for saying so, but I had decided that you had the comprehension of a bullock. I was mistaken. You understand me perfectly well. That's right. A little more. A little to the right. Aaah. Now you're there. In shade, in shadow. Good-o. Now I can get down to brass tacks. Can't I?
[*Pause.*]

No doubt you're wondering why I invited you into this
house? You may think I was alarmed by the look of you.
You would be quite mistaken. I was not alarmed by the
look of you. I did not find you at all alarming. No, no.
Nothing outside this room has ever alarmed me. You dis-
gusted me, quite forcibly, if you want to know the truth.
[*Pause.*]
Why did you disgust me to that extent? That seems to be
a pertinent question. You're no more disgusting than
Fanny, the squire's daughter, after all. In appearance you
differ but not in essence. There's the same . . .
[*Pause.*]
The same . . .
[*Pause.*]
[*In a low voice.*] I want to ask you a question. Why do you
stand outside my back gate, from dawn till dusk, why do
you pretend to sell matches, why . . . ? What is it, damn
you. You're shivering. You're sagging. Come here, come
here . . . mind your tray! [EDWARD *rises and moves behind
a chair.*] Come, quick quick. There. Sit here. Sit . . . sit
in this.

The MATCHSELLER *stumbles and sits. Pause.*

Aaaah! You're sat. At last. What a relief. You must be
tired. [*Slight pause.*] Chair comfortable? I bought it in a
sale. I bought all the furniture in this house in a sale. The
same sale. When I was a young man. You too, perhaps.
You too, perhaps.
[*Pause.*]
At the same time, perhaps!
[*Pause.*]
[*Muttering.*] I must get some air. I must get a breath of air.

He goes to the door.

Flora!

FLORA: Yes?

EDWARD [*with great weariness*]: Take me into the garden.

Silence. They move from the study door to a chair under a canopy.

FLORA: Come under the canopy.

EDWARD: Ah. [*He sits.*]

[*Pause.*]

The peace. The peace out here.

FLORA: Look at our trees.

EDWARD: Yes.

FLORA: Our own trees. Can you hear the birds?

EDWARD: No, I can't hear them.

FLORA: But they're singing, high up, and flapping.

EDWARD: Good. Let them flap.

FLORA: Shall I bring your lunch out here? You can have it in peace, and a quiet drink, under your canopy.

[*Pause.*]

How are you getting on with your old man?

EDWARD: What do you mean?

FLORA: What's happening? How are you getting on with him?

EDWARD: Very well. We get on remarkably well. He's a little . . . reticent. Somewhat withdrawn. It's understandable. I should be the same, perhaps, in his place. Though, of course, I could not possibly find myself in his place.

FLORA: Have you found out anything about him?

EDWARD: A little. A little. He's had various trades, that's certain. His place of residence is unsure. He's . . . he's not a drinking man. As yet, I haven't discovered the reason for his arrival here. I shall in due course . . . by nightfall.

FLORA: Is it necessary?

EDWARD: Necessary?

FLORA [*quickly sitting on the right arm of the chair*]: I could show him out now, it wouldn't matter. You've seen him, he's harmless, unfortunate . . . old, that's all. Edward—

listen—he's not here through any . . . design, or anything, I know it. I mean, he might just as well stand outside our back gate as anywhere else. He'll move on. I can . . . make him. I promise you. There's no point in upsetting yourself like this. He's an old man, weak in the head . . . that's all. [*Pause.*]

EDWARD: You're deluded.

FLORA: Edward—

EDWARD [*rising*]: You're deluded. And stop calling me Edward.

FLORA: You're not still frightened of him?

EDWARD: Frightened of him? Of *him*? Have you *seen* him? [*Pause.*]

He's like jelly. A great bullockfat of jelly. He can't see straight. I think as a matter of fact he wears a glass eye. He's almost stone deaf . . . almost . . . not quite. He's very nearly dead on his feet. Why should he frighten me? No, you're a woman, you know nothing. [*Slight pause.*] But he possesses other faculties. Cunning. The man's an imposter and he knows I know it.

FLORA: I'll tell you what. Look. Let me speak to him. I'll speak to him.

EDWARD [*quietly*]: And I know he knows I know it.

FLORA: I'll find out all about him, Edward. I promise you I will.

EDWARD: And he knows I know.

FLORA: Edward! Listen to me! I can find out all about him, I promise you. I shall go and have a word with him now. I shall . . . get to the bottom of it.

EDWARD: You? It's laughable.

FLORA: You'll see—he won't bargain for me. I'll surprise him. He'll . . . he'll admit everything.

EDWARD [*softly*]: He'll admit everything, will he?

FLORA: You wait and see, you just—

EDWARD [*hissing*]: What are you plotting?

FLORA: I know exactly what I shall—

EDWARD: What are you plotting?

He seizes her arms.

FLORA: Edward, you're hurting me!
[*Pause.*]
[*With dignity.*] I shall wave from the window when I'm ready. Then you can come up. I shall get to the truth of it, I assure you. You're much too heavy-handed, in every way. You should trust your wife more, Edward. You should trust her judgment, and have a greater insight into her capabilities. A woman . . . a woman will often succeed, you know, where a man must invariably fail.

Silence. She goes into the study.

Do you mind if I come in?

The door closes.

Are you comfortable?
[*Pause.*]
Oh, the sun's shining directly on you. Wouldn't you rather sit in the shade?

She sits down.

It's the longest day of the year today, did you know that? Actually the year has flown. I can remember Christmas and that dreadful frost. And the floods! I hope you weren't here in the floods. We were out of danger up here, of course, but in the valleys whole families I remember drifted away on the current. The country was a lake. Everything stopped. We lived on our own preserves, drank elderberry wine, studied other cultures.
[*Pause.*]
Do you know, I've got a feeling I've seen you before, somewhere. Long before the flood. You were much younger. Yes, I'm really sure of it. Between ourselves, were you ever

a poacher? I had an encounter with a poacher once. It was
a ghastly rape, the brute. High up on a hillside cattle track.
Early spring. I was out riding on my pony. And there on the
verge a man lay—ostensibly injured, lying on his front, I
remember, possibly the victim of a murderous assault, how
was I to know? I dismounted, I went to him, he rose, I
fell, my pony took off, down to the valley. I saw the sky
through the trees, blue. Up to my ears in mud. It was a
desperate battle.
[*Pause.*]
I lost.
[*Pause.*]
Of course, life was perilous in those days. It was my first
canter unchaperoned.
[*Pause.*]
Years later, when I was a Justice of the Peace for the county,
I had him in front of the bench. He was there for poaching.
That's how I know he was a poacher. The evidence though
was sparse, inadmissible, I acquitted him, letting him off
with a caution. He'd grown a red beard, I remember. Yes.
A bit of a stinker.
[*Pause.*]
I say, you are perspiring, aren't you? Shall I mop your
brow? With my chiffon? Is it the heat? Or the closeness?
Or confined space? Or . . .? [*She goes over to him.*]
Actually, the day is cooling. It'll soon be dusk. Perhaps it
is dusk. May I? You don't mind?
[*Pause. She mops his brow.*]
Ah, there, that's better. And your cheeks. It is a woman's
job, isn't it? And I'm the only woman on hand. There.

Pause. She leans on the arm of chair.

[*Intimately.*] Tell me, have you a woman? Do you like
women? Do you ever . . . think about women?
[*Pause.*]

Have you ever . . . stopped a woman?

[*Pause.*]

I'm sure you must have been quite attractive once. [*She sits.*] Not any more, of course. You've got a vile smell. Vile. Quite repellent, in fact.

[*Pause.*]

Sex, I suppose, means nothing to you. Does it ever occur to you that sex is a very vital experience for other people? Really, I think you'd amuse me if you weren't so hideous. You're probably quite amusing in your own way. [*Seductively.*] Tell me all about love. Speak to me of love.

[*Pause.*]

God knows what you're saying at this very moment. It's quite disgusting. Do you know when I was a girl I loved . . . I loved . . . I simply adored . . . what *have* you got on, for goodness sake? A jersey? It's clogged. Have you been rolling in mud? [*Slight pause.*] You haven't been rolling in mud, have you? [*She rises and goes over to him.*] And what have you got under your jersey? Let's see. [*Slight pause.*] I'm not tickling you, am I? No. Good . . . Lord, is this a vest? That's quite original. Quite original. [*She sits on the arm of his chair.*] Hmmnn, you're a solid old boy, I must say. Not at all like a jelly. All you need is a bath. A lovely lathery bath. And a good scrub. A lovely lathery scrub. [*Pause.*] Don't you? It will be a pleasure. [*She throws her arms round him.*] I'm going to keep you. I'm going to keep you, you dreadful chap, and call you Barnabas. Isn't it dark, Barnabas? Your eyes, your eyes, your great big eyes.

Pause.

My husband would never have guessed your name. Never. [*She kneels at his feet. Whispering.*] It's me you were waiting for, wasn't it? You've been standing waiting for me. You've seen me in the woods, picking daisies, in my apron, my pretty daisy apron, and you came and stood, poor creature, at my gate, till death us do part. Poor Barnabas. I'm going to put you to bed. I'm going to put you to bed and watch over you. But first you must have a good whacking great bath. And I'll buy you pretty little things that will suit you. And little toys to play with. On your deathbed. Why shouldn't you die happy?

A shout from the hall.

EDWARD: Well?
[*Footsteps upstage.*]
Well?
FLORA: Don't come in.
EDWARD: Well?
FLORA: He's dying.
EDWARD: Dying? He's not dying.
FLORA: I tell you, he's very ill.
EDWARD: He's not dying! Nowhere near. He'll see you cremated.
FLORA: The man is desperately ill!
EDWARD: Ill? You lying slut. Get back to your trough!
FLORA: Edward . . .
EDWARD [*violently*]: To your trough!

She goes out. Pause.

[*Coolly.*] Good evening to you. Why are you sitting in the gloom? Oh, you've begun to disrobe. Too warm? Let's open these windows, then, what?

He opens the windows.

Pull the blinds.

He pulls the blinds.

And close . . . the curtains . . . again.

He closes the curtains.

Ah. Air will enter through the side chinks. Of the blinds.
And filter through the curtains. I hope. Don't want to
suffocate, do we?

[*Pause.*]

More comfortable? Yes. You look different in darkness.
Take off all your togs, if you like. Make yourself at home.
Strip to your buff. Do as you would in your own house.

[*Pause.*]

Did you say something?

[*Pause.*]

Did you say something?

[*Pause.*]

Anything? Well then, tell me about your boyhood. Mmnn?

[*Pause.*]

What did you do with it? Run? Swim? Kick the ball?
You kicked the ball? What position? Left back? Goalie?
First reserve?

[*Pause.*]

I used to play myself. Country house matches, mostly.
Kept wicket and batted number seven.

[*Pause.*]

Kept wicket and batted number seven. Man called—
Cavendish, I think had something of your style. Bowled
left arm over the wicket, always kept his cap on, quite a
dab hand at solo whist, preferred a good round of prop and
cop to anything else.

[*Pause.*]

On wet days when the field was swamped.

[*Pause.*]

Perhaps you don't play cricket.

[*Pause.*]

Perhaps you never met Cavendish and never played cricket.
You look less and less like a cricketer the more I see of you.
Where did you live in those days? God damn it, I'm en-
titled to know something about you! You're in my blasted

house, on my territory, drinking my wine, eating my duck!
Now you've had your fill you sit like a hump, a mouldering
heap. In my room. My den. I can rem . . . [*He stops
abruptly.*]

[*Pause.*]

You find that funny? Are you grinning?

[*Pause.*]

[*In disgust.*] Good Christ, is that a grin on your face?
[*Further disgust.*] It's lopsided. It's all—down on one side.
You're grinning. It amuses you, does it? When I tell you
how well I remember this room, how well I remember
this den. [*Muttering.*] Ha. Yesterday now, it was clear,
clearly defined, so clearly.

[*Pause.*]

The garden, too, was sharp, lucid, in the rain, in the sun.

[*Pause.*]

My den, too, was sharp, arranged for my purpose . . .
quite satisfactory.

[*Pause.*]

The house too, was polished, all the banisters were polished,
and the stair rods, and the curtain rods.

[*Pause.*]

My desk was polished, and my cabinet.

[*Pause.*]

I was polished. [*Nostalgic.*] I could stand on the hill and
look through my telescope at the sea. And follow the path
of the three-masted schooner, feeling fit, well aware of my
sinews, their suppleness, my arms lifted holding the
telescope, steady, easily, no trembling, my aim was perfect,
I could pour hot water down the spoon-hole, yes, easily, no
difficulty, my grasp firm, my command established, my
life was accounted for, I was ready for my excursions to the
cliff, down the path to the back gate, through the long
grass, no need to watch for the nettles, my progress was
fluent, after my long struggling against all kinds of usurpers,

disreputables, lists, literally lists of people anxious to do me down, and my reputation down, my command was established, all summer I would breakfast, survey my landscape, take my telescope, examine the overhanging of my hedges, pursue the narrow lane past the monastery, climb the hill, adjust the lens [*he mimes a telescope*], watch the progress of the three-masted schooner, my progress was as sure, as fluent . . .

Pause. He drops his arms.

Yes, yes, you're quite right, it is funny.
[*Pause.*]
Laugh your bloody head off! Go on. Don't mind me. No need to be polite.
[*Pause.*]
That's right.
[*Pause.*]
You're quite right, it is funny. I'll laugh with you!

He laughs.

Ha-ha-ha! Yes! You're laughing with me, I'm laughing with you, we're laughing together!

He laughs and stops.

[*Brightly.*] Why did I invite you into this room? That's your next question, isn't it? Bound to be.
[*Pause.*]
Well, why not, you might say? My oldest acquaintance. My nearest and dearest. My kith and kin. But surely correspondence would have been as satisfactory . . . more satisfactory? We could have exchanged postcards, couldn't we? What? Views, couldn't we? Of sea and land, city and village, town and country, autumn and winter . . . clocktowers . . . museums . . . citadels . . . bridges . . . rivers . . .

[*Pause.*]

Seeing you stand, at the back gate, such close proximity, was not at all the same thing.

[*Pause.*]

What are you doing? You're taking off your balaclava . . . you've decided not to. No, very well then, all things considered, did I then invite you into this room with express intention of asking you to take off your balaclava, in order to determine your resemblance to—some other person? The answer is no, certainly not, I did not, for when I first saw you you wore no balaclava. No headcovering of any kind, in fact. You looked quite different without a head—I mean without a hat—I mean without a headcovering, of any kind. In fact every time I have seen you you have looked quite different to the time before.

[*Pause.*]

Even now you look different. Very different.

[*Pause.*]

Admitted that sometimes I viewed you through dark glasses, yes, and sometimes through light glasses, and on other occasions bare eyed, and on other occasions through the bars of the scullery window, or from the roof, the roof, yes in driving snow, or from the bottom of the drive in thick fog, or from the roof again in blinding sun, so blinding, so hot, that I had to skip and jump and bounce in order to remain in one place. Ah, that's good for a guffaw, is it? That's good for a belly laugh? Go on, then. Let it out. Let yourself go, for God's . . . [*He catches his breath.*] You're crying . . .

[*Pause.*]

[*Moved.*] You haven't been laughing. You're crying.

[*Pause.*]

You're weeping. You're shaking with grief. For me. I can't believe it. For my plight. I've been wrong.

[*Pause.*]

[*Briskly.*] Come, come, stop it. Be a man. Blow your nose for goodness sake. Pull yourself together.

He sneezes.

Ah.

He rises. Sneeze.

Ah. Fever. Excuse me.

He blows his nose.

I've caught a cold. A germ. In my eyes. It was this morning. In my eyes. My eyes.

Pause. He falls to the floor.

Not that I had any difficulty in seeing you, no, no, it was not so much my sight, my sight is excellent—in winter I run about with nothing on but a pair of polo shorts—no, it was not so much any deficiency in my sight as the airs between me and my object—don't weep—the change of air, the currents obtaining in the space between me and my object, the shades they make, the shapes they take, the quivering, the eternal quivering—please stop crying—nothing to do with heat-haze. Sometimes, of course, I would take shelter, shelter to compose myself. Yes, I would seek a tree, a cranny of bushes, erect my canopy and so make shelter. And rest. [*Low murmur.*] And then I no longer heard the wind or saw the sun. Nothing entered, nothing left my nook. I lay on my side in my polo shorts, my fingers lightly in contact with the blades of grass, the earthflowers, the petals of the earth-flowers flaking, lying on my palm, the underside of all the great foliage dark, above me, but it is only afterwards I say the foliage was dark, the petals flaking, then I said nothing, I remarked nothing, things happened upon me, then in my times of shelter, the shades, the petals, carried themselves, carried their bodies upon me, and nothing entered my nook, nothing left it.

[*Pause.*]

But then, the time came. I saw the wind. I saw the wind, swirling, and the dust at my back gate, lifting, and the long grass, scything together . . . [*Slowly, in horror.*] You *are* laughing. You're laughing. Your face. Your body. [*Overwhelming nausea and horror.*] Rocking . . . gasping . . . rocking . . . shaking . . . rocking . . . heaving . . . rocking . . . You're laughing at me! Aaaaahhhh!

The MATCHSELLER *rises. Silence.*

You look younger. You look extraordinarily . . . youthful. [*Pause.*]

You want to examine the garden? It must be very bright, in the moonlight. [*Becoming weaker.*] I would like to join you . . . explain . . . show you . . . the garden . . . explain . . . The plants . . . where I run . . . my track . . . in training . . . I was number one sprinter at Howells . . . when a stripling . . . no more than a stripling . . . licked . . . men twice my strength . . . when a stripling . . . like yourself.

[*Pause.*]

[*Flatly.*] The pool must be glistening. In the moonlight. And the lawn. I remember it well. The cliff. The sea. The three-masted schooner.

[*Pause.*]

[*With great, final effort—a whisper.*] Who are you?

FLORA [*off*]: Barnabas?

[*Pause.*]

She enters.

Ah, Barnabas. Everything is ready.

[*Pause.*]

I want to show you my garden, your garden. You must see my japonica, .my convolvulus . . . my honeysuckle, my clematis.

[*Pause.*]

The summer is coming. I've put up your canopy for you. You can lunch in the garden, by the pool. I've polished the whole house for you.

[*Pause.*]

Take my hand.

Pause. The MATCHSELLER *goes over to her.*

Yes. Oh, wait a moment.

[*Pause.*]

Edward. Here is your tray.

She crosses to EDWARD *with the tray of matches, and puts it in his hands. Then she and the* MATCHSELLER *start to go out as the curtain falls slowly.*

THE HOTHOUSE

Author's Note

I wrote *The Hothouse* in the winter of 1958. I put it aside for further deliberation and made no attempt to have it produced at the time. I then went on to write *The Caretaker*. In 1979 I re-read *The Hothouse* and decided it was worth presenting on the stage. I made a few changes during rehearsal, mainly cuts.

HAROLD PINTER

Characters

ROOTE, *in his fifties*

GIBBS, *in his thirties*

LAMB, *in his twenties*

MISS CUTTS, *in her thirties*

LUSH, *in his thirties*

TUBB, *fifty*

LOBB, *fifty*

The Hothouse was first presented at Hampstead Theatre, London, on 24 April 1980 in a production directed by Harold Pinter. It moved to the Ambassador Theatre, London, on 25 June 1980.

The cast was as follows:

ROOTE	Derek Newark
GIBBS	James Grant
LAMB	Roger Davidson
MISS CUTTS	Angela Pleasence
LUSH	Robert East
TUBB	Michael Forrest
LOBB	Edward de Souza

Director Harold Pinter
Set Designer Eileen Diss
Costume Designer Elizabeth Walker
Lighting Gerry Jenkinson
Sound Dominic Muldowney

Sets

ROOTE's *office*
A stairway
A sitting room
A soundproof room
LOBB's *office in the Ministry*

Act One

ROOTE's office. Morning.
ROOTE is standing at the window, looking out.
GIBBS is at the filing cabinet, examining some papers.

ROOTE

Gibbs.

GIBBS

Yes, sir?

ROOTE

Tell me ...

GIBBS

Yes, sir?

ROOTE

How's 6457 getting on?

GIBBS

6457, sir?

ROOTE

Yes.

GIBBS

He's dead, sir.

ROOTE

Dead?

GIBBS

He died on Thursday, sir.

ROOTE

Thursday? What are you talking about? What's today?

GIBBS

Saturday, sir.

ROOTE

Saturday . . . Well, for goodness sake, I had a talk with him, when was it? (*Opens his desk diary.*) Recently. Only the other day. Yesterday, I think. Just a minute.

GIBBS

I hardly think yesterday, sir.

ROOTE

Why not?

GIBBS

I supervised the burial arrangements myself, sir.

ROOTE

This is ridiculous. What did he die of?

GIBBS

I beg your pardon, sir?

ROOTE

If he's dead, what did he die of?

GIBBS

Heart failure, sir.

ROOTE *stares at him, sits at the desk and consults the diary.*

ROOTE

Wait ... here we are. Got it. Conversation with 6457 ten o'clock Friday morning. That was yesterday. Well, what do you make of that?

GIBBS

I'm afraid there seems to be a slight discrepancy, sir.

ROOTE

Discrepancy! I'm damn sure there's a discrepancy! You come and tell me that a man has died and I've got it down here that I had a conversation with him yesterday morning. According to you he was in his grave. There does seem to be a slight discrepancy, I agree with you.

GIBBS

I meant ... about the dates, sir.

ROOTE

Dates? What dates?

GIBBS

In your diary, sir. (*He moves to the desk.*) I must point out that you are in fact referring to Friday, the 17th. (*He indicates a date on the page.*) There, sir. Yesterday was Friday the 24th. (*He turns the pages forward and indicates a date.*) Here, sir. You had a conversation with 6457 on the 17th. He died on the 23rd. (*Indicates a date.*) Here.

ROOTE

What! (*He turns the pages back.*) Good Lord, you're right.
You're quite right. How extraordinary. I haven't written a
single thing down in this diary for a whole week.

GIBBS

You've held no interviews with any of the patients, sir,
during the last week.

ROOTE

No, I haven't, have I? Why not?

GIBBS

You decided on the ... 18th, sir, that you would cancel all
interviews until further notice.

ROOTE (*slowly*)

Oh yes. So I did.

GIBBS *moves round the desk.*

GIBBS

For the sake of accuracy, sir, I'd like, if I may, to point out to
you what is apparently another discrepancy.

ROOTE

Another one?

GIBBS

Yes, sir.

ROOTE

You're very keen this morning, aren't you, Gibbs?

GIBBS

I do try to keep my powers of observation well exercised, sir.

ROOTE

Don't stand so close to me. You're right on top of me. What's the matter with you?

GIBBS

I'm so sorry, sir. (*He steps away from the desk.*)

ROOTE

There's plenty of room in here, isn't there? What are you breathing down my neck for?

GIBBS

I do apologise, sir.

ROOTE

Nothing's more irritating.

GIBBS

It was thoughtless of me, sir.

Pause

ROOTE

Well . . . what was this *other* discrepancy, anyway?

GIBBS (*flatly*)

It was not 6457, sir, whom you interviewed on the 17th.

ROOTE

Gibbs.

GIBBS

Sir?

ROOTE

One question.

GIBBS

Sir.

ROOTE

Are you taking the piss out of me?

GIBBS

Most decidedly not, sir.

Slight pause

ROOTE

All right. You have just said it was not 6457 I interviewed on the 17th. What evidence have you got to support your contention?

GIBBS

The figures in your diary, sir.

ROOTE

Figures?

GIBBS

One figure, sir. If I may . . . (*He bends over the desk.*) . . . this one.

ROOTE

Which one?

GIBBS

This one. It's not a seven, sir. It's a nine.

ROOTE

Nine?

GIBBS

Nine, sir. The number is 645 . . . 9.

ROOTE

Good God, so it is. Nine. Well, it's not a very clear nine, is it?

GIBBS

It was in fact 6459 whom you interviewed, sir.

ROOTE

Must have been. That's funny. I wonder why I thought it was seven. (*He rises abruptly.*) The whole thing's ridiculous! The system's wrong. (*He walks across the room.*) We shouldn't use these stupid numbers at all. Only confuses things. Why don't we use their names, for God's sake? They've got names, haven't they?

GIBBS

It was your predecessor who instituted the use of numbers, sir.

ROOTE

How do you know?

GIBBS

So I understand, sir.

ROOTE

You weren't even here then.

GIBBS

No, sir.

ROOTE

I was.

GIBBS

Quite, sir.

ROOTE

I was standing where you're standing now. I can tell you that. Saying yes sir, no sir and certainly sir. Just as you are now. I didn't bribe anyone to get where I am. I worked my way up. When my predecessor ... retired ... I was invited to take over his position. And have you any idea why you call me sir now?

GIBBS

Yes, sir.

ROOTE

Why?

GIBBS

Because you called him sir then, sir.

ROOTE

Right!

Pause

But I sometimes think I've been a bit slow in making
changes. Change is the order of things, after all. I mean it's *in*
the order of things, it's not *the* order of things, it's *in* the order
of things.

Slight pause

Still, I sometimes think I could have instituted a few more
changes — if I'd had time. I'm not talking about many changes
or drastic changes. That's not necessary. But on this numbers
business, for instance. It would make things so much simpler
if we called them by their names. Then we'd all know where
we were. After all, they're not criminals. They're only people
in need of help, which we try to give, in one way or another,
to the best of our discretion, to the best of our judgement, to
help them regain their confidence, confidence in themselves,
confidence in others, confidence in ... the world. What?
They're all people specially recommended by the Ministry,
after all. They're not any Tom, Dick or ... or ... er ... Harry.

He stops, brooding.

I often think it must depress them ... somewhat ... to have a
number rapped at them all the time. After some of them have
been here a few years they're liable to forget what names their
fathers gave them. Or their mothers.

Pause

One of the purposes of this establishment is to instil that confidence in each and every one of them, that confidence which will one day enable them to say 'I am . . . Gubbins', for example. Not easy, not easy, agreed, but it makes it doubly difficult if they're constantly referred to as 5244, doesn't it? We lose sight of their names and they lose sight of their names. I sometimes wonder if it's the right way to go about things. (*He sits at the desk.*)

GIBBS

Would you like me to place further consideration of this matter on the agenda, sir?

ROOTE (*sharply*)

Certainly not. We can't.

GIBBS

Can't, sir?

ROOTE

You know damn well we can't. That was one of the rules of procedure laid down in the original constitution. The patients are to be given numbers and called by those numbers. And that's how it's got to remain. You understand?

GIBBS

Perfectly, sir.

GIBBS *goes to the filing cabinet.*

ROOTE

A death on the premises?

GIBBS

Sir?

ROOTE

A death? You say this man has died?

GIBBS

6457, sir? Yes, sir.

ROOTE

Which one was he?

GIBBS

You had quite a lot to do with him, actually, sir.

ROOTE

He was a man I dealt with personally?

GIBBS

Yes, sir.

ROOTE

Well, which one was he, for God's sake?

GIBBS

You knew him well, sir.

ROOTE

You keep saying that! But I can't remember a damn thing about him. What did he look like?

Pause

GIBBS

Thinnish.

ROOTE

Fairheaded?

GIBBS (*sitting*)

Not darkheaded, sir.

Pause

ROOTE

Tall?

GIBBS

Certainly not small.

Pause

ROOTE

Quite a sharp sort of face?

GIBBS

Quite sharp, yes, sir.

ROOTE

Yes.

Pause

Yes, he had a sharp sort of face, didn't he?

GIBBS

I should say it was sharp, sir, yes.

ROOTE

Limped a bit?

GIBBS

Oh, possibly a trifle, sir.

ROOTE

Yes, he limped. He limped on his left leg.

GIBBS

His left, sir?

ROOTE

Well, one of them. I'm sure of it.

GIBBS

Yes, he had a slight limp, sir.

ROOTE

Yes, of course he had.

Pause

He had a slight limp. Whenever he walked anywhere . . . he limped. Prematurely grey, he was. Prematurely grey.

Pause

Yes, I remember him very well.

Pause

He's dead, you say?

GIBBS

Yes, sir.

ROOTE

Then why wasn't I told? It's your job to keep me informed of all developments in this building, no matter how slight, no matter how trivial. I demand an answer. Why wasn't I told?

GIBBS

You signed the death certificate, sir.

GIBBS *goes to the filing cabinet.*

ROOTE

Did he get a decent burial?

GIBBS

Oh, very decent, sir.

ROOTE

I don't see why I wasn't invited. Who said the last words over
him?

GIBBS

There were no last words, sir.

ROOTE (*appalled*)

No last words?

ROOTE *rises, walks to the window, looks out.*

Snowing. Isn't it the patients' exercise time?

GIBBS

Not today, sir.

ROOTE

Why not?

GIBBS

It's Christmas day, sir.

ROOTE *goes back to the desk and sits.*

ROOTE
All right, that's all for now. Bear everything in mind.

He examines some papers. GIBBS *does not move.* ROOTE *looks up.*

What is it? What are you waiting for?

GIBBS
You asked me a question earlier, sir, which I haven't yet had a chance to answer.

ROOTE
Haven't had a chance? What do you mean? That I've been talking too much or something?

GIBBS
Not at all, sir. We simply passed on to another topic.

ROOTE (*regarding him*)
Gibbs.

GIBBS
Sir?

ROOTE (*confidentially*)
Between ourselves, man to man, you're not by any chance taking the old wee-wee out of me, are you?

GIBBS
Most assuredly not, sir. By no means. I merely feel it incumbent upon me to answer any questions you put to me, or to do

my best to do so. You are dependent upon me for certain information and I feel it in the line of duty to supply you with it, especially when it is by specific request.

ROOTE

Stop mouthing! This has been a most exhausting morning. If the morning's like this what's the rest of the day going to be like? There's no system, that's the trouble. Look. The next time I ask you a question answer it and we won't waste so much time fiddling about. Things are getting much too slack around here.

Pause

Well, come on, what was this question?

GIBBS

You asked me, sir –

ROOTE

Wait!

He leans forward on the desk.

(*Quietly.*) Before you go on, Gibbs, let me say one thing. Be sure that what you say is accurate. You are about to quote a question you say I put to you. I don't know what you're going to say, but immediately you've said it I shall know whether I said it, or whether I didn't. I shall know.

GIBBS

Yes, sir.

ROOTE

I didn't get this job for nothing, I can assure you. I shall know. Have no doubt whatsoever on that point.

GIBBS

No, sir.

ROOTE

Stick to the facts, man, and we won't go far wrong.

GIBBS

Yes, sir.

Pause

ROOTE

Well, what was this question?

GIBBS

You asked me how 6459 was getting on, sir.

Pause

ROOTE (*expressionless*)

Did I?

GIBBS

To be quite accurate, sir, it was 6457 you inquired after, but, of course, 6457 is dead. We agreed, after examining certain discrepancies, that it was 6459 you were referring to.

Pause

ROOTE (*expressionless*)

Did we?

The lights fade on the office. They go up on the sitting room. MISS
CUTTS *and* LAMB *enter the sitting room.*

LAMB

That was fun, I must say. You know you really play extraordinarily well, Miss Cutts.

CUTTS

Do I?

LAMB

Oh, excellent. I enjoyed it immensely.

MISS CUTTS *sits.* LAMB *goes to the coffee machine.*

LAMB

Black or white?

CUTTS

Black.

LAMB (*chuckling*)

I must say I got the surprise of my life, you know, when you
came up to me this morning and asked me if I played table
tennis. What I mean is, considering we've never spoken to
each other before.

He gives her a coffee.

It was really very nice of you.
Do you play often?

CUTTS

Not often.

LAMB

Well, it's a damn good piece of luck that our rotas coincide at this time of the morning, isn't it? It'll be something to look forward to, a game of ping-pong. I haven't played for ages.

Pause. He sits with his coffee.

Do you like it here?

CUTTS

Oh, I do. It's so rewarding.

LAMB

Your work?

CUTTS

Terribly rewarding.

LAMB

You've been here some time, of course?

CUTTS

Mmnn. Oh yes.

LAMB

What about Mr. Roote? How do you get on with him?

CUTTS

Oh, such a charming person. So genuine.

LAMB

Yes, I'm sure he is. I haven't really . . . spoken to him yet. Although I expect I will be meeting him, very soon now.

He stands, walks about.

I only wish I had a bit more to do. I'm a very energetic sort of chap, you know. Tremendous mental energy. I'm the sort of chap who's always *thinking* – you know what I mean? Then, when I've thought about something, I like to put it into action. I mean, I think a lot about the patients, you see.

Pause

You have quite a bit to do with them, I suppose?

CUTTS

Mmmn . . . . . .

LUSH *walks quickly into the sitting room.*

LUSH

Have you seen Gibbs?

LAMB

Gibbs?

LUSH *goes.*

What a curious thing. Did you hear that, Miss Cutts? That was Lush. He asked if we'd seen Gibbs.

MISS CUTTS *is leaning back in her chair.*

CUTTS

Mmnn?

LAMB

Lush. Popped his head in the door just now. Asked if we'd seen Gibbs.

CUTTS

And have we?

LAMB

I haven't.

Pause

You know, I ... I haven't really got used to this place.

Pause

Do you know what I mean? I wouldn't say this to anyone else but you, of course. The fact is, I haven't made much contact with any of the others. Hogg said good morning to me in a very nice way about a week ago when I bumped into him near the gym, but I haven't seen him since. (*With sudden brisk-ness.*) No, you see, what happened was this – the Ministry said to me, I was working in one of their other departments at the time, doing something quite different – well, anyway, they called me up and they said to me – 'You've been posted'. Well, I'd heard about this place, of course. I was delighted. But ... but what exactly is the post, I said. You'll learn that when you get down there, they said, but we think you've got the right qualifications.

Pause

That's what they said. That was over a year ago.

Pause

And I've never learned who the man was I took over from, and I've never found out why he left, either. Anyway I'm pretty sure he wasn't doing the job I'm doing. Or if he was doing the same job he wasn't doing it in exactly the same way. The whole rota's been altered since he left, for a start. He couldn't have been doing my rota, and if he wasn't doing my rota he can hardly be said to have been doing my job. Rotas make all the difference.

Pause

I mean, my job, for instance. I have to see that all the gates are locked outside the building and that all the patients' doors are locked inside the building. It gives me exercise, I'll say that. It takes me two hours and six minutes, approximately, to try every gate and every door, then I can stand still for ten minutes, then off I go again. I have the regulation breaks, of course. Breakfast, lunch, tea and dinner. Still, I feel a bit whacked when my shift's over, I must admit. But as I said it gives me time to think — not when I'm testing the locks, of course — but in between locks — it gives me time to think, and mostly I think about the patients. I get some very good ideas while I think, honestly. As a matter of fact, I hear one receives a little token of esteem, sometimes — I mean after a certain period. I've got a feeling that mine's almost due.

Pause

Perhaps it might even be promotion.

Pause

Quite frankly, I can't make much more progress with this job I was allocated. There's not enough scope. I wish I could deal with the patients — directly. I've thought out a number of schemes, you know, ideas, for a really constructive, progressive approach to the patients — in fact, I've sent them in to the office. Haven't heard anything yet. I think possibly what's happening is that on the evidence of these schemes I sent in they're considering promotion. Look, I want to ask you, these schemes of mine — you know, the ones I've sent in to the office — do you think that was the right place to send them, or should I have handed them in personally to someone? The point is, who?

MISS CUTTS *looks at her watch. She stands.*

CUTTS
Will you excuse me? I'm afraid I have an appointment.

She goes to the door. LAMB *follows.*

LAMB
You're the only friend I've got here, to be quite frank. I don't seem to be able to . . . reach the others. Don't know why. After all, I share their interests. Wouldn't you say?

They go out.

The lights fade on the sitting room. They go up on the office. ROOTE *and* GIBBS *are in the same positions.*

ROOTE *(deliberately)*
Well, how is 6459 getting on?

GIBBS
She's given birth to a boy, sir.

Pause

ROOTE

She ... has ... what?

GIBBS

Given birth, sir.

ROOTE

To ... a what?

GIBBS

A boy, sir.

Pause

ROOTE

I think you've gone too far, Gibbs.

GIBBS

Not me, sir, I assure you.

ROOTE *leans across the desk.*

ROOTE

Given birth?

GIBBS

Yes, sir.

ROOTE

To a child?

GIBBS

Yes, sir.

ROOTE

On these premises?

GIBBS

On the fourth floor, sir.

ROOTE *rises, leans over the desk to* GIBBS, *about to speak, unable to speak, turns, leaves the desk, walks heavily across the room.*

ROOTE

Sex?

GIBBS

Male.

ROOTE *sinks on to the sofa.*

ROOTE

This has made my morning. It really has made my morning.

He takes a pair of glasses out of his pocket, puts them on and looks across the room to GIBBS.

I'm dumbstruck. Quite thunderstruck. Absolutely thunderstruck! This has never happened before. Never! In all the years I've been here, in all the years my predecessor was here. And I'm quite certain never before him. To spend years and years, winter after winter, trying to perfect the working of an institution so fragile in its conception and execution, so fragile the boundary between the achievement of one's aspirations and their collapse, not only one's own aspirations; rather the aspirations of a whole community, a tradition, an ideal; such a delicately wrought concept of participation between him who is to be treated and him who is to treat that it defies analysis; trying to sustain this fine, fine balance, finer than a ... finer than a ...... far, far finer. Year after year, and so refined the operation that the softest breath, the breath of a ... feather ... can send the whole thing tottering into chaos, into ignominy, to the death and cancellation of all our hopes. Goodness gracious.

He stands.

As my predecessor said, on one unforgettable occasion: 'Order, gentlemen, for God's sake, order!' I remember the silence, row upon row of electrified faces, he with his golden forelock, his briar burning, upright and commanding, a soldier's stance, looking down from the platform. The gymnasium was packed to suffocation, standing room only. The lucky ones were perched on vaulting horses, hanging without movement from the wallbars. 'Order, gentlemen,' he said, 'for the love of Mike!' As one man we looked out of the window at Mike, and gazed at the statue – covered in snow, it so happened, then as now. Mike! The predecessor of my predecessor, the predecessor of us all, the man who laid the foundation stone, the man who introduced the first patient, the man who, after the incredible hordes of patients, or would-be patients, had followed him through town and country, hills and valleys, waited under hedges, lined the bridges and sat six feet deep in the ditch, opened institution after institution up and down the country, rest homes, nursing homes, convalescent homes, sanatoria. He was sanctioned by the Ministry, revered by the populace, subsidised by the State. He had set in motion an activity for humanity, of humanity and by humanity. And the keyword was order.

He turns to GIBBS.

I, Gibbs, have tried to preserve that order. A vocation, in fact. And you choose Christmas morning to come and tell me this. I tell you quite frankly I smell disaster.

GIBBS

With respect, sir, I can't see that the matter is of such extreme significance.

ROOTE

You can't? Have we ever, to your knowledge, given birth to a child on these premises before?

GIBBS

Not to my knowledge, sir.

ROOTE

Therefore we have no yardstick. As a mathematician you will appreciate that we have nothing to measure this event by so that we can with ease assess its implications.

GIBBS

I am not a mathematician, sir.

ROOTE

Well, you look like one!

He pockets his glasses, sits at the desk.

Right! There's work to be done. Find the culprit. Who is he?

GIBBS

That, sir, we have not yet been able to ascertain.

ROOTE

Why not? Have you asked the patient?

GIBBS

Yes, sir.

ROOTE

What did she say?

GIBBS

She was ... noncommital, sir. She said she couldn't be entirely sure since most of the staff have had relations with her in this last year.

ROOTE

Most of the staff?

GIBBS

According to her statement, sir.

ROOTE *rubs his mouth.*

ROOTE

Which one *is* 6459?

GIBBS

She's a woman in her thirties –

ROOTE

That means nothing to me, get on with it, what does she look like? Perhaps I know her.

GIBBS

Oh, there's no doubt that you know her, sir.

ROOTE

What does she look like?

Pause

GIBBS

Fattish.

ROOTE

Darkheaded?

GIBBS (*sitting*)

Not fairheaded, sir.

Pause

ROOTE

Small?

GIBBS

Certainly not tall.

Pause

ROOTE

Quite a sensual sort of face?

GIBBS

Quite sensual, yes, sir.

ROOTE

Yes.

Pause

Yes, she's got a sensual sort of face, hasn't she?

GIBBS

I should say it was sensual, sir, yes.

ROOTE

Wobbles when she walks?

GIBBS

Oh, possibly a trifle, sir.

ROOTE

Yes, she wobbles. She wobbles in her left buttock.

GIBBS

Her left, sir?

ROOTE

Well, one of them. I'm sure of it.

GIBBS

Yes, she has a slight wobble, sir.

ROOTE

Yes, of course she has.

Pause

She's got a slight wobble. Whenever she walks anywhere . . .
she wobbles. Likes eating toffees, too . . . when she can get
any.

GIBBS

Quite true, sir.

Pause

ROOTE

No – I don't think I know her.

Pause

And you say a number of the staff have had relations with this woman, do you?

GIBBS

Apparently, sir.

ROOTE (*standing*)

Well, one of them's slipped up, hasn't he? One of them's not been using his head! His know-how! Common or garden horsesense! I don't mind the men dipping their wicks on occasion. It can't be avoided. It's got to go somewhere. Besides that, it's in the interests of science. If a member of the staff decides that for the good of a female patient some degree of copulation is necessary then two birds are killed with one stone! It does no harm to either party. At least, that's how I've found it in my experience. (*With emphasis.*) But we all know the rule! Never ride barebacked. Always take precautions. Otherwise complications set in. Never ride barebacked and always send in a report. After all, the reactions of the patient have to be tabulated, compared with others, filed, stamped and if possible verified! It stands to reason. (*Grimly.*) Well, I can tell you something, Gibbs, one thing is blatantly clear to me. *Someone* hasn't been sending in his report!

GIBBS

Quite, sir.

ROOTE

Who?

GIBBS *sits on the sofa and puts his hand to his mouth.*

GIBBS

I think I know the man.

ROOTE

Who?

GIBBS (*thoughtfully*)

Yes, it's suddenly come to me. How absurd I didn't realise it
before.

ROOTE

Who, for God's sake?

GIBBS

I'd prefer to have the matter verified, sir, before I . . . bring
him before you.

ROOTE

All right. But find him. The good name of this establishment
depends on it.

ROOTE *sits at the desk.* GIBBS *goes to the door.*

GIBBS

What shall I do about the baby, sir?

ROOTE

Get rid of it.

GIBBS

The mother would have to go with it, sir.

ROOTE

Why?

GIBBS

Can't live without the mother.

ROOTE

Why not?

GIBBS

The mother feeds it.

ROOTE

I know that! Do you think I'm an idiot? My mother fed me, didn't she?

GIBBS

Mine fed me.

ROOTE

But mine fed me!

Pause

I remember.

Pause

Isn't there a wet nurse in the house? If there's a wet nurse in the house the baby can go with the wet nurse and the mother can stay here.

GIBBS

There's no wet nurse among the staff, sir.

ROOTE

I should hope not. I'm thinking about the understaff, the kitchen staff, the cleaning staff. Find out if there's a wet nurse among the understaff and get the thing in motion.

GIBBS

Don't you think the mother might miss the baby, sir?

ROOTE

I won't miss it. Will you miss it?

GIBBS

No, sir. I won't miss it.

ROOTE

Then why should the mother miss it?

They stare at each other. There is a knock on the door.

ROOTE

Who is it?

CUTTS

Me.

ROOTE

Gibbs, find that father. Come in!

Enter MISS CUTTS.

CUTTS (*to* GIBBS)

Hullo.

GIBBS

I'll keep you in touch with developments, sir.

ROOTE

That's very thoughtful of you.

GIBBS *goes out.* MISS CUTTS *sits on the sofa.* ROOTE *rises, goes to the sofa and sits next to her.*

ROOTE

I'm exhausted.

CUTTS

You know, I think that man's frightened of me.

ROOTE

Rubbish.

CUTTS

He never speaks to me. He never says a single word to me.
And not only that, he never ... he never looks at me. I can
only think I must frighten him in some way.

ROOTE

What do you mean, never speaks to you? He's obliged to
speak to you. You're working together, aren't you?

CUTTS

Oh yes, he talks shop to me. We discuss the patients, naturally. We were discussing one of the patients ... only yesterday. But he never speaks to me socially.

ROOTE

Which patient?

CUTTS

Or do you think he's taken with me? Do you think that he just
finds me too attractive to look at?

ROOTE

Which patient were you discussing?

CUTTS

But I can't say I like him. He's so cold. Oh, I like men to be cold — but not as cold as that. Oh, no, he's much too cold. You know, I think I'll ask him. I think I'll ask him whether he's taken with me or whether I frighten him. I mean, one might as well know.

ROOTE

Do you know what I've just heard? One of the patients has just had a baby.

CUTTS

A baby? But how?

ROOTE

As large as life. And under my auspices. It's nothing short of criminal.

CUTTS

But how did she manage it?

ROOTE

She had an accomplice.

CUTTS

No? Who?

ROOTE

That's what we've got to find out.

CUTTS

But which patient? Who is she?

ROOTE
I don't know her.

MISS CUTTS *leans back.*

CUTTS *(dreamily)*
I bet she feels very feminine now.

ROOTE *(vacantly, staring into space)*
She's always been feminine.

CUTTS
Do you think I'm feminine enough, darling? Or do you think
I should be more feminine?

ROOTE *is still abstracted.*

Darling. You don't think I'm too masculine, do you? I mean,
you don't think I could go even further? Do you?

ROOTE *(absently, muttering)*
Yes, yes why not?

CUTTS
You *do* think I should be more feminine?

ROOTE
What?

CUTTS
But you always say I'm feminine enough!

ROOTE

You are feminine enough.

CUTTS

Then if I'm feminine enough why do you want me to be more feminine?

ROOTE

I don't, I don't.

CUTTS

But you just said you did!

ROOTE

I don't, I don't!

CUTTS (*at a great pace*)

Because it would be awful if you really thought that I was letting you down in the most important aspect of the relationship between any man and any woman –

ROOTE

You're quite feminine enough!!

Pause

CUTTS

You really mean it?

ROOTE

Yes. (*He runs his hand through his hair.*) I've had the most wearing morning. On top of everything else one of the patients has died.

CUTTS

Died?

ROOTE

Dead.

CUTTS

Oh my poor sweet, and I've been nasty to you.

She kisses him.

Let me massage you. Come into the bedroom. Let me do your neck.

ROOTE

Yes. Do my neck.

They go into the bedroom.
The lights go down on the office. They go up on the sitting room.

GIBBS *enters. He sits at the low table, takes out a pack of cards and begins to play patience, very deliberately.*
LUSH *appears at the head of the stairway and descends.*
Suddenly a long sigh is heard, amplified.
LUSH *stops.* GIBBS, *about to place a card, stops. A long keen is heard, amplified.*
LUSH *looks up.* GIBBS, *card in hand, looks up.*
A laugh is heard, amplified, dying away.
Silence.
LUSH *descends the steps, enters the room.*

LUSH

Hullo, Charlie.

He closes the door and comes to the table. GIBBS, *after a glance at him, places another card.* LUSH, *inspects the state of the game.* GIBBS *scatters the cards.*

How's tricks, Charlie? (*Pause.*) What you been doing with yourself? (*Pause.*) Mmnn? (*Pause.*) Having a nice Christmas?

GIBBS

What do you want?

LUSH

What do you think of the weather?

GIBBS *collects the cards and puts them into a card case.*

GIBBS

You want something. What is it?

LUSH

I don't want anything, Gibbs. I've got something to report, that's all.

GIBBS

What is it?

LUSH

Don't get tense, Gibbs. After all, we're all buddies, aren't we? We're all in the game together.

GIBBS

You want to report something. What is it?

LUSH

Actually I want to ask you something first.

GIBBS

What?

LUSH

How's 6459 getting on?

Pause

GIBBS

You want to report something. What is it?

LUSH

I hear she's given birth.

GIBBS

It's none of your business.

LUSH

Oh, we're all concerned, you know. We're all concerned.

GIBBS

Listen, Lush. I'm not prepared to have any kind of conversation with you whatsoever. If you've got something to report report it and don't make a fool of yourself.

LUSH

Are you the father, Gibbs?

GIBBS *sits back and folds his arms.*

LUSH

Or the old man. Is the old man the father?

LUSH *sits*.

Who's going to carry the can? Miss Cutts? Do you think she's the father? We're all terribly excited, you know. Can't think what to call it. The kid's got to have a name, after all. What do you think yourself? I think something that'll remind him of this establishment when he grows up, don't you? His birth place. Of course, it depends on the father's name, doesn't it? I mean, the father might like the boy to be named after him. You know, if the father's name was John then the boy would be named John too. Do you see what I mean? The same name as the father.

GIBBS

You know, Lush, I don't know how you've lasted here. You're incompetent, you're unwholesome and you're offensive. You're the most totally bloody useless bugger I've ever come across.

LUSH

I can see you're in one of your moods today, Gibbs, so I suppose I'd better report to you what I came to report to you.

GIBBS

What is it?

LUSH

The mother of 6457 came to see me today.

GIBBS

The mother of 6457?

LUSH

Yes, you know. The one who died. He died last Thursday. From heart failure.

GIBBS

His mother?

LUSH

Yes.

GIBBS

How did she get in?

LUSH

That's what baffled me. It did. It quite baffled me. How on
earth did she get in? I wondered. How did she do it? Why
wasn't she stopped? Why did no-one demand her creden-
tials? It baffled me. Then – in a flash! – the answer came.
She'd been hiding all night in the shrubbery, waiting for
Tubb to leave his cubby-hole and take a leak, which eventu-
ally he did, and then she just darted in, like a shot off a shovel.
Simple. We really tend to overlook the simple cunning of the
simple. Would you like her description?

GIBBS

No. What did she want?

LUSH

She wanted to know how her son was getting on. She said that
when her son came here she was told he needed peace and
expert attention and that she would be hearing from us in due
course, and that in fact it was now a year since she had seen
him and she wanted to know how he was getting on.

GIBBS

What did you say?

LUSH

I said – A year? You haven't seen him for a year? But that's ridiculous. Didn't you come down for Mother's Day, or Thanksgiving Day, or for the annual summer picnic for patients, staff, relatives and friends? Weren't you invited to the Halloween Feast, the May Dance, the October Revival, the Old Boys and Girls supper and social? Dancing on the lawn, cold buffets on the flat roof, midnight croquet, barbecued boar by the lake? None of this? I never knew about it, she said. What! I said. The autumn art exhibition, the monthly concert of orchestral music in the bandroom, the half-yearly debate on a selected topic, held traditionally in the men's changing room? The pageant? The unveiling? The Festival of One-Act Plays, judged by Miss Daisy Cutts, L.R.M.B., A.C.A., our dramatic instructor? You came down, I said, for none of these activities and ceremonies through which we from time immemorial engage and channel our patients' energies? Oh dear, she said, I was never told. Obviously a clerical error, I said, I shall have it looked into. But, I said, it is a shame that you haven't seen him, since he is now departed from us.

GIBBS

What!

LUSH

He was moved some time ago, I said, to a convalescent home. But I thought this was a convalescent home, said 6457's mother. (*He laughs.*) Silly woman. A convalescent home? I countered, no, no, no, not at all, not at all, whatever gave you that idea? This is a rest home. Oh, said 6457's mother. I see. Well, wasn't he getting enough rest here that they had to send him to a convalescent home? Ah, Mrs 6457, I said, it's not quite so simple as that. It's not *quite* so *simple* as *that*. In a rest home, you see, you do not merely rest. Nor, in a convalescent home, do you merely convalesce. No, no, in both institutions, you see, you are obliged to work and play and join in daily communal activity to the greatest possible extent. Otherwise the concepts of rest and convalescence are rendered meaningless. Don't for a moment either imagine that the terms rest and convalescence are synonymous. No, no, no, no. They represent, you see, stages. Sometimes one must rest first and then convalesce. Sometimes the reverse. Either course, of course, is only decided after the best interests of the patient have been taken into account. So, I continued, you can rest assured that if your son was moved from here to another place it was in his best interests, and only after the most extensive research into his case, the wealth and weight of all the expert opinion in this establishment, where some of the leading brains in this country are concentrated; after a world of time, care, gathering and accumulating of mass upon mass upon mass of relevant evidence, document, affidavit, tape recordings, played both backwards and forwards, deep into the depth of the night; hours of time, attention to the most minute detail, unstinting labour, unflagging effort, scrupulous attachment to the matter in hand and meticulous examination of all aspects of the question had determined the surest and most beneficial course your son's case might take. The conclusion, after this supreme example of applied dedication, was to send your son to a convalescent home, where we are sure he will be content.

Pause

I also pointed out that we had carte blanche from the Ministry. She left much moved by my recital.

Pause

GIBBS
Thank you for your report, Mr. Lush.

LUSH

No congratulations?

GIBBS *consults his watch and goes to the internal telephone.*

GIBBS

Will you excuse me?

LUSH

I'll excuse you for the time being, Gibbs.

He goes out.

GIBBS (*into the phone*)

22, please. (*Pause.*) Sir? Gibbs here. I'd like to speak with Miss Cutts, if I may, with reference to that matter we were discussing earlier. Thank you. (*Pause.*) Miss Cutts? I believe you know a man called Lamb. He's on the staff. Yes. I would be obliged if you would collect him and bring him to number one interviewing room. When I join you, perhaps you would be so kind as to go to 1A control room. I shall be glad of your participation. Thank you.

He replaces the receiver, and leaves the room.
The lights fade on the sitting room.
The lights go up on the left stage area, including the stairway.
MISS CUTTS, *followed by* LAMB, *appears at the foot of the stairway. They ascend.* MISS CUTTS *is wearing a white coat.*

LAMB

But what do you think it's all about? I mean, he wanted to see me particularly, did he?

CUTTS

Oh yes. Particularly.

LAMB (*stopping*)

But he didn't say why?

CUTTS

No.

LAMB

You know, I don't know why, but as soon as you said 'Mr Gibbs wants to see you,' I felt an extraordinary *uplift*. Isn't it amazing? Really, I felt uplifted. I still do, I must say . . .

They go out of sight. The lights come up on the sound-proof room. MISS CUTTS *and* LAMB *enter the sound-proof room.*

It's very curious, I know, but I really feel it's . . . significant. I mean, why should I suddenly feel uplifted . . . You know, I can't help thinking, I know it's very silly of me, but I can't help thinking this is something to do with my promotion. Do you think he's read my schemes? I mean, why else would he send for me when I was on duty?

GIBBS *enters the room from another door. He wears a white coat.*

CUTTS

Mr Gibbs, have you met Mr Lamb?

GIBBS

How do you do?

LAMB

How do you do?

CUTTS

Would you excuse me a minute, please?

She leaves the room by the other door.

GIBBS

Would you take a seat, Mr Lamb?

LAMB

This one?

GIBBS

Yes, this one.

LAMB *sits.*

GIBBS

I'm delighted to meet you.

LAMB

Thank you. I must say I've always enjoyed my work here
tremendously . . . I mean, you really get the feeling here that
something . . . *important* is going on, something really valuable, and to be associated with it in any way can't be seen in
any other light than as a privilege.

GIBBS

That's a very heartening attitude.

LAMB

Oh, I really mean it, quite sincerely.

GIBBS

Good. I've heard a great deal about you, you know.

LAMB

Really?

GIBBS

Yes, there's quite a lot I'd like to talk to you about, when we have the time. But in the meanwhile I wonder ... if you'd give me a helping hand?

LAMB

I'd be quite delighted!

GIBBS

That's the spirit! (*With no undue emphasis.*) Miss Cutts, could you come down, please?

LAMB

What did you say?

GIBBS

I beg your pardon?

LAMB

Did you speak to Miss Cutts just now?

GIBBS

Yes, I asked her to come down.

LAMB

But where from?

GIBBS

From room 1A.

LAMB

But did she hear you?

GIBBS

Oh yes.

LAMB

How?

GIBBS (*pointing*)

That mike. It's just been switched on.

LAMB (*laughing*)

Oh, I see.

Pause

Curious kind of room, isn't it?

GIBBS

It's a sound-proof room.

Enter MISS CUTTS.

Ah, Miss Cutts. Now, Lamb, what I'd like is for you to help us with some little tests. Will you do that?

LAMB

Tests? I'd be delighted. That's what I hoped I'd be doing when I first came down here.

GIBBS

Really? Good.

LAMB

What kind of tests are they?

GIBBS

Experiments.

LAMB

Oh, I see.

GIBBS

Well, we have a very willing subject, Miss Cutts.

CUTTS

We do.

GIBBS

Oh by the way, Lamb, Merry Christmas.

LAMB

Thanks. Merry Christmas to you. And to you, Miss Cutts.

CUTTS

Thank you. And to you. (*To* GIBBS.) And to you too.

GIBBS

And to you. (*Briskly.*) Now — perhaps you would fit the electrodes to Mr. Lamb's wrists.

LAMB

Electrodes?

GIBBS

Yes.

CUTTS

Could I have your hand, Mr. Lamb?

MISS CUTTS *brings an electrode from her pocket and attaches it to* LAMB's *wrist.*

CUTTS

Now the other one.

She attaches a second electrode.

LAMB

What are they . . . exactly?

GIBBS

They're electric. You don't feel anything, of course. Best thing to do is forget all about them.

CUTTS

Now I'm going to plug in.

She bends at the wall, where, through a hole, three leads protrude. She picks up two and returns to LAMB.

GIBBS

Now she's going to plug in. You see the little socket on each of those electrodes? They're for the plug. (*He watches* MISS CUTTS *plug in.*) That's right. First plug in A, then plug in B. Right. Now you're plugged in.

LAMB

Oh, you've . . . got to be plugged in, have you?

GIBBS (*with a chuckle*)

Oh yes, got to be plugged in. The leads go right through the
wall and up to the control room, you see. We're plugged in
the other end.

LAMB

You?

GIBBS (*laughing*)

No, no, not me. You. Into the receiving set.

LAMB

Oh, I see. What are these . . . what are these electrodes for,
exactly?

GIBBS

They measure electrical potential on the skin.

LAMB

Oh.

GIBBS

Engendered by neural activity, of course.

LAMB

Oh, of course.

GIBBS

Electrical impulses, in a word. You can imagine how

important they are and yet how little we know about them.
Right. Now the earphones.

MISS CUTTS *stoops, picks up the earphones, attaches them to*
LAMB's *head.*

LAMB

Earphones?

GIBBS

Yes, same principle. Plugged in at the socket on your head,
plugged in at the other end in our control room. (*Cheeringly.*)
Don't worry, they're nice long leads, all of them. Plenty of
leeway. No danger of strangulation.

LAMB (*laughing*)

Oh yes. Good.

GIBBS

By the way, your predecessor used to give us a helping hand
occasionally, too, you know. Before you came, of course.

LAMB

My predecessor?

CUTTS

Could you just keep still a second, Mr Lamb, while I plug in
the earphones?

LAMB *is still. She plugs.*

Thank you.

GIBBS

Comfortable?

LAMB

Yes, thank you. My predecessor, did you say?

GIBBS

Yes, the chap you took over from.

LAMB

Oh! Did he really? Oh, good. I've often wondered what he ... did, exactly. Oh good, I'm ... glad I'm following in a tradition.

They all chuckle.

Have you any idea where he is now?

GIBBS

No, I don't think I do know where he is now. Do you know where he is, Miss Cutts?

CUTTS

No, I'm afraid I don't.

GIBBS

No, I'm afraid we don't really know. He's not here, anyway. That's certain. Now what I want you to do is to sit perfectly still. Relax completely. Don't think about a thing. That's right. Now you see that light up there. Ignore it. It might go on and off at regular or irregular intervals. Take no notice. Sit perfectly still. Quite comfortable?

LAMB

Yes, thanks.

GIBBS

Jolly good. Don't go to sleep, will you? We're awfully grateful to you, old chap, for helping us.

LAMB

It's a pleasure.

GIBBS *places his hand briefly on* LAMB*'s shoulder.*
MISS CUTTS *and* GIBBS *go out.*
LAMB *sits. Silence. He shifts, concentrates. The light, which is
red, flicks on and off.*
Silence. Suddenly LAMB *jolts rigid, his hands go to his earphones, he is propelled from the chair, falls to his knees, twisting
from side to side, still clutching his earphones, emitting highpitched cries.*

He suddenly stops still.

The red light is still flickering.
He looks up. He sits in the chair, emits a short chuckle.
The red light stops.

The voice of MISS CUTTS *is heard.*

CUTTS

Would you say you were an excitable person?

LAMB *looks up.*

LAMB

Not . . . not unduly, no.

The voice of GIBBS *is heard.*

GIBBS

Would you say you were a moody person?

LAMB

Moody? No, I wouldn't say I was moody – well, sometimes occasionally I –

CUTTS

Do you ever get fits of depression?

LAMB

Well, I wouldn't call them depression, exactly –

GIBBS

Would you say you were a sociable person?

LAMB

Well, that's not a very easy question to answer, really. I try, I certainly try to be sociable, I mean I think it should be the aim of any one interested in human nature to try to mix, to better his understanding of it. I –

CUTTS

Do you find yourself unaccountably happy one moment and unaccountably unhappy the next?

LAMB

It's strange you should say that because –

GIBBS

Do you often do things which you regret in the morning?

LAMB

Regret? Things I regret? Well, it depends what you mean by often, really. I mean, when you say often –

CUTTS

Are you often puzzled by women?

LAMB

Women?

GIBBS

Men.

LAMB

Men? Well, I was just going to answer the question about
women –

GIBBS

Do you often feel puzzled?

LAMB

Puzzled?

GIBBS

By women.

LAMB

Women?

CUTTS

Men.

LAMB

Uh – now just a minute, I . . . do you want separate answers or
a joint answer?

CUTTS

After your day's work, do you ever feel tired, edgy?

GIBBS

Fretty?

CUTTS

Irritable?

GIBBS

At a loose end?

CUTTS

Morose?

GIBBS

Frustrated?

CUTTS

Morbid?

GIBBS

Unable to concentrate?

CUTTS

Unable to sleep?

GIBBS

Unable to eat?

CUTTS

Unable to remain seated?

GIBBS

Unable to stand upright?

CUTTS

Lustful?

GIBBS

Indolent?

CUTTS

On heat?

GIBBS

Randy?

CUTTS

Full of desire?

GIBBS

Full of energy?

CUTTS

Full of dread?

GIBBS

Drained?

CUTTS

Of energy?

GIBBS

Of dread?

CUTTS

Of desire?

Pause

LAMB

Well, it's difficult to say, really —

LAMB *jolts rigid, his hands go to his earphones, he is propelled from the chair, falls to his knees, twisting from side to side, still*

clutching his earphones, emitting highpitched cries.
The red light flicks on and off.

He suddenly stops still.

The red light is still flickering.
He looks up. He sits in the chair, emits a short chuckle.
The red light stops.

CUTTS

Are you virgo intacta?

LAMB

What?

CUTTS

Are you virgo intacta?

LAMB

Oh, I say, that's rather embarrassing. I mean, in front of a
lady—

CUTTS

Are you virgo intacta?

LAMB

Yes, I am, actually. I'll make no secret of it.

CUTTS

Have you always been virgo intacta?

LAMB

Oh yes, always. Always.

CUTTS

From the word go?

LAMB

Go? Oh yes. From the word go.

GIBBS

What is the law of the Wolf Cub Pack?

LAMB

The cub gives in to the Old Wolf, the cub does not give in to himself.

GIBBS

When you were a boy scout were you most proficient at somersault, knots, leap frog, hopping, skipping, balancing, cleanliness, recitation or ball games?

LAMB

Well, actually, I never became a boy scout proper. I was a wolf cub, of course, but I never became a boy scout. I don't know why, actually. I've forgotten . . . to be frank. But I was a cub.

CUTTS

Do women frighten you?

GIBBS

Their clothes?

CUTTS

Their shoes?

GIBBS

Their voices?

CUTTS

Their laughter?

GIBBS

Their stares?

CUTTS

Their way of walking?

GIBBS

Their way of sitting?

CUTTS

Their way of smiling?

GIBBS

Their way of talking?

CUTTS

Their mouths?

GIBBS

Their hands?

CUTTS

Their legs?

GIBBS

Their teeth?

CUTTS

Their shins?

GIBBS

Their cheeks?

CUTTS

Their ears?

GIBBS

Their calves?

CUTTS

Their arms?

GIBBS

Their toes?

CUTTS

Their eyes?

GIBBS

Their knees?

CUTTS

Their thighs?

Pause

LAMB

Well, it depends what you mean by frighten –

GIBBS

Do you ever wake up in the middle of the night?

LAMB

Sometimes, yes, for a glass of water.

GIBBS

Do you ever feel you would like to join a group of people in which group common assumptions are shared and common principles observed?

LAMB

Well, I am a member of such a group, here, in this establishment.

GIBBS

Which establishment?

LAMB

This one.

GIBBS

Which establishment?

LAMB

This one.

GIBBS

You are a member of this establishment?

LAMB

Of course.

Silence

(*Looking up*.) Mmnn?

Any more questions?

I'm quite ready for another question.

I'm quite ready.

I'm rather enjoying this, you know.

Oh, by the way, what was that extraordinary sound?

It gave me quite a start, I must admit.

Are you all right up there?

You haven't finished your questions, have you?

I'm ready whenever you are.

Silence

LAMB *sits.*
The red light begins to flick on and off.
LAMB *looks up, stares at it.*
We hear the loud click of a switch from the control room.
The microphone in the room has been switched off.
The red light gradually grows in strength, until it consumes the room.
LAMB *sits still.*

Curtain

Act Two

ROOTE's *office. Night.*
ROOTE *is at his desk, examining some papers.*
LUSH *is at the window, looking out.*

> ROOTE (*without looking up*)

What are you looking at, Lush?

> LUSH

The yard, sir.

> ROOTE

Anyone about?

> LUSH

Not a soul.

> ROOTE

What's the weather like?

> LUSH

The snow has turned to slush.

> ROOTE

Ah.

Pause

Has the wind got up?

> LUSH

No. No wind at all.

ROOTE *turns a page.*

ROOTE (*muttering*)

No wind, eh? (*He examines the page, then slams it onto the desk.*) I can't read a word of this! It's indecipherable. What's the matter with this man Hogg? Why can't he type his reports out like everyone else? I can't read this writing. It's unreadable.

LUSH

His typewriter's out of action, sir.

ROOTE

What's the matter with it?

LUSH

It seems to have got stuck, sir.

ROOTE

Stuck?

LUSH

It just won't move at all.

ROOTE

Well, there must be an obstacle somewhere, or something.

LUSH

It looked like rust to me.

ROOTE

Rust? What are you talking about? It's a brand new typewriter. It's a Ministry typewriter. We had a whole cartload sent down from the Ministry – when was it? – a couple of

months ago. Brand new. I've still got the invoice somewhere.
Rust. Never heard such rubbish. Anyway, I can't sit here all
night trying to work this out. (*He puts the papers in a drawer,
goes to the drinks cabinet, takes out a bottle of whisky and pours
himself a drink.*) I've had enough this week. I never leave this
desk, do you know that? Sun up to sundown. Day in day out.
It's the price you have to pay for being in command, for being
responsible for the whole shoot. As I am. The whole damn
shoot. (*He drinks.*)

LUSH *walks to the cabinet, collects a glass and pours himself a
drink.*

                          LUSH
You do leave this desk quite often, though, don't you, sir?

                          ROOTE
What?

                          LUSH
I say, in point of fact, you do leave this desk quite often, don't
you?

                          ROOTE
When?

                          LUSH
When you go and visit the patients, for instance.

                          ROOTE
That's purely in the line of duty. It's not relaxation. I meant
relaxation. I wasn't talking about the line of duty.

                          LUSH
Oh.

ROOTE

Anyway, I've given up visiting the patients. It's not worth it.
A waste of energy.

LUSH

What an extraordinary thing to say, Mr Roote.

ROOTE

Don't Mr Roote me.

LUSH

But I never expected to hear you say a thing like that, Mr
Roote.

ROOTE

I said don't Mr Roote me!

LUSH

But I always understood that you looked upon visits to the
patients from the head of this establishment as one of the
most important features in the running of this establishment
... Mr. Roote.

ROOTE

Listen! I give you leeway. But don't think I give you that
much leeway.

LUSH

No, sir.

ROOTE

Don't think I can't squash you on a plate as easy as look at
you.

LUSH

Yes, sir.

ROOTE

As easy as look at you, Lush.

LUSH

Quite, sir.

ROOTE

So don't give me any more lip, you understand me? Otherwise you're liable to find yourself in trouble.

LUSH

You know I harbour no illusions about my position, Colonel.

ROOTE

Don't call me Colonel!

LUSH

But you were a Colonel once, weren't you, Colonel?

ROOTE

I was. And a bloody good one too.

LUSH

If I may say so, you still possess considerable military bearing.

ROOTE

Really?

LUSH

Oh yes.

ROOTE

Well, it's not surprising.

LUSH

And the ability to be always one thought ahead of the next man.

ROOTE

It's a military characteristic.

LUSH

Really?

ROOTE

Oh yes. Of course, some of them aren't very bright, I must admit.

LUSH

Who?

ROOTE

Military men.

LUSH

Really? I'm sorry to hear that.

ROOTE

Yes, some of them tend to let the side down. They've got no foresight, that's what it is. They can't think clearly. They've got no vision. Vision's very important.

LUSH

You must have been quite a unique kind of man, sir, in your regiment.

ROOTE

Yes, well I . . . What do you mean?

LUSH

The age of the specialist is dead.

ROOTE

What?

LUSH

The age of the specialist is dead.

ROOTE

Oh. Dead. Yes.

LUSH

That's why I say you must have been quite a unique kind of man, sir, in your regiment, being such an all-round man.

ROOTE

Yes, yes, there's something in that.

He perches on the desk.

LUSH

I mean, not only are you a scientist, but you have literary ability, musical ability, knowledge of most schools of philosophy, philology, photography, anthropology, cosmology, theology, phytology, phytonomy, phytotomy –

ROOTE

Oh, no, no, not phytotomy.

LUSH

Not phytotomy?

ROOTE

I was always meaning to get round to phytotomy, of course, but ... well, I've had so many other things to think about.

LUSH

Naturally.

ROOTE

But anyway, once you know something about phytonomy you're halfway there.

LUSH

Halfway where, sir?

ROOTE

To phytotomy!

Pause

Give us a drink.

LUSH *fills the glasses.*

LUSH

Why have you given up visiting the patients?

ROOTE

I've given up, that's all.

> LUSH

But I thought you were getting results?

> ROOTE (*staring at him*)

Cheers.

> LUSH

Weren't you getting results?

> ROOTE (*staring at him*)

Drink your whisky.

> LUSH

But surely you achieved results with one patient very recently. What was the number? 6459, I think.

ROOTE *throws his whisky in* LUSH's *face.* LUSH *wipes his face.*

> LUSH

Let me fill you up. (*He takes* ROOTE's *glass, pours, brings the glass to* ROOTE, *gives it to him.*) Yes, quite a substantial result, I should have thought.

ROOTE *throws his whisky in* LUSH's *face.* LUSH *wipes his face.* LUSH *takes* ROOTE's *glass, pours, brings the glass to* ROOTE, *gives it to him.*

But perhaps I'm thinking of 6457.

LUSH *grabs* ROOTE's *glass and holds it above his head, with his own. Slowly he lowers his own.*

Cheers.

He drinks, and then gives ROOTE *his glass.*

ROOTE (*taking the glass, in a low voice*)
You're neglecting to call me sir, Lush. You're supposed to
call me sir when you address me.

Pause

ROOTE *suddenly takes off his jacket, hangs it on the back of his
chair and sits.*

God, the heat of this place. It's damn hot, isn't it? It's like a
crematorium in here. Why is it suddenly so hot?

LUSH
The snow has turned to slush, sir.

ROOTE
Has it?

LUSH
Very dangerous.

ROOTE
It's a heatwave, that's what it is. (*A knock on the door.*) Who is
it?

Enter GIBBS.

Oh no, what is it? Business at this hour? You sit down to have
a quiet drink and what happens?

GIBBS

I have something to report, sir.

ROOTE

What? (GIBBS *looks at* LUSH.) Oh, never mind about him! What is it?

GIBBS

I don't approve of divulging official secrets to all and sundry, sir.

ROOTE

I know you don't approve! I don't approve! Nobody approves! But you've no alternative, have you?

GIBBS

Mr Lush could leave the room, sir.

ROOTE

Good God, what an impertinence! The man's my guest, do you understand that? Which is more than you bloodywell are! I've never heard of such a thing in all my life. He barges in here and tells me to chuck my own guest out of the room. Who do you think you are?

Pause

(*To* LUSH.) He gets on my wick sometimes – doesn't he you?

GIBBS

I ... apologise, sir, if I have been presumptuous.

ROOTE

Well, what's your business?

GIBBS

The father has been found.

ROOTE

No?

GIBBS

Found.

ROOTE (*rising*)

Found? So soon? In so short a space of time? Jiminy Cricket,
that's quick work, Gibbs! (*He stands, shakes hands with*
GIBBS.) Absolutely first class! (*He moves to* LUSH.) What do
you think of that, eh, for a bit of quick work?

LUSH

Remarkable.

ROOTE

You see the way I train my staff? Alacrity! First and fore-
most, alacrity! Get on with it, don't muck about, don't
dither, pick your man and pin him to the wall. Let your nose
do your thinking for you and you won't go far wrong. That's
what we try to do here, cultivate the habit of split second
decisions. Right? Right, Gibbs?

GIBBS

Quite, sir.

ROOTE

Right, Lush?

LUSH

Quite, sir.

ROOTE

And it never fails. I'm pleased with you, Gibbs. Who is he?

GIBBS

A man called Lamb, sir.

ROOTE

Never heard of him.

ROOTE *sits, pours a drink and drinks*.

LUSH

Lamb? Surely not Lorna Lamb? Lorna Lamb in the dispensary department?

ROOTE

A man, not a woman, you bloody fool!

LUSH

Oh, I'm so sorry, I didn't quite ... What exactly has this person done?

Pause

ROOTE

Tell him what this person has done, Mr Gibbs.

GIBBS

A child has been born to one of the patients. It was considered a matter of the first importance to locate the father. This has now been done.

ROOTE

Lamb? Who the hell's Lamb? Do I know him?

GIBBS

I think it doubtful that you've ever met him, sir.

ROOTE

I don't even know what he looks like. A rapist on my own staff and I don't know what he looks like!

LUSH

Was it rape?

ROOTE

Of course it was rape. You don't think that sort of thing happens by consent, do you?

GIBBS

He's not a very important member of your staff, sir.

ROOTE

Well, if he's not important how did he get into the patient's room? You know as well as I do that only a very select handful of the personnel are allowed in the patients' rooms. How did he get in?

GIBBS

He tests the locks, sir, of all the rooms in the building. Either this particular lock was ... not locked, or he forced it.

ROOTE

It's unbelievable, isn't it, Lush, the things that go on?

LUSH

It almost is, sir.

ROOTE

The sabotage that goes on, under your very nose. Open the window. I'm suffocating. (LUSH *opens the window*.) Is that radiator hot?

LUSH *bends to the radiator and touches it.*

LUSH
Scalding, sir.

ROOTE
That's why I'm so hot.

LUSH
The night is warm, Mr Roote. The snow has turned to slush.

ROOTE
That's about the fifth time you've said the snow has turned to slush!

GIBBS
It's quite true, sir. I noticed it myself.

ROOTE
I don't care whether it's true or not. I don't like to have a thing repeated and repeated and repeated! Anyone would think I was slow on the uptake. The snow has turned to slush. I heard it. I understand it. That's enough.

He pours a drink, drinks.

You think I'm past my job, do you? You think I'm a bit slow? Don't you believe it. I'm as quick as a python.

LUSH
An adder.

ROOTE
What?

LUSH

An adder.

ROOTE

What do you mean, an adder?

GIBBS

Do you think I deserve a little tipple of whisky, sir?

ROOTE

Good God, Gibbs is being jocular. Did you hear that, Lush? He's just made a pleasantry. Didn't you, son? Oh, that's better. I can feel a draught. See if you can turn that radiator off. If we can't turn it off here we'll have to get hold of Tubb and tell him to turn it off at the mains.

LUSH *bends to the radiator.*

Well?

LUSH

It won't budge. It's stiff.

ROOTE

It'll have to be turned off at the mains.

LUSH

It's a very cold building, sir, it's perishing on the upper floors.

ROOTE

I tell you it's too bloody hot and the damned heating's got to go off! Who's the boss here, for Christ's sake, you or me?

LUSH

Not me.

ROOTE

I do ten times as much work as the whole lot of you put together. I deserve a bit of comfort, a bit of consideration. The heating will have to be turned off! Every single pipe of it. That's what causes the laxity, the skiving, the inefficiency in this place. It's overheated! Always has been. (*To* GIBBS.) What's the matter with you, standing there like a tit in a trance? Tip the bottle, for the love of Mike. Deserved or undeserved.

GIBBS *pours himself a glass of whisky.*

What do you mean, you deserve it, anyway? You deserve nothing.

GIBBS

I meant for locating the father, sir.

ROOTE

You deserve nothing. Either of you. You've got a job to do. Do it. You won't get any tulips from me. Come on, fill it up, we'll drink a toast. Got yours, Lush?

LUSH

Just a minute.

LUSH *pours a glass of whisky.*

ROOTE (*solemnly*)

I'd like to drink a toast.

LUSH

To whom, sir?

ROOTE

I'd like to drink a toast, gentlemen, to our glorious dead.

LUSH

Which ones are they, sir?

ROOTE

The chaps who died for us in the field of action.

LUSH

Oh yes.

ROOTE

The men who gave their lives so that we might live. Who sacrificed themselves so that we might continue. Who helped keep the world clean for the generations to come. The men who died in our name. Let us drink to them. After all, it's Christmas. Couldn't be more appropriate.

LUSH

My glass is ready, sir.

ROOTE

Is yours ready, Gibbs?

GIBBS

It is.

ROOTE

Gentlemen, I give you a toast. To our glorious dead. (*Rising*.)

GIBBS *and* LUSH

To our glorious dead.

They drink.

ROOTE

A rapist on my own staff and I don't know what he looks like.
It's ridiculous. What sort of man is he?

GIBBS

Lamb, sir? Nondescript.

ROOTE

Tall?

GIBBS

No, sir. Small.

LUSH

Tall.

GIBBS

Small.

Pause

ROOTE

Do you know him, Lush?

LUSH

I've seen him.

ROOTE

Is he fat?

                              GIBBS

Thin, sir.

                              LUSH

Fat.

                              GIBBS

Thin.

Pause

                              ROOTE

Brown eyes?

                              GIBBS

Blue, sir.

                              LUSH

Brown.

                              GIBBS

Blue.

Pause

                              ROOTE

Curly hair?

GIBBS *and* LUSH *eye each other.*

                              LUSH

Straight, sir.

                              GIBBS

Curly.

LUSH

Straight.

Pause

ROOTE

What colour teeth?

GIBBS

Lemon, sir.

LUSH

Nigger.

GIBBS

Lemon.

LUSH

Nigger.

Pause

ROOTE

Any special peculiarities?

GIBBS

None.

LUSH

One.

GIBBS

None.

Pause

ROOTE

These descriptions don't tally. Next time bring me a photo-graph. Or you've got a cine-camera. You could devote a halfhour film to the man. A documentary – for educational purposes. It's still stifling in here. We'll have to get hold of Tubb. It's uncommonly warm in here for this time of the year, isn't it?

LUSH

It's warm out too. The snow has turned to slush.

ROOTE *turns, expostulating.*

GIBBS

Shall I call Tubb on the intercom, sir?

LUSH

I tried the intercom before. It sounded a bit clogged up.

ROOTE

Clogged up? What's the matter with this place? Everything's clogged up, bunged up, stuffed up, buggered up. The whole thing's running down hill. I don't like the look of it. Let's see.

He switches on the intercom on his desk and sits. A voice is heard.

VOICE

Number 84. A duck. Who's got ticket number 84? A duck ready for the oven. No-one? Unclaimed, Fred. Next one coming up. Ticket number 21. Number 21. Ten Portuguese cigars. Ten beautiful Portuguese cigars. No-one? Unclaimed, Fred. Number 38. Two tickets to the circus. Two tickets to the circus. Unclaimed, Fred. Number 44. A lovely crockery, cutlery, china and cookery set. A lovely crockery, cutlery, china and cookery set. Number 44. Unclaimed, Fred.

ROOTE *switches off*.

ROOTE
Yes, it does sound a bit clogged up, I must admit.

He fills the glasses.

What's it all about?

LUSH
It's the Christmas raffle, held by the understaff in the understaff canteen.

ROOTE
Raffle? Did we get any tickets?

GIBBS
I was approached, sir, but on behalf of the staff declined to purchase any.

ROOTE
Did you? Well, there's a bloody big amount of unclaimed stuff down there, isn't there?

LUSH
Must be a whole pile of it.

ROOTE
Well, who gets it?

LUSH
I expect there'll be another raffle at Easter, sir.

ROOTE

What about that duck? You can't keep a duck until Easter! It's . . . it's just not sensible! There's not much I don't know about poultry. Lush, make an immediate inquiry as to what's to become of that duck.
He sits.

LUSH

Yes, sir. What about the two tickets to the circus?

ROOTE

Christmas, eh? And I haven't received one present. Not one gift, of any kind. It's most upsetting.

LUSH

Actually, I've seen the duck, sir.

ROOTE

You have? What's it like?

LUSH

It's a dead duck, sir.

ROOTE

Dead?

LUSH

Quite dead, sir.

ROOTE

Good God, I didn't know it was dead.

LUSH

Yes, as dead as patient 6457. If not deader.

Silence

GIBBS

Is this Ministry whisky, sir? It's quite excellent.

ROOTE (*to* LUSH)

What do you know about 6457?

GIBBS

I wouldn't advise any further discussion of that matter, sir.

ROOTE

What do you know about 6457?

LUSH

I know that he's dead.

ROOTE

What do you know about it?

GIBBS

It is inadvisable to discuss the matter any further, sir.

ROOTE (*to* LUSH)

You're damned clever, aren't you?

LUSH

As a matter of fact, I met a relation of 6457's today.

ROOTE

You what?

GIBBS

Lush. The matter is closed.

ROOTE

What relation?

LUSH

His mother.

ROOTE

How do you know she was his mother?

LUSH

She said so.

ROOTE

She was a liar!

LUSH

No, she wasn't.

ROOTE

How do you know?

LUSH

She looked like a mother.

ROOTE

How do you know what mothers look like?

LUSH

I had one myself.

ROOTE

Do you think I didn't?

LUSH (*pointing at* GIBBS)

He didn't.

GIBBS

Oh yes, I did, damn you!

ROOTE

I was fed, Mister Cleverboots, at my mother's breast.

GIBBS

So was I.

LUSH

Me too.

Sudden silence

ROOTE

WELL? AND WHAT ABOUT IT?

ROOTE *sinks back in his seat. He looks at his glass, picks it up and swallows the glassful. He chokes, stands, writhes about in a fit of coughing.* GIBBS *and* LUSH *go to his aid.*

GIBBS (*taking his left arm*)

Come and sit in the armchair, sir.

LUSH (*taking his right arm*)

Come and sit on the sofa, sir.

A short tug-of-war commences, ROOTE *still coughing.*

ROOTE *shakes them off. He stands, shaking and panting.*

LUSH *goes to the desk, picks up a glass of whisky, takes it to* ROOTE.

LUSH

Here, drink this, sir.

ROOTE *viciously knocks the glass out of his hand. He stands, glaring at them, then goes back to his desk, sits.* LUSH *picks up the glass and places it on* ROOTE'*s desk.* LUSH *fills his glass.*

ROOTE

6457's mother, eh? How did she get in? Wasn't the porter on duty at the gate?

LUSH

Don't you want to know what she wanted?

ROOTE

I want to know why the porter wasn't on duty at the gate!

GIBBS

He's in charge of the raffle, sir, in the understaff canteen.

ROOTE

Tubb? That was Tubb just now, on the intercom?

LUSH

Oh, very much Tubb, sir.

ROOTE

Holding a raffle when he should have been on duty at the gate? Honestly, things are going from bad to worse. (*Pouring.*) Down the hatch. (*He raises his glass.*)

GIBBS

Happy Christmas, sir.

ROOTE

Happy Christmas to you, Gibbs.

LUSH

Happy Christmas, sir.

ROOTE

Thank you. Happy Christmas to you, Lush. A happy Christmas to you both.

GIBBS *and* LUSH (*raising their glasses*)

And to you, sir.

ROOTE

Thanks. And the best of luck for the new year.

GIBBS *and* LUSH

The best of luck for the new year to you, sir.

A knock at the door.

ROOTE

Who's that?

TUBB

Tubb, sir.

ROOTE

Come in.

Enter TUBB, *carrying a small box.*

Tubb! I thought you were on the intercom.

TUBB

Merry Christmas to you, Colonel.

ROOTE

Thank you, Tubb. And to you.

TUBB

How did you enjoy your Christmas dinner, sir?

ROOTE

Disappointing.

TUBB

Oh, I'm sorry to hear that, Colonel.

ROOTE

Too much gravy.

LUSH

Really? Mine was bone dry.

ROOTE

What?

LUSH

Honestly. Bone dry.

ROOTE

Well, mine was swimming in gravy.

LUSH

That's funny, isn't it, Gibbs? His was swimming in gravy and mine was bone dry.

TUBB

I'm surprised to hear yours was wet, Colonel.

ROOTE

Well, it was. Very wet.

He looks at the box.

What have you got there, Tubb?

TUBB

It's a Christmas present for you, Colonel.

ROOTE

A present?

TUBB

Just a little token of the understaff's regard, Colonel. Just a little something for Christmas.

ROOTE

Not a duck, by any chance?

TUBB

A duck, Colonel?

ROOTE

I just wondered whether it might have been a duck.

TUBB

Oh no, we haven't got any duck, sir.

ROOTE

No duck?

TUBB

No, sir.

ROOTE

What about number 84 then? Eh? Unclaimed. Ready for the oven. What? That was a duck wasn't it? And what's more it was unclaimed.

TUBB

Oh, that duck. Oh, that was claimed.

ROOTE (*startled*)

Claimed? Who by?

TUBB

Well, it wasn't exactly claimed, sir. But we found out who owned the ticket, so we're keeping it for him till he turns up, it's only fair.

ROOTE

Who is it?

TUBB

A man called Lamb, sir.

Silence

But anyway, what I've got here, Colonel, is a little token of regard from the understaff and the compliments of the season from all of us in the understaff, wishing you all the very best of luck in the year to come.

ROOTE

Thanks very much, Tubb. What is it?

TUBB

It's a Christmas cake, Colonel, cooked by the cook.

ROOTE

A cake? For me?

LUSH

That's very nice, isn't it, Gibbs?

ROOTE

A cake? For me?

TUBB

For you, sir.

ROOTE

How kind. How very kind. I'm most touched. Most touched.
More than touched. Deeply moved. It's a long time, a very
long time, since I had a Christmas cake. A long long time.

Pause

This ... was from the cook?

TUBB

From the cook, sir, from me, sir, from the kitchen staff, sir,
from the portering staff, sir, from the cleaning staff, sir, from
the very whole of the understaff, sir, from the very all of us
... to you, sir.

ROOTE

How very kind. How very very kind. I'm deeply moved.
Deeply moved. More than moved ...

LUSH

What an awfully nice gesture.

TUBB

The understaff, Colonel, and I'm sure the patients, would be even more deeply moved if you were to give them a Christmas address, sir.

ROOTE

An address?

TUBB

They would be most touched, sir. They're all clustered up now in the canteen and I've fitted up the loudspeaker system with an extension to all the corridors leading onto the patients' rooms as well.

LUSH

What a splendid idea.

ROOTE

An address? Your people would appreciate an address, would they?

TUBB

Oh, they would, sir. I know they would. Just a little word for Christmas.

LUSH

What an exciting innovation.

ROOTE

And the patients ... they haven't expressed any desire ... themselves ... have they?

TUBB

Well, not exactly expressed one, sir, as far as I know, but I've
fitted up the loudspeaker system to their rooms and I'm sure
they'd be deeply moved.

Pause

ROOTE

What do you think, Gibbs?

Pause

Gibbs!

GIBBS

I beg pardon, sir?

ROOTE

I said what do you think?

GIBBS

I ... I think it's an excellent idea, sir.

ROOTE

Lush?

LUSH

I think it would be deeply moving, sir.

Pause

ROOTE (*briskly*)

Where's the mike?

TUBB

In the cake, sir.

ROOTE

In the cake!

TUBB

I just shoved it in with the cake, sir.

ROOTE

Well, it's got no business to be anywhere near the cake!
What's the matter with you? (*Muttering.*) What a place to put
a mike!

TUBB (*extracting mike*)

Here we are, Colonel.

ROOTE

Well, plug it in, let's get on with it.

TUBB *plugs in by the wall.* ROOTE *sits, clears his throat.*

TUBB (*with mike*)

On here on the blotting paper all right, sir?

ROOTE

Move out of it.

TUBB

Switch this switch when you're ready, Colonel.

ROOTE (*slowly*)

Yes.

TUBB

They're all ready. They're all clustered up in the understaff
canteen.

Pause

ROOTE

What are you looking at, Gibbs?

GIBBS

Nothing in particular, sir.

ROOTE

You were looking at me! Do you call that nothing in particular?

Pause

I can't do it now. I'll do it later on. Later on. You can't make a
speech like that without some thought. Tell them not to be
disappointed. Tell them they'll hear my Christmas address
later on. Later on.

The lights go down on the office. They go up on the sitting room.
MISS CUTTS *comes in. She sits, takes a table tennis ball from
her pocket, tosses it up and catches it.*
GIBBS *descends the stairs.*
Suddenly a long sigh is heard, amplified.
GIBBS *stops.* MISS CUTTS *, about to toss the ball, stops.*
A long keen is heard, amplified.
GIBBS *looks up.* MISS CUTTS *looks up.*
A laugh is heard, amplified, dying away.
Silence.

MISS CUTTS *puts the ball to her mouth.*
GIBBS *is still a moment, then turns and enters the sitting room.*
MISS CUTTS *throws the ball at him. It falls at his feet.*

CUTTS

Catch!

GIBBS *looks down at the ball and stamps on it.*

GIBBS

Don't do that.

He takes out a packet of pills and swallows one.

CUTTS

What's the matter, Charlie?

GIBBS

Headache.

He sits, closes his eyes.
MISS CUTTS *goes to him.*

CUTTS

Have you got a headache, darling? Come to room 1A. (*She kisses him.*) I'll make it better for you. Are you coming?

GIBBS

I've got to go back.

CUTTS

What! Why?

GIBBS

To hear his Christmas address.

CUTTS

Another one? Oh, God, I thought he'd forgotten all about it.

GIBBS

He hadn't forgotten.

CUTTS

Every year. Sometimes I could scream.

GIBBS

I can't stand screaming.

CUTTS

Charlie, what is it? Don't I please you any more? Tell me. Be honest. Am I no longer the pleasure I was? Be frank with me. Am I failing you?

GIBBS

Stop it. I'm not in the mood.

CUTTS

Let me massage your neck.

She touches his neck.

GIBBS (*throwing her off*)

You and your necks! You love to get your hands round someone's neck!

CUTTS

So do you.

GIBBS

I'm not in the habit of touching people's necks.

CUTTS

It was such fun working with you this morning.

She sits.

You're so clever. I think you're the cleverest man I've ever had anything to do with. We don't work together nearly enough. It's such fun in room 1A. I think that's my favourite room in the whole place. It's such an intimate room. You can ask the questions and be so intimate. I love your questions. They're so intimate themselves. That's what makes it so exciting. The intimacy becomes unbearable. You keep waiting for the questions to stop, to pass from one intimacy into another, beautifully, and just when you know you can't ask another one, that they must stop, that you must stop, that it must stop—they stop!—and we're alone, and we can start, we can continue, in room 1A, because you know, you always know, your sense of timing is perfect, you know when the questions must stop, *those* questions, and you must start asking me questions, other questions, and I must start asking you questions, and it's question time, question time, question time, forever and forever and forever.

GIBBS (*standing*)

I tell you I'm not in the mood.

CUTTS

Come to 1A, Charlie.

GIBBS *stands, looking at the door.*

GIBBS

Did you hear anything, just now?

CUTTS

What?

GIBBS

Something. Sounds. Sounds. Just now. Just before.

CUTTS

Nothing. Not a thing. Nothing.

She looks at him.

What was it?

GIBBS

I don't know.

CUTTS (*a nervous chuckle*)

Don't tell me something's going to happen?

GIBBS

Something's *happening*. But I don't know what. I can't . . . define it.

CUTTS

How absurd.

GIBBS

It is absurd. Something's happening, I feel it, I know it, and I can't define it. It's ... it's ridiculous.

CUTTS

I know what's going to happen.

GIBBS

That old fool in there, he sees nothing, getting drunk with that ... bitch.

CUTTS

I know what's going to happen. You're going to kill him.

GIBBS

What?

CUTTS

Aren't you? You promised. You promised you would. Didn't you? Do it now. Now. Before he makes his Christmas speech.

GIBBS

Oh, stow it, for God's sake!

CUTTS

But you said you would!

GIBBS

Did I?

CUTTS

You said you'd stab him and pretend it was someone else.

GIBBS

Really? Who?

CUTTS

Lush.

GIBBS

Lush? Lush could never be taken for a murderer. He's scum but he's not a murderer.

CUTTS

No, but you are.

GIBBS *stares at her.*

GIBBS (*quietly*)

What did you say?

Pause

What did you call me?

CUTTS

Nothing.

GIBBS

You called me a murderer.

CUTTS

No, I didn't call you anything –

GIBBS (*ice*)

How dare you call me a murderer?

CUTTS

But I didn't!

GIBBS

Who do you know that I've murdered?

CUTTS

No-one!

GIBBS

Then how dare you call me a murderer?

CUTTS

You're not a murderer!

GIBBS (*hissing*)

I'm not a murderer, he's a murderer, Roote is a murderer!

Pause

You dare to call me a murderer?

CUTTS (*moaning*)

No, Charlie.

GIBBS

You know what that is, don't you? Slander. Defamation of character.

Pause

And on top of that, you try to incite me to kill my chief, Mr Roote. The man in charge. You, his own mistress. Just to satisfy your own personal whim.

Pause

CUTTS
Charlie . . .

GIBBS
Shut up!

MISS CUTTS *falls out of her chair onto the floor.*

CUTTS (*whispering*)
Oh, I wish I was in room 1A. I shall never get to room 1A again. I know I won't. Ever.

Blackout.
A drone is heard.
The drone stops.
Lights go up on the office.
ROOTE *and* LUSH *are still drinking.*
ROOTE *is at the desk,* LUSH *is seated, drooping.*
ROOTE *rises and perches on the front of the desk.*

ROOTE
Women! I've known them all. Did I ever tell you about the woman in the blue dress? She was a spy. A spy in a blue dress. I met her in Casablanca. Believe it or believe it not that woman was an agent for a foreign power. She was tattooed on her belly with a pelican. Yes. Her belly was covered with a pelican. She could make that pelican waddle across the room to you. On all fours, sideways, feet first, arse-upwards, any way you like. Her control was superhuman. Only a woman could possess it. Under her blue dress she wore a shimmy. And under that shimmy she wore a pelican.

Pause

My cake! We haven't cut the cake! My God, and it's nearly midnight.

He unwraps the cake, holds it.

A beauty. (*Going to his desk drawer.*) Wait a minute. Where are we? Just the thing in here.

Takes a bayonet from the drawer.

Now. Right down the middle.

He cuts the cake.

I remember the day my walls used to be hung with Christmas cards, I used to walk knee deep in presents, all my aunties and uncles popping in for a drink, a log fire in the grate, bells on the Christmas tree, garlands, flowers, floral decoration, music, flowers ... floral decoration ... laughter ... (*Abruptly.*) I didn't notice a card from you, did I? Didn't expect it either. Because you've no sense of decorum, it sticks out a mile. No heart. It's not so much the language, it's the attitude of mind that's nasty, unwholesome, putrid.

LUSH

The snow has turned to slush.

ROOTE

The temperature must have dropped. (*Thrusting a piece of cake at him.*) Well, here you are, have a piece of this cake.

LUSH *stares at it.*

Go on. Eat it!

They both munch. LUSH *spits his out.* ROOTE *grabs him by the neck.*

What are you doing? That's my cake!

                    LUSH
I can't!

            ROOTE (*shaking him*)
That's my Christmas cake! You can't spit out my Christmas cake!

            LUSH (*violently, breaking away*)
Stuff it!

ROOTE *regards him.*

                    ROOTE (*gravely*)
You've insulted me, you've insulted the cook, and you've insulted Jesus Christ.

Pause

We've got no room for unhealthy minds in this establishment.

            LUSH (*muttering*)
Muck and slush.

                    ROOTE
Lush!

                    LUSH
Colonel?

ROOTE (*grimly*)

I said you'd better watch your step. Everyone had better watch their step! (*He begins to move about the room.*) I don't like the look of things. You can't trust a soul. And there's something going on here that I haven't quite cottoned on to. There's something funny afoot. I can feel it. Some people think I'm old, but oh no, not by a long chalk. I've got second sight. I can see through walls. (*He considers.*) I don't mean that that's second sight, seeing through walls. I mean I've got second sight *and* I can see through walls!

LUSH

And your knowledge of phytotomy, sir.

ROOTE

That's more than a passing acquaintance. I can see right through them. I can hear a whisper in the basement. I didn't waste my youth. I exercised my faculties – to the hilt! And I spent a lot of time pondering. Pondering. For instance, this stupid business of the world going round. It's all a lot of balls. If the world was going round we'd be falling about all over the room. (*Bending over* LUSH.) But are we? Are we?

LUSH *considers*.

And today I feel something in my bones. I know it. Something's going on which I can't define. It's ridiculous. But I don't damn well know what it is. Do you think I'm going to be murdered?

LUSH

That's it.

ROOTE *brings the bottle to the desk and pours.*

The day got off to a lousy start! A death and a birth.
Absolutely bloody scandalous! Is it too much to ask — to keep
the place clean?

LUSH *goes to the desk, pours a drink, goes back to the armchair.*

You know who you remind me of? You remind me of Whipper Wallace, back in the good old days.

The door opens. GIBBS *enters and stands still.*

He used to hang about with a chap called House-Peters.
Boghouse-Peters we used to call him. I remember one day the
Whipper and Boghouse — he had a scar on his left cheek,
Boghouse — caught in some boghouse brawl, I suppose. (*He
laughs.*) Well, anyway, there they were, the Whipper and
Boghouse, rolling down the banks of the Euphrates this
night, when up came a policeman . . .

He dissolves in laughter.

up came this policeman . . . up came a policeman . . . this
policeman . . . approached . . . Boghouse . . . and the Whipper . . . were questioned . . . this night . . . the Euphrates . . . a
policeman . . .

GIBBS *moves.* ROOTE *jumps.*

Aaaaahhhh! (*To him.*) What the bloody hell do you think
you're doing, creeping up behind me like a snake! Eh? You
frightened the life out of me.

GIBBS

I've come to hear the Christmas speech, sir.

ROOTE

Well, why don't you make it? You're dying to make it, aren't you? Why don't you make it?

GIBBS

It's your privilege, sir.

ROOTE

Well, I'm sick to death of it! The patients, the staff, the understaff, the whole damn thing!

GIBBS

I'm sorry to hear that, sir.

ROOTE

It's bleeding me to death.

LUSH

Then why do you continue?

ROOTE *looks at him.*

ROOTE

Because I'm a delegate.

LUSH

A delegate of what?

ROOTE (*calmly*)

I tell you I'm a delegate.

LUSH

A delegate of what?

They stare at each other.

ROOTE

Not only me. All of us. That bastard there. (*To* GIBBS.)
Aren't you?

GIBBS

I am.

ROOTE

There you are.

LUSH

You haven't explained yourself.

ROOTE

Who hasn't?

LUSH

You can't explain yourself.

ROOTE

I can't?

LUSH

Explain yourself.

GIBBS

He's drunk.

ROOTE (*moving to him*)
Explain yourself, Lush.

LUSH
No, you! You explain yourself!

ROOTE
Be careful, sonny.

LUSH (*rising*)
You're a delegate, are you?

ROOTE (*facing him squarely*)
I am.

LUSH
On whose authority? With what power are you entrusted? By
whom were you appointed? Of *what* are you a delegate?

ROOTE *hits him in the stomach.*

ROOTE
I'm a delegate! (*He hits him in the stomach.*)
I was entrusted! (*He hits him in the stomach.*)
I'm a delegate! (*He hits him in the stomach.*)
I was appointed!

LUSH *backs, crouched, slowly across the stage,* ROOTE *following
him.*

Delegated! (*He hits him in the stomach.*)
Appointed! (*He hits him in the stomach.*)
Entrusted!

He hits him in the stomach. LUSH *sinks to the floor.*
ROOTE *stands over him and shouts:*

I AM AUTHORISED!

LUSH *remains heaped on the floor.* ROOTE *goes back to the desk,*
pours a drink for himself and GIBBS.

ROOTE (*to* GIBBS, *sourly*)
What do you want?

GIBBS
I came to hear your Christmas speech, Colonel.

ROOTE
You're sure you didn't come here to murder me?

GIBBS
Murder you?

ROOTE
Yes, wasn't that why you came?

GIBBS
Certainly not. What an idea.

ROOTE
Yes, you did! I can see it in your eyes! Can you see it, Lush, in
his eyes? This chap came here to do me in. You can see it in
his eyes.

GIBBS
I did no such thing.

ROOTE

You went cross-eyed, man, don't argue with me. Guilty! It
was written all over your face.

GIBBS

This is ridiculous.

ROOTE

Yes, well, you're not much good at it, are you? You're pretty
poor at it. I twigged it like that! (*He clicks his fingers, laughs.*)
Didn't I? You won't get very far as a murderer, will he,
Lush?

LUSH *begins to stand, slowly.*

Will you?

GIBBS

I resent this levity, sir.

ROOTE

Do you?

GIBBS

I resent it very strongly.

ROOTE

He resents it. (*Going behind the desk with his drink.*) Well, if he
resents it he resents it. (*Drinks.*) You're just too sensitive,
that's your trouble.

GIBBS (*sitting*)

A foul insinuation.

ROOTE

Oh, don't be so touchy!

LUSH *walks carefully to* GIBBS.

LUSH

He was only having a little joke, Gibbs old man.

ROOTE

Of course I was.

GIBBS

I found it less than funny.

LUSH

He didn't mean it. Honestly. Don't be downhearted. Now give me the knife and we won't say another word.

Sudden silence.
All still. GIBBS *and* LUSH *stare at each other.*
LUSH *makes a tiny movement to his jacket.*
Immediately GIBBS *rises, with a knife in his hand.*
LUSH *faces him, a knife in his hand.*
ROOTE *seizes the bayonet from his desk, comes above them, covering them both, grinning.*
Silence. All knives up.
Suddenly a long sigh is heard, amplified.
The knives go down.
A long keen is heard, amplified.
They look up.
A laugh is heard, amplified, dying away.
Silence.

LUSH

What was that?

ROOTE

I don't know. What was it?

GIBBS

I don't know.

Pause

ROOTE

I heard something, didn't you?

LUSH

Yes, I did.

GIBBS

Yes, I heard something.

Pause

ROOTE

Well, what was it?

Pause

GIBBS

I don't know.

LUSH

Nor do I.

Pause

ROOTE

Well, is there any way of finding out?

GIBBS

Something's happening, sir. I don't like it. There's something going on ... which I can't quite define.

ROOTE

How odd you should say that. I was only saying the same before, wasn't I, Lush? I was saying the same before. Just before you came in.

Pause

GIBBS

We'll investigate. Come on, Lush.

LUSH

Go yourself.

ROOTE

Go with him.

LUSH

I don't want to go with him.

ROOTE

Go with him! What's the matter? Are you frightened of the dark?

LUSH (*shyly*)

No ... well, you see, the fact is, Colonel, I've ... I've got a present for you.

ROOTE

A present?

LUSH

A Christmas present.

ROOTE (*suspiciously*)

Oh yes? What sort of a present?

LUSH

Just a little something, sir, for Christmas.

He takes a cigar from his pocket and hands it to ROOTE.

This is it.

ROOTE

I say! That looks a fine one.

LUSH

Just a little token, sir.

ROOTE

Well, that's a very nice thought, Lush my lad. I'm deeply
gratified.

LUSH

I'm glad you like it, sir.

ROOTE (*beaming*)

Yes, very nice. I shall smoke it before I go to bed. Now off
you go, about your business.

GIBBS

When would you like to see Lamb, sir?

ROOTE

Lamb?

GIBBS

The father, sir.

ROOTE

Oh, him. In the morning, son, in the morning. I can't be bothered to bother with him now. Can I?

GIBBS

In the morning then. Thank you for the drink, sir.

LUSH

And the cake.

ROOTE

Goodnight, gentlemen.

GIBBS *and* LUSH *go out.*
ROOTE *walks, with the cigar, to the sofa.*
MISS CUTTS *appears behind him from the bedroom door, watches him. She wears a nightdress.*
ROOTE *lights the cigar, puffs.*
The cigar explodes.
MISS CUTTS *rushes to him.* ROOTE *throws the cigar down, sees* MISS CUTTS.

CUTTS

Are you all right?

ROOTE *stares at her.*

What's the matter with that cigar?

ROOTE

You remind me of someone.

CUTTS

In my new nightie? Who?

ROOTE

Where did you get that thing?

CUTTS

It's a gift. Who do I remind you of?

ROOTE

Where did you get it?

CUTTS

From a friend. Do you like it? She just gave it to me. I had tea with her today. She's a nursing mother. She doesn't need it. She insisted I should have it. She's so sweet, and she's got such a bonny baby. I said to her, now we're friends, I can't go on calling you 6459, can I? What's your name? Do you know, she wouldn't tell me? Well, what does your lover call you? I said, what little nickname? She blushed to the roots of her hair. I must say I'm very curious. What could he have called her? She's sweet, but she said the baby misses his Daddy. Babies do miss Daddy, you know. Archie, can't the baby see his Daddy, just for a little while, just to say hello?

ROOTE (*quietly*)

No. Daddy will stay where he is.

CUTTS

Where is he?

ROOTE

You're supposed to be on nightshift.

CUTTS

Oh, it's Christmas, I knocked off early.

ROOTE

You're supposed to be working.

CUTTS

You're not pleased to see me.

Pause. ROOTE *sighs, looks at her.*

ROOTE

Are you ...

He sits on the sofa with her.

Are you ... happy?

CUTTS

Happy? Of course I am.

ROOTE

Are you ... are you happy with me?

CUTTS

Of course I'm happy. With you. When you're not silly.

ROOTE

You're really happy with me?

CUTTS

Not when you want me to go out into the cold with my nightie on.

ROOTE (*taking her hand*)

Don't go out.

He caresses her hand. She regards him gravely.

CUTTS

You know, sometimes I think I'm not feminine enough for you.

ROOTE

You are, you are feminine enough for me.

CUTTS

Perhaps if I was more feminine you wouldn't want me to go out in the cold.

ROOTE

I don't want you to go out. I want you to stay.

CUTTS

Or perhaps ... perhaps it's because you think you're not masculine enough.

ROOTE

I am!

CUTTS

Perhaps you're not.

ROOTE

You can't want me to be *more* masculine?

CUTTS (*urgently*)

It's not what *I* want. It's what *you* really *think*. It's what you really *deeply* think and *feel*. It's what *you* want, it's what you truly *are*, can't you see that, Archie? I mean, if you're suddenly worried that you're not masculine enough – I mean, that I'm not feminine enough and that you're too feminine – well, it's not going to work, is it?

ROOTE

Now, wait a minute, I never said anything–

CUTTS (*intensely*)

If I didn't love you so much it wouldn't matter. Do you remember the first time we met? On the beach? In the night? All those people? And the bonfire? And the waves? And the spray? And the mist? And the moon? Everyone dancing, somersaulting, laughing? And you – standing silent, staring at a sandcastle in your sheer white trunks. The moon was behind you, in front of you, all over you, suffusing you, consuming you, you were transparent, translucent, a beacon. I was struck dumb, dumbstruck. Water rose up my legs. I could not move. I was rigid. Immovable. Our eyes met. Love at first sight. I held your gaze. And in your eyes, bold and unashamed, was desire. Brutal, demanding desire. Bestial, ruthless, remorseless. I stood there magnetised, hypnotised. Transfixed. Motionless and still. A spider caught in a web.

ROOTE *stands, goes to the desk, sits, switches on the microphone.*

ROOTE (*into the mike*)

Patients, staff and understaff. A merry Christmas to you all, and a happy and prosperous new year. And on behalf of all the staff I'd like to wish all the understaff the very best of luck for the year to come and a very happy Christmas. And to the

patients I should like to send a personal greeting, to each and
every one of them, wishing them the heartiest compliments
of the season, and very best wishes, on behalf of the staff, the
understaff and myself, not forgetting the Ministry, which I
know would be glad to be associated with these words, for a
healthy, happy and prosperous new year.

Pause

We have had our little difficulties, in the year that is about to
die, our little troubles, our little sorrows as well as our little
joys, but through working together, through each and every
one of us pulling his weight, no matter how lowly or apparently trivial his job, by working, by living, by pulling
together as one great family, we stand undaunted. ‾

Pause

We say goodbye to the old year very soon now, and hail the
new, but I say to you, as we stand before these embers, that
we carry with us from the old year ... things ... which will
stand us in good stead in the new, and we are not daunted.

Pause

Some of you, sitting at your loudspeakers tonight, may sometimes find yourselves wondering whether the little daily
hardships, the little daily disappointments, the trials and
tribulations which seem continually to dog you are, in the
end, worth it. To you I would say one simple thing. Have
faith.

Pause

Yes, I think if I were asked to convey to you a special message this Christmas it would be that: Have faith.

Pause

Remember that you are not alone, that we here, for example, in this our home, are inextricably related, one to another, the staff to the understaff, the understaff to the patients, the patients to the staff. Remember this, as you sit by your fires, with your families, who have come from near and from far, to share this day with you, and may you be content.

He switches off the microphone and sits.
The lights go down on the office.
Darkness.
A low light on the stairway and the forestage.
Squeaks are heard, of locks turning.
The rattle of chains.
A great clanging, reverberating, as of iron doors opening.
Shafts of light appear abruptly about the stage, as of doors opening into corridors and into rooms.
Whispers, chuckles, half-screams of the patients grow.
The clanging of locks and doors grows in intensity.
The lights shift from area to area, rapidly.
The sounds reach a feverish pitch and stop.
Lights up on the office in the ministry.
LOBB *rises as* GIBBS *enters.*

LOBB

Ah, come in, Gibbs. How are you?

They shake hands.

Have a good journey down?

GIBBS

Not at all bad, thank you, sir.

LOBB

Sit down.

They sit.

LOBB

Cigarette?

GIBBS

No thank you, sir.

LOBB

You haven't been waiting long, have you?

GIBBS

Oh, no sir, not at all.

LOBB

My secretary's down with flu. Rather disorganised. What's the weather like up there?

GIBBS

Quite sharp, sir.

LOBB

Been fair to middling down here, for the time of year. Treacherous, though. My secretary, for instance, quite a stalwart sort of chap, strong as an ox, went down like a log over the weekend.

GIBBS

It's certainly treacherous.

LOBB

Dreadful. How are you feeling yourself?

GIBBS

Oh, I'm quite fit, thank you, sir.

LOBB

Yes, you look fit. Remarkably fit, really. You wear a vest, don't you?

GIBBS

Yes, sir.

LOBB

There you are. Very sensible. My secretary, for instance, strong as an ox, but he never wore a vest in his life. That's what did it.

Pause

Well, I'm glad you got down to see me, Gibbs.

GIBBS

So am I, sir.

LOBB

Rather unfortunate business. You've made out your report, I take it?

GIBBS

Yes, sir.

LOBB

I haven't seen it yet.

GIBBS

No, sir. I have it with me.

LOBB

Hand it in to the office on the way out, will you?

GIBBS

Yes, sir.

LOBB

Got any definite figures?

GIBBS

Yes, I ... have, sir.

LOBB

What are they?

Pause

GIBBS

The whole staff was slaughtered, sir.

LOBB

The whole staff?

GIBBS

With one exception, of course.

LOBB

Who was that?

GIBBS

Me, sir.

LOBB

Oh yes, of course.

Pause

The whole staff, eh? A massacre, in fact?

GIBBS

Exactly.

LOBB

Most distressing.

Pause

How did they . . . how did they do it?

GIBBS

Various means, sir. Mr Roote and Miss Cutts were stabbed in their bed. Lush –

LOBB

Excuse me, did you say bed, or beds?

GIBB

Bed, sir.

LOBB

Oh, really? Yes, go on.

GIBBS

Lush, Hogg, Beck, Budd, Tuck, Dodds, Tate and Pett, sir, were hanged and strangled, variously.

LOBB

I see. Well, I should think there's going to be quite a few questions asked about this, Gibbs.

GIBBS

Yes, sir.

LOBB

What's the position now?

GIBBS

The patients are all back in their rooms. I've left the head porter, Tubb, in charge of things. He's very capable. All the understaff, of course, are still active.

LOBB

They didn't touch the understaff?

GIBBS

No. Just the staff.

LOBB

Ah. Look here, Gibbs, there's something I'd like to know. How did the patients get out?

GIBBS

I'm not sure that I can give an absolutely conclusive answer to that, sir, until the proper inquiry has been set in motion.

LOBB

Naturally, naturally.

GIBBS

One possibility though is that one of their doors may not have been properly locked, that the patient got out, filched the keys from the office, and let the others out.

LOBB

Good Lord.

GIBBS

You see, the locktester who should have been on duty – we always had a locktester on duty –

LOBB

Of course, of course.

GIBBS

Was absent from duty.

LOBB

Absent? I say, well ... that's rather ... significant, isn't it?

GIBBS

Yes, sir.

LOBB

What happened to him?

GIBBS

He's ... not to be found, sir.

LOBB

Well, it would be a good thing if he were found, wouldn't it?

GIBBS

I shall do my best, sir.

LOBB

Good-o. (*Slight pause.*) Tell me. Why weren't you killed? Just as a matter of interest.

GIBBS

I was engaged on some research, sir, alone. I was probably the only member of the staff awake, so was able to take measures to protect myself.

LOBB

I see. Well, it's all most unfortunate, but we can't really do anything until the report has gone in and the inquiry set up. Meanwhile you'd better try to get hold of that locktester of yours. I think we shall probably want to have a word with him. What's his name?

GIBBS

Lamb, sir.

LOBB (*making a note of the name*)

Lamb. Well, Gibbs, I would like to say on behalf of the Ministry how very much we commend the guts you've shown.

GIBBS

Thank you, sir. My work means a great deal to me.

LOBB

That's the spirit. (*Slight pause.*) You can carry on now, I suppose? We'll have some reinforcements down in a few days. Can't be sooner, I'm afraid. We've got to get hold of some properly qualified people. Not as easy as all that.

GIBBS

I can carry on, sir.

LOBB

You'll be in charge, of course.

GIBBS

Thank you, sir.

LOBB (*rising*)

Don't thank me. It's we have to thank you.

They walk to the door.

One last question. Why do you think they did it? I mean . . .
why did they feel so strongly?

GIBBS

Well, Mr. Lobb, it's a little delicate in my position . . .

LOBB

Go on, my boy, go on. It's the facts that count.

GIBBS

One doesn't like to speak ill of the dead.

LOBB

Naturally, naturally.

GIBBS

But there's no doubt that Mr Roote was unpopular.

LOBB

With good cause?

GIBBS

I'm afraid so, sir. Two things especially had made him rather unpopular. He had seduced patient 6459 and been the cause of her pregnancy, and he had murdered patient 6457. That had not gone down too well with the rest of the patients.

Blackout on office.

Lights rise on sound-proof room.

LAMB *in chair. He sits still, staring, as in a catatonic trance.*

Curtain.

A NIGHT OUT

A Night Out was first performed on the B.B.C. Third Programme on 1 March 1960, with the following cast:

ALBERT STOKES	Barry Foster
MRS. STOKES, *his mother*	Mary O'Farrell
SEELEY	Harold Pinter
KEDGE	John Rye
BARMAN AT THE COFFEE STALL	Walter Hall
OLD MAN	Norman Wynne
MR. KING	David Bird
MR. RYAN	Norman Wynne
GIDNEY	Nicholas Selby
JOYCE	Jane Jordan Rogers
EILEEN	Auriol Smith
BETTY	Margaret Hotine
HORNE	Hugh Dickson
BARROW	David Spenser
THE GIRL	Vivien Merchant

Produced by Donald McWhinnie

The play was televised by A.B.C. Armchair Theatre on 24 April 1960, with the following cast:

ALBERT STOKES	Tom Bell
MRS. STOKES, *his mother*	Madge Ryan
SEELEY	Harold Pinter
KEDGE	Philip Locke
BARMAN AT THE COFFEE STALL	Edmond Bennett
OLD MAN	Gordon Phillott
MR. KING	Arthur Lowe
MR. RYAN	Edward Malin
GIDNEY	Stanley Meadows
JOYCE	José Read
EILEEN	Maria Lennard
BETTY	Mary Duddy
HORNE	Stanley Segal
BARROW	Walter Hall
THE GIRL	Vivien Merchant

Produced by Philip Saville

Act One

SCENE ONE

The kitchen of MRS. STOKES' *small house in the south of London.
Clean and tidy.*

ALBERT, *a young man of twenty-eight, is standing in his shirt
and trousers, combing his hair in the kitchen mirror over the
mantelpiece. A woman's voice calls his name from upstairs.
He ignores it, picks up a brush from the mantelpiece and brushes
his hair. The voice calls again. He slips the comb in his pocket,
bends down, reaches under the sink and takes out a shoe
duster. He begins to polish his shoes.* MRS. STOKES *descends
the stairs, passes through the hall and enters the kitchen.*

MOTHER: Albert, I've been calling you. [*She watches him.*]
What are you doing?

ALBERT: Nothing.

MOTHER: Didn't you hear me call you, Albert? I've been
calling you from upstairs.

ALBERT: You seen my tie?

MOTHER: Oh, I say, I'll have to put the flag out.

ALBERT: What do you mean?

MOTHER: Cleaning your shoes, Albert? I'll have to put the
flag out, won't I?

ALBERT *puts the brush back under the sink and begins to search
the sideboard and cupboard.*

What are you looking for?

ALBERT: My tie. The striped one, the blue one.

MOTHER: The bulb's gone in Grandma's room.

ALBERT: Has it?

MOTHER: That's what I was calling you about. I went in and switched on the light and the bulb had gone.

She watches him open the kitchen cabinet and look into it.

Aren't those your best trousers, Albert? What have you put on your best trousers for?

ALBERT: Look, Mum, where's my tie? The blue one, the blue tie, where is it? You know the one I mean, the blue striped one, I gave it to you this morning.

MOTHER: What do you want your tie for?

ALBERT: I want to put it on. I asked you to press it for me this morning. I gave it to you this morning before I went to work, didn't I?

She goes to the gas stove, examines the vegetables, opens the oven and looks into it.

MOTHER [*gently*]: Well, your dinner'll be ready soon. You can look for it afterwards. Lay the table, there's a good boy.

ALBERT: Why should I look for it afterwards? You know where it is now.

MOTHER: You've got five minutes. Go down to the cellar, Albert, get a bulb and put it in Grandma's room, go on.

ALBERT [*irritably*]: I don't know why you keep calling that room Grandma's room, she's been dead ten years.

MOTHER: Albert!

ALBERT: I mean, it's just a junk room, that's all it is.

MOTHER: Albert, that's no way to speak about your Grandma, you know that as well as I do.

ALBERT: I'm not saying a word against Grandma—

MOTHER: You'll upset me in a minute, you go on like that.

ALBERT: I'm not going on about anything.

MOTHER: Yes, you are. Now why don't you go and put a bulb in Grandma's room and by the time you come down I'll have your dinner on the table.

ALBERT: I can't go down to the cellar, I've got my best trousers on, I've got a white shirt on.

MOTHER: You're dressing up tonight, aren't you? Dressing up, cleaning your shoes, anyone would think you were going to the Ritz.

ALBERT: I'm not going to the Ritz.

MOTHER [*suspiciously*]: What do you mean, you're not going to the Ritz?

ALBERT: What do you mean?

MOTHER: The way you said you're not going to the Ritz, it sounded like you were going somewhere else.

ALBERT [*wearily*]: I am.

MOTHER [*shocked surprise*]: You're going out?

ALBERT: You know I'm going out. I told you I was going out. I told you last week. I told you this morning. Look, where's my tie? I've got to have my tie. I'm late already. Come on, Mum, where'd you put it?

MOTHER: What about your dinner?

ALBERT [*searching*]: Look . . . I told you . . . I haven't got the . . . wait a minute . . . ah, here it is.

MOTHER: You can't wear that tie. I haven't pressed it.

ALBERT: You have. Look at it. Of course you have. It's beautifully pressed. It's fine.

He ties the tie.

MOTHER: Where are you going?

ALBERT: Mum, I've told you, honestly, three times. Honestly, I've told you three times I had to go out tonight.

MOTHER: No, you didn't.

ALBERT *exclaims and knots the tie.*

I thought you were joking.

ALBERT: I'm not going . . . I'm just going to Mr. King's. I've told you. You don't believe me.

MOTHER: You're going to Mr. King's?

ALBERT: Mr. Ryan's leaving. You know Ryan. He's leaving the firm. He's been there years. So Mr. King's giving a sort of party for him at his house . . . well, not exactly a party, not a party, just a few . . . you know . . . anyway, we're all invited. I've got to go. Everyone else is going. I've got to go. I don't want to go, but I've got to.

MOTHER [*bewildered, sitting*]: Well, I don't know . . .

ALBERT [*with his arm round her*]: I won't be late. I don't want to go. I'd much rather stay with you.

MOTHER: Would you?

ALBERT: You know I would. Who wants to go to Mr. King's party?

MOTHER: We were going to have our game of cards.

ALBERT: Well, we can't have our game of cards.

[*Pause.*]

MOTHER: Put the bulb in Grandma's room, Albert.

ALBERT: I've told you I'm not going down to the cellar in my white shirt. There's no light in the cellar either. I'll be pitch black in five minutes, looking for those bulbs.

MOTHER: I told you to put a light in the cellar. I told you yesterday.

ALBERT: Well, I can't do it now.

MOTHER: If we had a light in the cellar you'd be able to see where those bulbs were. You don't expect me to go down to the cellar?

ALBERT: I don't know why we keep bulbs in the cellar!

[*Pause.*]

MOTHER: Your father would turn in his grave if he heard you raise your voice to me. You're all I've got, Albert. I want you to remember that. I haven't got anyone else. I want you . . . I want you to bear that in mind.

ALBERT: I'm sorry . . . I raised my voice.

He goes to the door.

[*Mumbling.*] I've got to go.

MOTHER [*following*]: Albert!

ALBERT: What?

MOTHER: I want to ask you a question.

ALBERT: What?

MOTHER: Are you leading a clean life?

ALBERT: A clean life?

MOTHER: You're not leading an unclean life, are you?

ALBERT: What are you talking about?

MOTHER: You're not messing about with girls, are you? You're not going to go messing about with girls tonight?

ALBERT: Don't be so ridiculous.

MOTHER: Answer me, Albert. I'm your mother.

ALBERT: I don't know any girls.

MOTHER: If you're going to the firm's party, there'll be girls there, won't there? Girls from the office?

ALBERT: I don't like them, any of them.

MOTHER: You promise?

ALBERT: Promise what?

MOTHER: That . . . that you won't upset your father.

ALBERT: My father? How can I upset my father? You're always talking about upsetting people who are dead!

MOTHER: Oh, Albert, you don't know how you hurt me, you don't know the hurtful way you've got, speaking of your poor father like that.

ALBERT: But he is dead.

MOTHER: He's not! He's living! [*Touching her breast.*] In here! And this is his house!

[*Pause.*]

ALBERT: Look, Mum, I won't be late . . . and I won't . . .

MOTHER: But what about your dinner? It's nearly ready.

ALBERT: Seeley and Kedge are waiting for me. I told you not to cook dinner this morning. [*He goes to the stairs.*] Just because you never listen . . .

He runs up the stairs and disappears. She calls after him from the hall.

MOTHER: Well, what am I going to do while you're out? I
  can't go into Grandma's room because there's no light. I
  can't go down to the cellar in the dark, we were going to
  have a game of cards, it's Friday night, what about our game
  of rummy?

SCENE TWO

*A coffee stall by a railway arch. A wooden bench is situated a
  short distance from it.*
SEELEY *and* KEDGE, *both about* ALBERT'S *age, are at the counter,
  talking to the barman. An old man leans at the corner of the
  counter.*

SEELEY: Give us a cheese roll as well, will you?
KEDGE: Make it two.
SEELEY: Make it two.
BARMAN: Two cheese rolls.
SEELEY: What are these, sausages?
BARMAN: Best pork sausages.
SEELEY [*to* KEDGE]: You want a sausage?
KEDGE [*shuddering*]: No, thanks.
SEELEY: Yes, you're right.
BARMAN: Two cheese rolls. What about these sausages, you
  want them or don't you?
SEELEY: Just the rolls, mate.
BARMAN: Two tea, two rolls, makes one and eightpence.

  SEELEY *gives him half a crown.*

KEDGE: There'll be plenty to eat at the party.
SEELEY: I'll bet.
OLD MAN: Eh! [*They turn to him.*] Your mate was by here not
  long ago.
SEELEY: Which mate?

OLD MAN: He had a cup of tea, didn't he, Fred? Sitting over there he was, on the bench. He said he was going home to change but to tell you he'd be back.

KEDGE: Uh-uh.

OLD MAN: Not gone more than above forty-five minutes.

BARMAN: One and eight from half a dollar leaves you ten pennies.

OLD MAN: Anyway, he told me to tell you when I see you he was coming back.

KEDGE: Thanks very much.

SEELEY: Well, I hope he won't be long. I don't want to miss the booze.

KEDGE: You think there'll be much there, do you?

OLD MAN: Yes, he was sitting over there.

KEDGE: Who was?

OLD MAN: Your mate.

SEELEY: Oh yes.

OLD MAN: Yes, sitting over there he was. Took his cup of tea and went and sat down, didn't he, Fred? He sat there looking very compressed with himself.

KEDGE: Very what?

OLD MAN: Compressed. I thought he was looking compressed, didn't you, Fred?

BARMAN: Depressed. He means depressed.

SEELEY: No wonder. What about that game on Saturday, eh?

KEDGE: You were going to tell me. You haven't told me yet.

BARMAN: What game? Fulham?

SEELEY: No, the firm. Firm's got a team, see? Play on Saturdays.

BARMAN: Who'd you play?

SEELEY: Other firms.

BARMAN: You boys in the team, are you?

KEDGE: Yes. I've been off sick though. I didn't play last week.

BARMAN: Sick, eh? You want to try one of my sausages, don't he, Henry?

OLD MAN: Oh, ay, yes.

KEDGE: What happened with the game, then?

They move to the bench.

SEELEY: Well, when you couldn't play, Gidney moved Albert to left back.

KEDGE: He's a left half.

SEELEY: I know he's a left half. I said to Gidney myself, I said to him, look, why don't you go left back, Gidney? He said, no, I'm too valuable at centre half.

KEDGE: He didn't, did he?

SEELEY: Yes. Well, you know who was on the right wing, don't you? Connor.

KEDGE: Who? Tony Connor?

SEELEY: No. You know Connor. What's the matter with you? You've played against Connor yourself.

KEDGE: Oh—whatsisname—Micky Connor.

SEELEY: Yes.

KEDGE: I thought he'd given up the game.

SEELEY: No, what are you talking about? He plays for the printing works, plays outside right for the printing works.

KEDGE: He's a good ballplayer, that Connor, isn't he?

SEELEY: Look. I said to Albert before the kick off, Connor's on the right wing, I said, play your normal game. I told him six times before the kick off.

KEDGE: What's the good of him playing his normal game? He's a left half, he's not a left back.

SEELEY: Yes, but he's a defensive left half, isn't he? That's why I told him to play his normal game. You don't want to worry about Connor, I said, he's a good ballplayer but he's not all that good.

KEDGE: Oh, he's good, though.

SEELEY: No one's denying he's good. But he's not all that good. I mean, he's not tip-top. You know what I mean?

KEDGE: He's fast.

SEELEY: He's fast, but he's not all that fast, is he?

KEDGE [*doubtfully*]: Well, not all that fast . . .

SEELEY: What about Levy? Was Levy fast?

KEDGE: Well, Levy was a sprinter.

SEELEY: He was a dasher, Levy. All he knew was run.

KEDGE: He could move.

SEELEY: Yes, but look how Albert played him! He cut him off, he played him out the game. And Levy's faster than Connor.

KEDGE: Yes, but he wasn't so clever, though.

SEELEY: Well, what about Foxall?

KEDGE: Who? Lou Foxall?

SEELEY: No, you're talking about Lou Fox, I'm talking about Sandy Foxall.

KEDGE: Oh, the winger.

SEELEY: Sure. He was a very smart ballplayer, Foxall. But what did Albert do? He played his normal game. He let him come. He waited for him. And Connor's not as clever as Foxall.

KEDGE: He's clever though.

SEELEY: Gawd blimey, I know he's clever, but he's not as clever as Foxall, is he?

KEDGE: The trouble is, with Connor, he's fast too, isn't he?

SEELEY: But if Albert would have played his normal game! He played a game foreign to him.

KEDGE: How many'd Connor get?

SEELEY: He made three and scored two.

Pause. They eat.

KEDGE: No wonder he's depressed, old Albert.

SEELEY: Oh, he was very depressed after the game, I can tell you. And of course Gidney was after him, of course. You know Gidney.

KEDGE: That birk.

[*Pause.*]

OLD MAN: Yes, he was sitting over where you are now, wasn't he, Fred? Looking very compressed with himself. Light-haired bloke, ain't he?

SEELEY: Yes, light-haired.

SCENE THREE

The house.

ALBERT *is coming down the stairs. He is wearing his jacket. He goes towards the door. His mother calls from the kitchen and goes into the hall.*

MOTHER: Albert! Where are you going?

ALBERT: Out.

MOTHER: Your dinner's ready.

ALBERT: I'm sorry. I haven't got time to have it.

MOTHER: Look at your suit. You're not going out with your suit in that state, are you?

ALBERT: What's the matter with it?

MOTHER: It needs a good brush, that's what's the matter with it. You can't go out like that. Come on, come in here and I'll give it a brush.

ALBERT: It's all right . . .

MOTHER: Come on.

They go into the kitchen. She gets the brush.

Turn round. No, stand still. You can't go out and disgrace me, Albert. If you've got to go out you've got to look nice. There, that's better.

She dusts his jacket with her hands and straightens his tie.

I didn't tell you what I made for you, did I? I made it specially. I made Shepherd's Pie tonight.

ALBERT [*taking her hand from his tie*]: The tie's all right.

He goes to the door.

Well, ta-ta.

MOTHER: Albert! Wait a minute. Where's your handkerchief?

ALBERT: What handkerchief?

MOTHER: You haven't got a handkerchief in your breast pocket.

ALBERT: That doesn't matter, does it?

MOTHER: Doesn't matter? I should say it does matter. Just a minute. [*She takes a handkerchief from a drawer.*] Here you are. A nice clean one. [*She arranges it in his pocket.*] You mustn't let me down, you know. You've got to be properly dressed. Your father was always properly dressed. You'd never see him out without a handkerchief in his breast pocket. He always looked like a gentleman.

SCENE FOUR

The coffee stall.
KEDGE *is returning from the counter with two teas.*

KEDGE: Time we were there.

SEELEY: We'll give him five minutes.

KEDGE: I bet his Mum's combing his hair for him, eh?

He chuckles and sits.

You ever met her, Seeley?

SEELEY: Who?

KEDGE: His . . . mother.

SEELEY: Yes.

KEDGE: What's she like?

SEELEY [*shortly*]: She's all right.

KEDGE: All right, is she?

SEELEY: I told you. I just said she was all right.

[*Pause.*]

KEDGE: No, what I mean is, he always gets a bit niggly when she's mentioned, doesn't he? A bit touchy. You noticed that?

SEELEY [*unwillingly*]: Yes.

KEDGE: Why's that, then?

SEELEY: I don't know. What're you asking me for?

KEDGE: I don't know. I just thought you might . . . sort of . . . well, I mean, you know him better than I do, don't you?

[*Pause.*]

Of course, he don't let much slip, does he, old Albert?

SEELEY: No, not much.

KEDGE: He's a bit deep really, isn't he?

SEELEY: Yes, he's a bit deep.

[*Pause.*]

KEDGE: Secretive.

SEELEY [*irritably*]: What do you mean, secretive? What are you talking about?

KEDGE: I was just saying he was secretive.

SEELEY: What are you talking about? What do you mean, he's secretive?

KEDGE: You said yourself he was deep.

SEELEY: I said he was deep. I didn't say he was secretive!

ALBERT *walks through the railway arch across to the bench.*

KEDGE: Hullo, Albert.

ALBERT: Hullo.

KEDGE: That's a nice bit of clobber you've got on there.

SEELEY: Very fair, very fair.

KEDGE: Yes, fits you like a glove.

SEELEY: Well, come on, catch a thirty-six round the corner.

ALBERT: Wait a minute, I . . . I don't think I feel like going, actually.

KEDGE: What are you talking about?

ALBERT: I don't feel like it, that's all.

SEELEY: What, with all that drink laid on?

ALBERT: No, I've just got a bit of a headache.

OLD MAN: That's the bloke! That's the bloke was here before, isn't it, Fred? I gave them your message, son.

ALBERT: Oh . . . thanks.

OLD MAN: Didn't I?

KEDGE: You did, you did, mate.

SEELEY: Well, what's going on, you coming or what?

ALBERT [*touching his forehead*]: No, I feel a bit . . . you know . . .

KEDGE: Don't you know who'll be there tonight, Albert?

ALBERT: Who?

KEDGE: Joyce.

ALBERT: Joyce? Well, what about it?

KEDGE: And Eileen.

ALBERT: Well, so what?

KEDGE: And Betty. Betty'll be there. They'll all be there.

SEELEY: Betty? Who's Betty?

KEDGE: Betty? What do you mean? You don't know Betty?

SEELEY: There's no girl in the office called Betty.

KEDGE: Betty! The dark bit! The new one. The one that came in last week. The little one, in the corner!

SEELEY: Oh, her. Is her name Betty? I thought it was—

KEDGE: Betty. Her name's Betty.

SEELEY: I've been calling her Hetty.

[*Pause.*]

KEDGE: Anywhat, she'll be there. She's raring to go, that one.

ALBERT: Well, you go then, I'll . . .

KEDGE: Albert, what's the matter with you, mate? It's wine, women and song tonight.

ALBERT: I see them every day, don't I? What's new in that?

KEDGE: You frightened Gidney'll be after you, then, because of the game?

ALBERT: What do you mean?

KEDGE: Go on, everyone has a bad game, Albert.

ALBERT: Yes, they do, don't they?

KEDGE: I played against Connor myself once. He's tricky. He's a very tricky ballplayer.

ALBERT: Yes.

SEELEY: Clever player, Connor.

ALBERT: What's Gidney got to do with it, Kedge?

KEDGE: Well, you know what he is.

ALBERT: What?

KEDGE: Well, he's captain of the team, isn't he, for a bang-off?

ALBERT: You think—?

SEELEY: Oh, scrub round it, will you? It's late—

ALBERT: You think I'm frightened of Gidney?

KEDGE: I didn't say you were—

SEELEY: Gidney's all right. What's the matter with Gidney?

ALBERT: Yes. What's wrong with him?

KEDGE: Nothing. There's nothing wrong with him. He's a nice bloke. He's a charmer, isn't he?

SEELEY: The cream of the cream. Well, come on, you coming or what?

ALBERT: Yes, all right. I'll come.

SEELEY: Just a minute. I'll get some fags.

He goes to the counter. ALBERT *and* KEDGE *are left standing.*

[*To the* BARMAN.] Twenty 'Weights', mate.

KEDGE *regards* ALBERT.

KEDGE: How's your Mum, Albert?

ALBERT: All right.

KEDGE: That's the idea.

BARMAN: Only got 'Woods'.

SEELEY: They'll do.

ALBERT [*quietly*]: What do you mean, how's my Mum?

KEDGE: I just asked how she was, that's all.

ALBERT: Why shouldn't she be all right?

KEDGE: I didn't say she wasn't.

ALBERT: Well, she is.

KEDGE: Well, that's all right then, isn't it?

ALBERT: What are you getting at?

KEDGE: I don't know what's the matter with you tonight, Albert.

SEELEY [*returning*]: What's up now?

ALBERT: Kedge here, suddenly asks how my mother is.

KEDGE: Just a friendly question, that's all. Gaw! You can't even ask a bloke how his mother is now without him getting niggly!

ALBERT: Well, why's he suddenly ask—?

SEELEY: He was just asking a friendly question, mate. What's the matter with you?

[*Pause*]

ALBERT: Oh.

SEELEY: Well, how is she, then?

ALBERT: She's fine. What about yours?

SEELEY: Fine. Fine.

[*Pause.*]

KEDGE: Mine's fine too, you know. Great. Absolutely great. A marvel for her age, my mother is. Of course, she had me very late.

[*Pause.*]

SEELEY: Well? Are you coming or not? Or what?

KEDGE: I'm coming.

ALBERT [*following*]: I'm coming.

SCENE FIVE

The kitchen. The MOTHER *is putting* ALBERT'S *dinner into the oven. She takes the alarm clock from the mantelpiece and puts it on the table. She takes out a pack of cards, sits at the table and begins to lay out a game of patience. Close up of her, broodingly setting out the cards. Close up of the clock. It is seven forty-five.*

Act Two

SCENE ONE

The lounge of MR. KING'S *house. The party is in progress.*
KEDGE *and* BETTY *are dancing. Music comes from a radio-
gram.* MR. KING, *an urbane man in his fifties,* GIDNEY, *the
chief accountant, in his late twenties,* SEELEY *and* ALBERT,
are standing in a group. JOYCE *and* EILEEN *are at the table
which serves as a bar. Two men and a woman of indeterminate
age sit holding drinks.* HORNE *and* BARROW, *two young
clerks, stand by the door.* MR. RYAN, *the old man, sits in the
centre of the room, smiling.*

JOYCE: You enjoying the party, Mr. Ryan?

RYAN *nods and smiles.*

EILEEN [*pleasantly*]: Enjoying the party, are you?

He nods, winks and smiles.

KING: I recommend a bicycle, honestly. It really keeps you
up to the mark. Out in the morning, on the bike, through
the town . . . the air in your lungs, muscles working . . .
you arrive at work . . . you arrive at work fresh . . . you
know what I mean? Uplifted.

GIDNEY: Not so good in the rain.

KING: Refreshes you! Clears the cobwebs. [*He laughs.*]

SEELEY: You don't walk to work, do you, Gidney?

GIDNEY: Me? I've got the car.

KING: I drive too, of course, but I often think seriously of taking up cycling again. I often think very seriously about it, you know.

JOYCE [*to* RYAN]: Nice party, isn't it, Mr. Ryan?

RYAN *nods and inclines his head, smiling.*

KEDGE [*dancing*]: You dance like a dream, Betty, you know that?

BETTY [*shyly*]: I don't.

KEDGE: You do. Honest. Like a dream. Like a dream come true.

BETTY: You're just saying that.

KING: Well, Kedge looks all right again, doesn't he? What was the matter with him? I've forgotten.

SEELEY: Stomach trouble.

KING: Not enough exercise. [*To* KEDGE.] You'll have to see you get more exercise, Kedge!

KEDGE [*passing*]: You never said a truer word, Mr. King.

SEELEY: Well, he don't look in bad trim to me, Mr. King.

They laugh.

KING: I must admit it.

GIDNEY: He'll never get to the last lap with that one, I can tell you.

KING [*smiling*]: Now, now, you young men, that's quite enough of that. No more of that.

GIDNEY [*pleasantly*]: What are you laughing at, Stokes?

ALBERT: What?

GIDNEY: Sorry. I thought you were laughing.

ALBERT: I was laughing. You made a joke.

GIDNEY: Oh yes, of course. Sorry.

[*Pause.*]

Well, we've got Kedge back at left back next Saturday.

KING: Yes. Excuse me.

SEELEY: That's a lovely pair of shoes you're wearing, Gidney.

GIDNEY: Do you think so?

SEELEY: Oh, they're the best, the very best, aren't they, Albert? Gidney always wears a nice pair of shoes, doesn't he, you noticed that? That's one thing I'll say about you, Gidney—you carry your feet well.

EILEEN: A mambo! Who's going to dance?

SEELEY: I'll give it a trot.

SEELEY *and* EILEEN *dance*.

GIDNEY: Don't you dance, Stokes?

ALBERT: Yes, sometimes.

GIDNEY: Do you? You will excuse me, won't you?

ALBERT: Yes.

ALBERT *is left standing*.

KING: Well, Ryan, enjoying the party?

RYAN *nods, smiles*.

Nice to see a lot of young people enjoying themselves, eh?

RYAN *nods, smiles*.

Of course, it's all in your honour, old man. Let's fill you up. I'll be the oldest man in the office after you've gone.

GIDNEY *and* JOYCE, *whispering*.

JOYCE: No. Why should I?

GIDNEY: Go on. Just for a lark.

JOYCE: What for?

GIDNEY: For a lark. Just for a lark.

JOYCE: You've got an evil mind, you have.

GIDNEY: No, it'll amuse me, that's all. I feel like being amused.

JOYCE: Well, I'm not going to.

GIDNEY: Gah, you wouldn't know how to, anyway.

JOYCE: Oh, wouldn't I?

GIDNEY [*taking her arm*]: Get hold of Eileen, don't tell her I told you though, and go over and lead him a dance, just lead him a dance, that's all, see what he does. I want to see his reaction, that's all, I just want to see how he takes it.

JOYCE: What, in front of everyone else, in front of—?

GIDNEY: Just talk to him, talk to him. I don't mean anything else, do I?

JOYCE: What do I get if I do?

GIDNEY: A toffee apple.

JOYCE: Oh, really? Thank you.

GIDNEY: I'll take you for a ride in the car. Honest.

SEELEY [*dancing*]: Hullo, Mr. Ryan. Enjoying the party?

EILEEN: You dance well, don't you?

SEELEY: I was going in for ballet once.

EILEEN: Go on!

SEELEY: Yes, true. They offered me the leading part in *Rigoletto*. When I was a boy soprano.

EILEEN: You're making it up.

GIDNEY [*to* JOYCE]: No, he just irritates me, that bloke. I . . . I haven't got any time for a bloke like that.

JOYCE: He's just quiet, that's all.

GIDNEY: Well, see if you can wake him up.

KING [*to* BETTY]: Well, Miss Todd, it hasn't taken you long to get to know everyone, has it?

BETTY: Oh no, Mr. King.

KEDGE: I've taken her under my wing, Mr. King.

KING: So I noticed.

KEDGE: Yes, I've been teaching her all about mortality tables. I told her in case of fire or burglary commission and damages come to her.

KING: I would hardly take Kedge's word as gospel, Miss Todd.

KEDGE: You know I've got the best interests of the firm at heart, Mr. King.

GIDNEY [*drinking, with* JOYCE]: Anyway, I'm thinking of moving on. You stay too long in a place you go daft. After all, with my qualifications I could go anywhere.

He sees ALBERT *at the bar.*

Couldn't I, Stokes?

ALBERT: What?

GIDNEY: I was saying, with my qualifications I could go anywhere. I could go anywhere and be anything.

ALBERT: So could I.

GIDNEY: Could you? What qualifications have you got?

ALBERT: Well, I've got a few, you know.

GIDNEY: Listen! Do you know that Chelsea wanted to sign me up a few years ago? They had a scout down to one of our games. They wanted to sign me up. And I'll tell you another thing as well. I could turn professional cricketer any day I wanted to, if I wanted to.

ALBERT: Then why don't you?

GIDNEY: I don't want to.

JOYCE: You'd look lovely in white.

GIDNEY: These people who talk about qualifications. Just makes me laugh, that's all.

KEDGE [*in the corner of the room, in an armchair with* BETTY]: Oh, you're lovely. You're the loveliest thing on four wheels.

KING [*to* HORNE *and* BARROW, *by the door*]: Well, I hope you'll both be in the team soon yourselves. I think it's a very good thing we've . . . that the firm's got a football team. And a cricket team, of course. It shows we look on the lighter side of things too. Don't you agree?

HORNE: Oh yes, Mr. King.

BARROW: Yes, Mr. King.

KING: Also gives a sense of belonging. Work together and play together. Office work can become so impersonal. We like to foster . . . to foster something . . . very different. You know what I mean?

HORNE: Oh yes, Mr. King.

BARROW: Yes, Mr. King.

KING: You interested in sailing, by any chance? You're quite welcome to come down to my boat at Poole any weekend— do a bit of sailing along the coast.

HORNE: Oh, thank you, Mr. King.

BARROW: Thank you, Mr. King.

JOYCE *and* EILEEN, *whispering*.

JOYCE [*slyly*]: Eh, what about going over and cheering up old Albert?

EILEEN: What for?

JOYCE: Well, he looks a bit gloomy, don't he?

EILEEN: I don't want to go over. You go over.

JOYCE: No, come on. You come over.

EILEEN: What for?

JOYCE: Cheer him up. For a bit of fun.

EILEEN: Oh, you're awful.

JOYCE: Come on. Come over.

KING [*to* RYAN]: Can I fill your glass, Ryan?

[RYAN *nods, and smiles*.]

Can't leave you without a drink, can we? The guest of honour.

JOYCE *and* EILEEN *sit either side of* ALBERT *on a divan.*

JOYCE: Mind if we join you?

ALBERT: Oh, hullo.

EILEEN: Enjoying the party?

JOYCE: What are you sitting all gloomy about?

ALBERT: I'm not gloomy, I'm just sitting, drinking. Feel a bit tired, actually.

JOYCE: Why, what have you been doing?

ALBERT: Nothing.

JOYCE: You just said you were tired. Eh, move up, I'm on the edge.

ALBERT: Sorry.

EILEEN: Eh, mind out, you're squashing me.

ALBERT: Oh . . .

JOYCE: You squash her, she won't mind.

EILEEN [*laughing*]: Oh, Joyce!

GIDNEY, *with a smile, watching.*

JOYCE: Come on, tell us, what are you tired about?

ALBERT: Oh, just work, I suppose.

JOYCE: I've been working too. I'm not tired. I love work. Don't you, Eileen? [*She leans across him to speak.*]

EILEEN: Oh yes, I love work.

ALBERT: No, I'm not tired, really. I'm all right.

EILEEN: He looks tired.

JOYCE: You've been living it up. Women.

EILEEN: I'll bet.

JOYCE: Females.

The girls giggle.

ALBERT [*with an uncertain smile*]: No, I wouldn't . . .

EILEEN: Eh, mind your drink. My best taffeta.

JOYCE: He's not bad looking when you get close.

EILEEN: Quite nice when you get close.

ALBERT: Thanks for the compliment.

EILEEN: You got a flat of your own?

ALBERT: No. Have you?

EILEEN [*forlornly*]: No.

JOYCE: You live with your mother, don't you?

ALBERT: Yes.

JOYCE: Does she look after you all right, then?

ALBERT: Yes, she . . . [*He stands.*] I'm just going to the bar.

JOYCE: So are we.

EILEEN: Me too.

They follow.

KING: Well, now everyone . . .

JOYCE: I'm having gin.

ALBERT: Gin? Wait a minute . . .

KING: Just a minute, everyone, can I have your attention?

GIDNEY [*to* JOYCE]: Didn't make much impression, did you?

JOYCE: Didn't I?

KING: Just for a moment, please . . .

GIDNEY: Eh, Stokes, pay attention, will you?

ALBERT: What?

GIDNEY: Mr. King wants your attention.

KING: I'd just like to propose a toast to our guest of honour, Mr. Ryan. Gidney!

GIDNEY: Yes?

ALBERT: Here's your gin, then.

JOYCE: Thanks.

KING [*to* GIDNEY]: Go and get Kedge out of that corner, will you? Now, as you know, we're all gathered here tonight to pay our respects to our old friend and colleague, Mr. Ryan . . .

KEDGE *and* BETTY *are locked together in the armchair.* GIDNEY *taps* KEDGE *on the shoulder.*

GIDNEY: Mr. King wants to know if you'll honour the party with your presence.

KEDGE [*jumping up*]: Oh, sorry. [BETTY, *thrown off, falls. He picks her up.*] Sorry.

KING: We've all known Mr. Ryan for a very long time. Of course, I've known him myself much longer than anyone here—

KEDGE: For he's a jolly good fellow—

KING: Wait! Very glad for your enthusiasm, Mr. Kedge. Your heart, I am quite sure, is in the right place.

General laughter.

ALBERT, EILEEN, JOYCE, SEELEY *and* GIDNEY *stand in a group around* MR. RYAN'S *chair.*

But please allow me to toast Mr. Ryan first and then the floor is yours. Well, as I was saying, the whole department is here tonight to pay tribute to a man who from time immemorial has become, how shall I put it, the very core of our little community. I remember Mr. Ryan sitting at his very own desk the first time my father brought me into the office—

A sharp scream and stiffening from EILEEN. *All turn to her.*

Good heavens!

GIDNEY: What is it?

AD LIB: What's happened? Eileen, what's the matter?

EILEEN: Someone touched me!

JOYCE: Touched you?

EILEEN: Someone touched me! Someone—!

BETTY: What did he do?

KEDGE: Touched you? What did he do?

JOYCE: What did he do, Eileen?

EILEEN: He . . . he . . . he took a liberty!

KEDGE: Go on! Who did?

EILEEN *turns and stares at* ALBERT. *Silence. All stare at* ALBERT.

ALBERT: What are you looking at me for?

GIDNEY [*muttering*]: Good God . . .

Tense, embarrassed pause.

HORNE [*at the door, whispering*]: What did he do, touch her?

BARROW [*open-mouthed*]: Yes.

HORNE [*wide-eyed*]: Where?

They look at each other, open-mouthed and wide-eyed.

ALBERT: What are you looking at me for?

KING: Please, now . . . can we possibly . . . I mean . . .

EILEEN [*in a voice of reproach, indignation and horror*]: Albert!

ALBERT: What do you mean?

SEELEY: How does she know it was Albert?

KEDGE: Wonder what he did. Made her jump didn't he?

ALBERT: Now look, wait a minute, this is absolutely ridiculous—

GIDNEY: Ridiculous, eh? I'll say it is. What do you think you're up to?

EILEEN: Yes, I was just standing there, suddenly this hand . . .

JOYCE: I could tell he was that sort.

The camera closes on MR. RYAN'S *hand, resting comfortably on his knee, and then to his face which, smiling vaguely, is inclined to the ceiling. It must be quite clear from the expression that it was his hand which strayed.*

GIDNEY: Come out here, Albert.

ALBERT: Don't pull me. What are you doing?

SEELEY: How do you know it was him?

ALBERT [*throwing off* GIDNEY'S *hand*]: Let go of me!

SEELEY: What are you pulling him for?

GIDNEY: You keep out of this.

KING [*nervously*]: Now please let me continue my toast, ladies and gentlemen. Really, you must settle this elsewhere.

SEELEY: We don't even know what he's supposed to have done.

ALBERT: I didn't do anything.

GIDNEY: We can guess what he did.

KING [*at speed*]: We are all collected here tonight in honour of Mr. Ryan and to present him with a token of our affection—

JOYCE [*to* ALBERT]: You snake!

SEELEY: Well, what did he do? What's he supposed to have done?

ALBERT: She doesn't know what she's talking about.

SEELEY: Come on, what's he supposed to have done, Eileen, anyway?

EILEEN: Mind you own business.

JOYCE: You don't think she's going to tell you, do you?

GIDNEY: Look, Seeley, why don't you shut up?

SEELEY: Now don't talk to me like that, Gidney.

ALBERT: Don't worry about him, Seeley.

KING: As I have been trying to say—

JOYCE: You come over here, Eileen, sit down. She's upset, aren't you?

EILEEN [to SEELEY]: So would you be!

KING: Miss Phipps, would you mind composing yourself?

EILEEN: Composing myself!

GIDNEY: Come outside a minute, Albert.

KING: As I have been trying to say—

KEDGE [brightly]: I'm listening, Mr. King!

KING: What?

KEDGE: I'm listening. I'm with you.

KING: Oh, thank you. Thank you, my boy.

ALBERT: I'm going, anyway.

ALBERT *goes into the hall, followed by* GIDNEY *and* SEELEY. *The door shuts behind them.*

GIDNEY: Wait a minute, Stokes.

ALBERT: What do you want?

GIDNEY: I haven't been satisfied with your . . . sort of . . . behaviour for some time, you know that, don't you?

ALBERT: You haven't . . . you haven't what?

GIDNEY: For instance, there was that bloody awful game of football you played when you threw the game away last Saturday that I've got on my mind, besides one or two other things!

SEELEY: Eh look, Gidney, you're talking like a prize—

GIDNEY [viciously]: I've told you to keep out of this.

ALBERT [tensely]: I'm going, anyway.

GIDNEY: Wait a minute, let's have it out. What do you think you're up to?

ALBERT: Look, I've told you—

GIDNEY: What did you think you were doing with that girl?

ALBERT: I didn't touch her.

GIDNEY: I'm responsible for that girl. She's a good friend of mine. I know her uncle.

ALBERT: Do you?

SEELEY: You know, you're being so stupid, Gidney—

GIDNEY: Seeley, I can take you any day, you know that, don't you?

SEELEY: Go on!

GIDNEY: Any day.

SEELEY: You can take me any day?

GIDNEY: Any day.

SEELEY: Well, go on, then. Go on . . . if you can take me . . .

ALBERT: Seeley—

SEELEY: No, if he says he can take me, if he can take me any day . . .

The door opens slightly. HORNE *and* BARROW *peer out.*

ALBERT: Gidney, why don't you . . . why don't you get back to the party?

GIDNEY: I was telling you, Albert—

ALBERT: Stokes.

GIDNEY: I was telling you, Albert, that if you're going to behave like a boy of ten in mixed company—

ALBERT: I told you my name's Stokes!

GIDNEY: Don't be childish, Albert.

A sudden silence. MR. KING'S *voice from the room.*

KING: . . . and for his unfailing good humour and cheeriness, Mr. Ryan will always be remembered at Hislop, King and Martindale!

Scattered applause. HORNE, *caught by their stares, shuts the door hastily.*

ALBERT [*going to the door.*]: Goodnight.

GIDNEY [*obstructing him*]: Go back and apologize.

ALBERT: What for?

GIDNEY: For insulting a lady. Mate. A lady. Something to do with breeding. But I suppose you're too bloody backward to know anything about that.

ALBERT: You're talking right out of your hat.

SEELEY: Right out of the bowler.

GIDNEY [*to* SEELEY]: No one invited you out here, did they?

SEELEY: Who invited you?

GIDNEY: I'm talking to this man on behalf of the firm! Unless I get a satisfactory explanation I shall think seriously about recommending his dismissal.

ALBERT: Get out of my way, will you?

GIDNEY: Acting like an animal all over the place—

ALBERT: Move out of it!

GIDNEY [*breathlessly*]: I know your trouble.

ALBERT: Oh, yes?

GIDNEY: Yes, sticks out a mile.

ALBERT: Does it?

GIDNEY: Yes.

ALBERT: What's my trouble then?

GIDNEY [*very deliberately*]: You're a mother's boy. That's what you are. That's your trouble. You're a mother's boy.

ALBERT *hits him. There is a scuffle.* SEELEY *tries to part them. The three rock back and forth in the hall: confused blows, words and grunts.*

The door of the room opens. Faces. MR. KING *comes out.*

KING: What in heaven's name is going on here!

The scuffle stops. A short silence. ALBERT *opens the front door, goes out and slams it behind him. He stands on the doorstep, breathing heavily, his face set.*

SCENE TWO

The kitchen.

MRS. STOKES *is asleep, her head resting on the table, the cards disordered. The clock ticks. It is twelve o'clock. The front door opens slowly.* ALBERT *comes in, closes the door softly, stops, looks across to the open kitchen door, sees his mother, and begins to creep up the stairs with great stealth. The camera follows him. Her voice stops him.*

MOTHER: Albert!

He stops.

Albert! Is that you?

She goes to the kitchen door.

What are you creeping up the stairs for? Might have been a burglar. What would I have done then?

He descends slowly.

Creeping up the stairs like that. Give anyone a fright. Creeping up the stairs like that. You leave me in the house all alone . . . [*She stops and regards him.*] Look at you! Look at your suit. What's the matter with your tie, it's all crumpled, I pressed it for you this morning. Well, I won't even ask any questions. That's all. You look a disgrace.

He walks past her into the kitchen, goes to the sink and pours himself a glass of water. She follows him.

What have you been doing, mucking about with girls?

She begins to pile the cards.

Mucking about with girls, I suppose. Do you know what the time is? I fell asleep, right here at this table, waiting for you. I don't know what your father would say. Coming in this time of night. It's after twelve o'clock. In a state like that. Drunk, I suppose. I suppose your dinner's ruined. Well, if you want to make a convenience out of your own home, that's your business. I'm only your mother, I don't suppose that counts for much these days. I'm not saying any more. If you want to go mucking about with girls, that's your business.

She takes his dinner out of the oven.

Well, anyway, you'll have your dinner. You haven't eaten a single thing all night.

She places a plate on the table and gets knife and fork. He stands by the sink, sipping water.

I wouldn't mind if you found a really nice girl and brought her home and introduced her to your mother, brought her home for dinner, I'd know you were sincere, if she was a really nice girl, she'd be like a daughter to me. But you've never brought a girl home here in your life. I suppose you're ashamed of your mother.
[*Pause.*]
Come on, it's all dried up. I kept it on a low light. I couldn't even go up to Grandma's room and have a look round because there wasn't any bulb, you might as well eat it.

He stands.

What's the matter, are you drunk? Where did you go, to one of those pubs in the West End? You'll get into serious trouble, my boy, if you frequent those places, I'm warning you. Don't you read the papers?
[*Pause.*]
I hope you're satisfied, anyway. The house in darkness, I wasn't going to break my neck going down to that cellar

to look for a bulb, you come home looking like I don't know what, anyone would think you gave me a fortune out of your wages. Yes. I don't say anything, do I? I keep quiet about what you expect me to manage on. I never grumble. I keep a lovely home, I bet there's none of the boys in your firm better fed than you are. I'm not asking for gratitude. But one things hurts me, Albert, and I'll tell you what it is. Not for years, not for years, have you come up to me and said, Mum, I love you, like you did when you were a little boy. You've never said it without me having to ask you. Not since before your father died. And he was a good man. He had high hopes of you. I've never told you, Albert, about the high hopes he had of you. I don't know what you do with all your money. But don't forget what it cost us to rear you, my boy, I've never told you about the sacrifices we made, you wouldn't care, anyway. Telling me lies about going to the firm's party. They've got a bit of respect at that firm, that's why we sent you there, to start off your career, they wouldn't let you carry on like that at one of their functions. Mr. King would have his eye on you. I don't know where you've been. Well, if you don't want to lead a clean life it's your lookout, if you want to go mucking about with all sorts of bits of girls, if you're content to leave your own mother sitting here till midnight, and I wasn't feeling well, anyway, I didn't tell you because I didn't want to upset you, I keep things from you, you're the only one I've got, but what do you care, you don't care, you don't care, the least you can do is sit down and eat the dinner I cooked for you, specially for you, it's Shepherd's Pie—

ALBERT *lunges to the table, picks up the clock and violently raises it above his head. A stifled scream from the* MOTHER.

Act Three

SCENE ONE

The coffee stall, shuttered.

ALBERT *is leaning against it. He is sweating. He is holding the butt of a cigarette. There is a sound of a foot on gravel. He starts, the butt burns his hand, he drops it and turns. A* GIRL *is looking at him. She smiles.*

GIRL: Good evening.
[*Pause.*]
What are you doing?
[*Pause.*]
What are you doing out at this time of night?

She moves closer to him.

I live just round the corner.

He stares at her.

Like to? Chilly out here, isn't it? Come on.
[*Pause.*]
Come on.

He goes with her.

SCENE TWO

The GIRL'S *room. The door opens. She comes in. Her manner has changed from the seductive. She is brisk and nervous.*

GIRL: Come in. Don't slam the door. Shut it gently. I'll light the fire. Chilly out, don't you find? Have you got a match?

He walks across the room.

GIRL: Please don't walk so heavily. Please. There's no need to let . . . to let the whole house know you're here. Life's difficult enough as it is. Have you got a match?

ALBERT: No, I . . . I don't think I have.

GIRL: Oh, God, you'd think you'd have a match.

He walks about.

I say, would you mind taking your shoes off? You're really making a dreadful row. Really, I can't bear . . . noisy . . . people.

He looks at his shoes, begins to untie one. The GIRL *searches for matches on the mantelpiece, upon which are a number of articles and objects, including a large alarm clock.*

I know I had one somewhere.

ALBERT: I've got a lighter.

GIRL: You can't light a gasfire with a lighter. You'd burn your fingers.

She bends down to the hearth.

Where are the damn things? This is ridiculous. I die without the fire. I simply die. [*She finds the box.*] Ah, here we are. At last.

She turns on the gas fire and lights it. He watches her. She puts the matchbox on the mantelpiece and picks up a photo.

Do you like this photo? It's of my little girl. She's staying with friends. Rather fine, isn't she? Very aristocratic features, don't you think? She's at a very select boarding school at the moment, actually. In . . . Hereford, very near Hereford. [*She puts the photo back.*] I shall be going down for the prize day shortly. You do look idiotic standing there with one shoe on and one shoe off. All lop-sided.

ALBERT *pulls at the lace of his other shoe. The lace breaks.*
He swears shortly under his breath.

GIRL [*sharply*]: Do you mind not saying words like that?

ALBERT: I didn't . . .

GIRL: I heard you curse.

ALBERT: My lace broke.

GIRL: That's no excuse.

ALBERT: What did I say?

GIRL: I'm sorry, I can't bear that sort of thing. It's just . . .
not in my personality.

ALBERT: I'm sorry.

GIRL: It's quite all right. It's just . . . something in my
nature. I've got to think of my daughter, too, you know.

She crouches by the fire.

Come near the fire a minute. Sit down.

He goes towards a small stool.

Not on that! That's my seat. It's my own stool. I did the
needlework myself. A long time ago.

He sits in a chair, opposite.

Which do you prefer, electric or gas? For a fire, I mean?

ALBERT [*holding his forehead, muttering*]: I don't know.

GIRL: There's no need to be rude, it was a civil question. I
prefer gas. Or a log fire, of course. They have them in
Switzerland.
[*Pause.*]
Have you got a headache?

ALBERT: No.

GIRL: I didn't realize you had a lighter. You don't happen to
have any cigarettes on you, I suppose?

ALBERT: No.

GIRL: I'm very fond of a smoke. After dinner. With a glass of
wine. Or before dinner, with sherry.

She stands and taps the mantelpiece, her eyes roaming over it.

You look as if you've had a night out. Where have you
been? Had a nice time?

ALBERT: Quite . . . quite nice.

GIRL [*sitting on the stool*]: What do you do?

ALBERT: I . . . work in films.

GIRL: Films? Really? What do you do?

ALBERT: I'm an assistant director.

GIRL: Really? How funny. I used to be a continuity girl. But
I gave it up.

ALBERT [*tonelessly*]: What a pity.

GIRL: Yes, I'm beginning to think you're right. You meet
such a good class of people. Of course, now you say you're
an assistant director I can see what you mean. I mean, I
could tell you had breeding the moment I saw you. You
looked a bit washed out, perhaps, but there was no mis-
taking the fact that you had breeding. I'm extremely particular, you see. I do like a certain amount of delicacy in
men . . . a certain amount . . . a certain degree . . .
a certain amount of refinement. You do see my point?
Some men I couldn't possibly entertain. Not even if I was
. . . starving. I don't want to be personal, but that word
you used, when you broke your lace, it made me shiver,
I'm just not that type, made me wonder if you were as
well bred as I thought . . .

He wipes his face with his hand.

You do look hot. Why are you so hot? It's chilly. Yes,
you remind me . . . I saw the most ghastly horrible fight
before, there was a man, one man, he was sweating . . .
sweating. You haven't been in a fight, by any chance? I
don't know how men can be so bestial. It's hardly much
fun for women, I can tell you. I don't want someone else's
blood on my carpet.

ALBERT *chuckles*.

What are you laughing at?
ALBERT: Nothing.
GIRL: It's not in the least funny.

ALBERT *looks up at the mantelpiece. His gaze rests there.*

What are you looking at?
ALBERT [*ruminatively*]: That's a nice big clock.

It is twenty past two.

GIRL [*with fatigue*]: Yes, it's late, I suppose we might as well
. . . Haven't you got a cigarette?
ALBERT: No.
GIRL [*jumping up*]: I'm sure I have, somewhere. [*She goes to
the table.*] Yes, here we are, I knew I had. I have to hide
them. The woman who comes in to do my room, she's very
light-fingered. I don't know why she comes in at all. Nobody wants her, all she does is spy on me, but I'm obliged
to put up with her, this room is serviced. Which means
I have to pay a pretty penny.

She lights her cigarette.

It's a dreadful area, too. I'm thinking of moving. The
neighbourhood is full of people of no class at all. I just don't
fit in.
ALBERT: Is that clock right?
GIRL: People have told me, the most distinguished people,
that I could go anywhere. You could go anywhere, they've
told me, you could be anything. I'm quite well educated,
you know. My father was a . . . he was a military man.
In the Army. Actually it was a relief to speak to you. I
haven't . . . spoken to anyone for some hours.

ALBERT *suddenly coughs violently*.

Oh, please don't do that! Use your handkerchief!

He sighs, and groans.

What on earth's the matter with you? What have you been doing tonight?

He looks at her and smiles.

ALBERT: Nothing.

GIRL: Really?

She belches.

Oh, excuse me. I haven't eaten all day. I had a tooth out. Hiccoughs come from not eating, don't they? Do you . . . do you want one of these?

She throws him a cigarette, which he slowly lights.

I mean, I'm no different from any other girl. In fact, I'm better. These so-called respectable girls, for instance, I'm sure they're much worse than I am. Well, you're an assistant director—all your continuity girls and secretaries, I'll bet they're . . . very loose.

ALBERT: Uh.

GIRL: Do you know what I've actually heard? I've heard that respectable married women, solicitors' wives, go out and pick men up when their husbands are out on business! Isn't that fantastic? I mean, they're supposed to be . . . they're supposed to be respectable!

ALBERT [*muttering*]: Fantastic.

GIRL: I beg your pardon?

ALBERT: I said it was fantastic.

GIRL: It is. You're right. Quite fantastic. Here's one thing, though. There's one thing that's always fascinated me. How far do men's girl friends go? I've often wondered.
[*Pause.*]
Eh?

ALBERT: Depends.

GIRL: Yes, I suppose it must.
  [*Pause.*]
  You mean on the girl?
ALBERT: What?
GIRL: You mean it depends on the girl?
ALBERT: It would do, yes.
GIRL: Quite possibly. I must admit that with your continuity
  girls and secretaries, I don't see why you . . . had to
  approach me. . . . Have you been on the town tonight,
  then? With a continuity girl?
ALBERT: You're a bit . . . worried about continuity girls,
  aren't you?
GIRL: Only because I've been one myself. I know what they're
  like. No better than they should be.
ALBERT: When were you a . . .?
GIRL: Years ago! [*Standing.*] You're nosey, aren't you?

She goes to the window.

Sometimes I wish the night would never end. I like
sleeping. I could sleep . . . on and on.

ALBERT *stands and picks up the clock.*

Yes, you can see the station from here. All the trains go
out, right through the night.

He stares at the clock.

I suppose we might as well . . . [*She turns and sees him.*]
What are you doing? [*She crosses to him.*] What are you
doing with that clock?

He looks at her, slowly.

Mmnn?
ALBERT: Admiring it.
GIRL: It's a perfectly ordinary clock. Give me it. I've seen too
  many people slip things into their pockets before now, as

soon as your back's turned. Nothing personal, of course.
[*She puts it back.*] Mind your ash! Don't spill it all over the
floor! I have to keep this carpet immaculate. Otherwise the
charlady, she's always looking for excuses for telling tales.
Here. Here's an ashtray. Use it, please.

She gives it to him. He stares at her.

Sit down. Sit down. Don't stand about like that. What are
you staring at me for?

He sits. She studies him.

Where's your wife?
ALBERT: Nowhere.

She stubs her cigarette.

GIRL: And what film are you making at the moment?
ALBERT: I'm on holiday.
GIRL: Where do you work?
ALBERT: I'm a free lance.
GIRL: You're . . . rather young to be in such a . . . high
position, aren't you?
ALBERT: Oh?
GIRL [*laughs*]: You amuse me. You interest me. I'm a bit of a
psychologist, you know. You're very young to be—what
you said you were. There's something childish in your face,
almost retarded. [*She laughs.*] I do like that word. I'm not
being personal, of course . . . just being . . . psycholo-
gical. Of course, I can see you're one for the girls. Don't
know why you had to pick on me, at this time of night,
really rather forward of you. I'm a respectable mother, you
know, with a child at boarding school. You couldn't call
me . . . anything else. All I do, I just entertain a few
gentlemen, of my own choice, now and again. What girl
doesn't?

His hand screws the cigarette. He lets it fall on the carpet.

[*Outraged.*] What do you think you're doing?

She stares at him.

Pick it up! Pick that up, I tell you! It's my carpet!

She lunges towards it.

It's not my carpet, they'll make me pay—

His hand closes upon hers as she reaches for it.

What are you doing? Let go. Treating my place like a
pigsty. [*She looks up at him as he bends over her.*] Let me go.
You're burning my carpet!

ALBERT [*quietly, intensely*]: Sit down.

GIRL: How dare you?

ALBERT: Shut up. Sit down.

GIRL [*struggling*]: What are you doing?

ALBERT [*erratically, trembling, but with quiet command*]: Don't
    scream. I'm warning you.

He lifts her by her wrist and presses her down on to the stool.

No screaming. I warn you.

GIRL: What's the—?

ALBERT [*through his teeth*]: Be quiet. I told you to be quiet.
    Now you be quiet.

GIRL: What are you going to do?

ALBERT [*seizing the clock from the mantelpiece*]: DON'T MUCK
    ME ABOUT!

She freezes with terror.

See this? One crack with this . . . just one crack . . .
[*Viciously.*] Who do you think you are? You talk too much,
you know that. You never stop talking. Just because you're
a woman you think you can get away with it. [*Bending over
her.*] You've made a mistake, this time. You've picked the
wrong man.

He begins to grow in stature and excitement, passing the clock from hand to hand.

You're all the same, you see, you're all the same, you're just a dead weight round my neck. What makes you think . . . [*He begins to move about the room, at one point half crouching, at another standing upright, as if exercising his body.*] . . . What makes you think you can . . . tell me . . . yes . . . It's the same as this business about the light in Grandma's room. Always something. Always something. [*To her.*] My ash? I'll put it where I like! You see this clock? Watch your step. Just watch your step.

GIRL: Stop this. What are you—?

ALBERT [*seizing her wrist, with trembling, controlled violence*]: Watch your step! [*Stammering.*] I've had—I've had—I've had—just about enough. Get it? . . . You know what I did?

He looks at her and chuckles.

Don't be so frightened.

GIRL: I . . .

ALBERT [*casually*]: Don't be so frightened.

He squats by her, still holding the clock.

I'm just telling you. I'm just telling you, that's all. [*Breathlessly.*] You haven't got any breeding. She hadn't either. And what about those girls tonight? Same kind. And that one. I didn't touch her!

GIRL [*almost inaudible*]: What you been doing?

ALBERT: I've got as many qualifications as the next man. Let's get that quite . . . straight. And I got the answer to her. I got the answer to her, you see, tonight. . . . I finished the conversation . . . I finished it . . . I finished her . . .

She squirms. He raises the clock.

With this clock! [*Trembling.*] One . . . crack . . . with

... this... clock ... finished! [*Thoughtfully.*] Of course, I loved her, really. [*He suddenly sees the photograph on the mantelpiece, puts the clock down and takes it. The* GIRL *half rises and gasps, watching him. He looks at the photo curiously.*] Uhhh? . . . Your daughter? . . . This a photo of your daughter? . . . Uuuh? [*He breaks the frame and takes out the photo.*]

GIRL [*rushes at him*]. Leave that!

ALBERT [*dropping the frame and holding the photo*]: Is it?

The GIRL *grabs at it.* ALBERT *clutches her wrist. He holds her at arm's length.*

GIRL: Leave that! [*Writhing.*] What? Don't—it's mine!

ALBERT [*turns the photo over and reads back*]: 'Class Three Classical, Third Prize, Bronze Medal, Twickenham Competition, nineteen thirty-three.' [*He stares at her. The* GIRL *stands, shivering and whimpering.*] You liar. That's you.

GIRL: It's not!

ALBERT: That's not your daughter. It's you! You're just a fake, you're just all lies!

GIRL: Scum! Filthy scum!

ALBERT, *twisting her wrist, moves suddenly to her. The* GIRL *cringing, falls back into her chair.*

ALBERT [*warningly*]: Mind how you talk to me. [*He crumples the photo.*]

GIRL [*moans*]: My daughter. My little girl. My little baby girl.

ALBERT: Get up.

GIRL: No . . .

ALBERT: Get up! Up!

She stands.

Walk over there, to the wall. Go on! Get over there. Do as you're told. Do as I'm telling you. I'm giving the orders here.

She walks to the wall.

Stop!

GIRL [*whimpering*]: What . . . do you want me to do?

ALBERT: Just keep your big mouth closed, for a start.

He frowns uncertainly.

Cover your face!

She does so. He looks about, blinking.

Yes. That's right. [*He sees his shoes.*] Come on, come on, pick up those shoes. Those shoes! Pick them up!

She looks for the shoes and picks them up.

That's right. [*He sits.*] Bring them over here. Come on. That's right. Put them on.

He extends his foot.

GIRL: You're . . .

ALBERT: On! Right on. That's it. That's it. That's more like it. That's . . . more like it! Good. Lace them! Good.

He stands. She crouches.

Silence.

He shivers and murmurs with the cold. He looks about the room.

ALBERT: It's cold.
[*Pause.*]
Ooh, it's freezing.

GIRL [*whispering*]: The fire's gone.

ALBERT [*looking at the window*]: What's that? Looks like light. Ooh, it's perishing. [*Looks about, muttering.*] What a dump. Not staying here. Getting out of this place.

He shivers and drops the clock. He looks down at it. She too. He kicks it across the room.

[*With a smile, softly.*] So you . . . bear that in mind. Mind how you talk to me.

He goes to door, then turns.

[*Flipping half a crown to her.*] Buy yourself a seat . . . buy yourself a seat at a circus.

He opens the door and goes.

SCENE THREE

The house.
The front door opens. ALBERT *comes in, a slight smile on his face. He saunters across the hall into the kitchen, takes off his jacket and throws it across the room. The same with his tie. He sits heavily, loosely, in a chair, his legs stretched out. Stretching his arms, he yawns luxuriously, scratches his head with both hands and stares ruminatively at the ceiling, a smile on his face. His mother's voice calls his name.*

MOTHER [*from the stairs*]: Albert!

His body freezes. His gaze comes down. His legs slowly come together. He looks in front of him.
His MOTHER *comes into the room, in her dressing gown. She stands, looking at him.*

Do you know what the time is?
[*Pause.*]
Where have you been?
[*Pause.*]
[*Reproachfully, near to tears.*] I don't know what to say to you, Albert. To raise your hand to your own mother. You've never done that before in your life. To threaten your own mother.
[*Pause.*]

That clock would have hurt me, Albert. And you'd have been . . . I know you'd have been very sorry. Aren't I a good mother to you? Everything I do is . . . is for your own good. You should know that. You're all I've got.

She looks at his slumped figure. Her reproach turns to solicitude.

[*Gently.*] Look at you. You look washed out. Oh, you look . . . I don't understand what could have come over you.

She takes a chair and sits close to him.

Listen, Albert, I'll tell you what I'm going to do. I'm going to forget it. You see? I'm going to forget all about it. We'll have your holiday in a fortnight. We can go away.

She strokes his hand.

We'll go away . . . together.
[*Pause.*]
It's not as if you're a bad boy . . . you're a good boy . . . I know you are . . . it's not as if you're really bad, Albert, you're not . . . you're not bad, you're good . . . you're not a bad boy, Albert, I know you're not . . .
[*Pause.*]
You're good, you're not bad, you're a good boy . . . I know you are . . . you are, aren't you?

THE BLACK AND WHITE

I always catch the all-night bus, six days out of the week.
I walk to Marble Arch and get the two-nine-four, that
takes me to Fleet Street. I never speak to the men on the
all-night buses. Then I go into the Black and White at
Fleet Street and sometimes my friend comes. I have a
cup of tea. She is taller than me but thinner. Sometimes
she comes and we sit at the top table. I always keep her
place but you can't always keep it. I never speak to them
when they take it. Some remarks I never listen to. A man
slips me the morning paper sometimes, the first one. He
told me what he was once. I never go down to the place
near the Embankment. I did go down there once. You
can see what goes on from the window by the top table if
you look. Mostly it's vans. They're always rushing.
Mostly they're the same van-drivers, sometimes they're
different. My brother was the same. He used to be in on
it. But I can do better without the night, when it's dark,
it's always light in the Black and White, sometimes it's
blue, I can't see much. But I can do better without the
cold when it's cold. It's always warm in the Black and
White, sometimes it's draughty, I don't kip. Five o'clock
they close down to give it a scrub round. I always wear
my grey skirt and my red scarf, you never see me without
lipstick. Sometimes my friend comes, she always brings
over two teas. If there's someone taken her place she tells
him. She's older than me but thinner. If it's cold I might
have soup. You get a good bowl. They give you the slice
of bread. They won't do that with tea but they do it with
soup. So I might have soup, if it's cold. Now and again
you can see the all-night buses going down. They all run
down there. I've never been the other way, not the way

some of them go. I've been down to Liverpool Street. That's where some of them end up. She's greyer than me. The lights get you down a bit. Once a man stood up and made a speech. A copper came in. They got him out. Then the copper came over to us. We soon told him off, my friend did. I never seen him since, either of them. They don't get many coppers. I'm a bit old for that, my friend told him. Are you, he said. Too old for you, she said. He went. I don't mind, there's not too much noise, there's always a bit of noise. Young people in cabs come in once. She didn't like the coffee. I've never had the coffee. I had coffee up at Euston, a time or two, going back. I like the vegetable soup better than the tomato. I was having a bowl then and this man was leaning from across the table, dead asleep, but sitting on his elbows, scratching his head. He was pulling the hairs out of his head into my soup, dead asleep. I pulled my bowl away. But at five o'clock they close down to give it a scrub round. They don't let you stay. My friend never stays, if she's there. You can't buy a cup of tea. I've asked but they won't let you sit, not even with your feet up. Still, you can get about four hours out of it. They only shut hour and a half. You could go down to that one near the Embankment, but I've only been down there once. I've always got my red scarf. I'm never without lipstick. I give them a look. They never pick me up. They took my friend away in the wagon once. They didn't keep her. She said they took a fancy to her. I've never gone in for that. You keep yourself clean. Still, she won't stand for any of it in the Black and White. But they don't try much. I see them look. Mostly nobody looks. I don't know many, some I've seen about. One woman in a big black hat and big black boots comes in. I never make out what she has. He slips her the morning paper. It's not long. You can go along, then come back. When it's light I

go. My friend won't wait. She goes. I don't mind. One
got me sick. Came in a fur coat once. They give you
injections, she said, it's all Whitehall, they got it all
worked out, she said, they can tap your breath, they
inject you in the ears. My friend came later. She was a bit
nervy. I got her quiet. They'd take her in. When it's light
I walk up to the Aldwych. They're selling the papers.
I've read it. One morning I went a bit over Waterloo
Bridge. I saw the last two-nine-six. It must have been the
last. It didn't look like an all-night bus, in daylight.

THE EXAMINATION

When we began, I allowed him intervals. He expressed no desire for these, nor any objection. And so I took it upon myself to adjudge their allotment and duration. They were not consistent, but took alteration with what I must call the progress of our talks. With the chalk I kept I marked the proposed times upon the blackboard, before the beginning of a session, for him to examine, and to offer any criticism if he felt so moved. But he made no objection, nor, during our talks, expressed any desire for a break in the proceedings. However, as I suspected they might benefit both of us, I allowed him intervals.

The intervals themselves, when they occurred, at whatever juncture, at whatever crucial point, preceded by whatever deadlock, were passed, naturally, in silence. It was not uncommon for them to be both preceded and followed by an equal silence, but this is not to say that on such occasions their purpose was offended. Frequently his disposition would be such that little could be achieved by insistence, or by persuasion. When Kullus was disposed to silence I invariably acquiesced, and prided myself on those occasions with tactical acumen. But I did not regard these silences as intervals, for they were not, and neither, I think, did Kullus so regard them. For if Kullus fell silent, he did not cease to participate in our examination. Never, at any time, had I reason to doubt his active participation, through word and through silence, between interval and interval, and I recognized what I took to be his devotion as actual and unequivocal, besides, as it seemed to me, obligatory. And so the nature of our silence within the frame of our examination, and the nature of our silence outside the frame of our examination, were entirely opposed.

Upon my announcement of an interval Kullus would change, or act in such a manner as would suggest change. His behaviour, on these occasions, was not consistent, nor, I am convinced, was it initiated by motives of resentment or enmity, although I suspect Kullus was aware of my watchfulness. Not that I made any pretence to be otherwise. I was obliged to remark, and, if possible, to verify, any ostensible change in his manner, whether it was outside the frame of our examination or not. And it is upon this point that I could be accused of error. For gradually it appeared that these intervals proceeded according to his terms. And where both allotment and duration had rested with me, and had become my imposition, they now proceeded according to his dictates, and became his imposition.

For he journeyed from silence to silence, and I had no course but to follow. Kullus's silence, where he was entitled to silence, was compounded of numerous characteristics, the which I duly noted. But I could not always follow his courses, and where I could not follow, I was no longer his dominant.

Kullus's predilection for windows was not assumed. At every interval, he retired to the window, and began from its vantage, as from a source. On approaching initially when the break was stated, he paid no attention to the aspect beyond, either in day-time or in night-time. And only in his automatic course to the window, and his lack of interest in the aspect beyond, did he prove consistent.

Neither was Kullus's predilection for windows a deviation from former times. I had myself suffered under his preoccupation upon previous occasions, when the order of his room had been maintained by particular arrangement of window and curtain, according to day and to night, and seldom to my taste or my comfort. But now he maintained no such order and did not determine their opening or closing. For we were no longer in Kullus's room.

And the window was always open, and the curtains were always open.

Not that Kullus displayed any interest in this constant

arrangement, in the intervals, when he might note it. But as I suspect he was aware of my watchfulness, so I suspect he was aware of my arrangement. Dependent on the intensity of his silence I could suspect and conclude, but where his silence was too deep for echo, I could neither suspect nor conclude. And so gradually, where this occurred, I began to take the only course open to me, and terminated the intervals arbitrarily, cutting short the proposed duration, when I could no longer follow him, and was no longer his dominant.

But this was not until later.

When the door opened. When Kullus, unattended, entered, and the interim ended. I turned from all light in the window, to pay him due regard and welcome. Whereupon without reserve or hesitation, he moved from the door as from shelter, and stood in the light from the window. So I watched the entrance become vacant, which had been his shelter. And observed the man I had welcomed, he having crossed my border.

Equally, now, I observed the selected properties, each in their place; the blackboard, the window, the stool. And the door had closed and was absent, and of no moment. Imminent upon opening and welcoming it had possessed moment. Now only one area was to witness activity and to suffer procedure, and that only was necessary and valid. For the door was closed and so closed.

Whereupon I offered Kullus the stool, the which I placed for him. He showed, at this early juncture, no disregard for my directions; if he did not so much obey, he extended his voluntary co-operation. This was sufficient for my requirements. That I detected in him a desire for a summation of our efforts spoke well for the progress of our examination. It was my aim to avoid the appearance of subjection; a common policy, I understand, in like examinations. Yet I was naturally dominant, by virtue of my owning the room; he having entered through the door I now closed. To be confronted with the

especial properties of my abode, bearing the seal and arrangement of their tenant, allowed only for recognition on the part
of my visitor, and through recognition to acknowledgement
and through acknowledgement to appreciation, and through
appreciation to subservience. At least, I trusted that such a
development would take place, and initially believed it to have
done so. It must be said, however, that his manner, from time
to time, seemed to border upon indifference, yet I was not
deluded by this, or offended. I viewed it as a utility he was
compelled, and entitled, to fall back on, and equally as a tribute
to my own incisiveness and patience. And if then I viewed it
as a tactical measure, it caused me little concern. For it seemed,
at this time, that the advantage was mine. Had not Kullus
been obliged to attend this examination? And was not his
attendance an admission of that obligation? And was not his
admission an acknowledgement of my position? And my position therefore a position of dominance? I calculated this to be
so, and no early event caused me to re-assess this calculation.
Indeed, so confident was I in the outcome of our talks, that I
decided to allow him intervals.

To institute these periods seemed to me both charitable and
politic. For I hoped he might benefit from a period of no
demand, so be better equipped for the periods of increased
demand which would follow. And, for a time, I had no reason
to doubt the wisdom of this arrangement. Also, the context
of the room in which Kullus moved during the intervals was
familiar and sympathetic to me, and not so to him. For Kullus
had known it, and now knew it no longer, and took his place
in it as a stranger, and when each break was stated, was compelled to pursue a particular convention and habit in his
course, so as not to become hopelessly estranged within its
boundaries. But gradually it became apparent that only in his
automatic course to the window, and his lack of interest in the
aspect beyond, did he prove consistent.

Prior to his arrival, I had omitted to establish one property

in the room, which I knew to be familiar to him, and so liable
to bring him ease. And never once did he remark the absence
of a flame in the grate. I concluded he did not recognize this
absence. To balance this, I emphasized the presence of the
stool, indeed, placed it for him, but as he never once remarked
this presence, I concluded his concern did not embrace it.
Not that it was at any time simple to determine by what
particular his concern might be engaged. However, in the
intervals, when I was able to observe him with possibly a finer
detachment, I hoped to determine this.

Until his inconsistency began to cause me alarm, and his
silence to confound me.

I can only assume Kullus was aware, on these occasions, of
the scrutiny of which he was the object, and was persuaded to
resist it, and to act against it. He did so by deepening the
intensity of his silence, and by taking courses I could by no
means follow, so that I remained isolated, and outside his
silence, and thus of negligible influence. And so I took the
only course open to me, and terminated the intervals arbitrarily, cutting short the proposed duration, when I could no
longer follow him, and was no longer his dominant.

For where the intervals had been my imposition, they had
now become his imposition.

Kullus made no objection to this adjustment, though without doubt he noted my anxiety. For I suffered anxiety with
good cause, out of concern for the progress of our talks, which
now seemed to me to be affected. I was no longer certain
whether Kullus participated in our examination, nor certain
whether he still understood that as being the object of our
meeting. Equally, the nature of our silences, which formerly
were distinct in their opposition: that is, a silence within the
frame of our examination, and a silence outside the frame of
our examination; seemed to me no longer opposed, indeed
were indistinguishable, and were one silence, dictated by
Kullus.

And so the time came when Kullus initiated intervals at his own inclination, and pursued his courses at will, and I was able to remark some consistency in his behaviour. For now I followed him in his courses without difficulty, and there was no especial duration for interval or examination, but one duration, in which I participated. My devotion was actual and unequivocal. I extended my voluntary co-operation, and made no objection to procedure. For I desired a summation of our efforts. And when Kullus remarked the absence of a flame in the gate, I was bound to acknowledge this. And when he remarked the presence of the stool, I was equally bound. And when he removed the blackboard, I offered no criticism. And when he closed the curtains I did not object.

For we were now in Kullus's room.